SEEK ME OUT

בקשו פני

Seek Me Out

TIMELESS LESSONS

FOR A TIME-BOUND WORLD

MOSHE M. EISEMANN

Rabbi Moshe M. Eisemann
403 Yeshiva Lane, Apt. 1B
Baltimore, MD 21208
(410) 484-7396

© Cover artwork by Raphael Polyakov
Composition by Eden Chachamtzedek
Edited by Muriel Jorgensen

This book was set in
Adobe Brioso Pro and Narkiss Classic MFO

ISBN 978-0-9817642-5-2

2 4 6 8 10 9 7 5 3 1

Printed in the USA

Contents

Introductory Remarks

"Welcome!" or "Welcome back!" as the case may be. This is the sixteenth book in as many years. Some of you may have just come on board; others, of course, are veterans. I am addressing these introductory remarks to all of you because this new book can use a bit of explaining.

Each of the first fourteen books dealt with a single topic. For example, *Parents and Penguins* discussed *Chinuch* issues, *Shelter Amongst the Shadows* zeroed in on Succos and Koheles, which, of course, belong together, and so on. Number 15, *Awake at the Wheel,* broke ranks and was simply a collection of essays on different subjects, some of which were loosely connected while others stood entirely on their own. Nevertheless the book, taken as a whole, had cohesion. It could be described as a collection of essays dealing with "everyday" kind of *mitzvos* in which we all engage, but which, being human, we often perform by rote. It was my hope that the insights that the book offered would let in a little fresh air and help improve our performance. I am sure that many of you readers have opinions about how successful the book was. I hope that you are able to share my impression that it did not do badly.

The current book, which also consists of unconnected essays, does not belong to either of the two genres we have described. Now that we have explained what it *isn't,* we need to come to grips with what it *is.* That is a little harder to get across. I hope that I will be able to capture your attention.

Consider the following situation. Somebody blessed with sufficient funds has decided that he wants to find out what Judaism is all about. He has heard that the purest Judaism is practiced among the ultra-Orthodox so he hires people armed with the latest in video and audio equipment to spend the time required to record the practice of Judaism in those communities. He expects to obtain a full picture.

Can he succeed?

Of course he cannot. He does not realize that in our *galus* situation, there are huge areas of mitzvos that simply cannot be fulfilled. Think of the Beis HaMikdash and the *Korbonos*. Think of the laws of *tum'ah* and *taharah*. Think of *Malchus Beis David* and the Sanhedrin. The list goes on and on. Even our most conscientious practitioners miss out on huge sections of Jewish performance. This is not because these *halachos* are in any way inferior to those that *Baruch HaShem* fill our lives even today, but because the circumstances under which they apply are simply not given in our present, tragic, exiled rootlessness.

Now, Dovid HaMelech told us in Tehilim 19:8–10 what the Torah's commands do for us. I will quote from Aaron Lichtenstein's rendering of this passage.[1] I think that he caught the spirit of these few verses perfectly.

> God's Torah is perfect, calming the soul.
> God's testament is trustworthy, enlightening the simple.
> God's laws are just, a cause for rejoicing.
> God's commandments sparkle, a delight to behold...
> All are more precious than gold,
> and sweeter than a honeycomb flow.

Can we even imagine what we are missing? With so many mitzvos fallen into disuse we are denied the lessons, the *hashkofos*, the simple inspirations that inhere in them. In the sense that I have now described, and only in that sense, the Judaism that we are able to practice today is truncated, and the pictures captured on our friend's video cameras will be sadly inadequate and perhaps even distorted.

In a number of essays in this book I have tried to discover some of the values on which, in practice, we are missing out. I assume — I see no reason not to — that there is no reason to suppose that because we are deprived of the practical fulfillment of these גופי תורה, we ought not to bask in the wisdom and sanctity that inheres in them.

So here we have the difference between this book and *Awake at the Wheel* that came out last year. That one dealt with contemporary practice and sought to enhance our approach to the mitzvos

1. *The Book of Psalms in Plain English. A Contemporary Reading of Tehillim* by Aaron Lichtenstein. Urim Publications, Jerusalem/New York.

that we do every day. I like to look at it as a happy book. It gives us a chance to spruce ourselves up in anticipation of meeting the Ribono shel Olam. It is like getting dressed for a *Chasunah*.

The current book is like flipping through an old and worn wedding album, full of sweet memories and still capable of stirring us to an appreciation of the bygone years that are still very much alive for us.

For this book I have chosen mainly such subjects as our friend with his video boys would have missed completely. For example, the third essay deals with *arachin/erchin*,[2] a topic of which I suspect even many yeshiva students are largely ignorant. This *sugia* is weighted with highly significant implications concerning Jewish thinking, ideas and ideals that for one reason or another are simply missing from Jewish living today and have been missing for a couple of thousand years. That is not because the ideals have expired — they are, on the contrary, alive and well — but because the practical conditions that would bring them to our minds are, today, not accessible.[3]

Now I have no intention of turning this introduction into a companion of the *Arachin* essay. To grasp what I have in mind you are going to have to read the essay. But just as a little taste of what you can expect, I am going to quote a short piece from the Midrash Tanchuma on BeChukosai.

אמר להן הקב"ה לישראל אם אתם מביאין לפני ערכים שלכם מעלה אני עליכם **כאלו נפשותיכם הקרבתם לפני** לכך נאמר איש כי יפליא נדר אמר הקב"ה לישראל **בזכות הערכין אני מציל אתכם מגיהנם**. אמר להם הקב"ה לישראל הן מעריכין לפני את נפשותיכם אני מציל אתכם מעריכת גיהנם שנאמר (ישעיה ל) כי ערוך מאתמול תפתה. **ואערוך לפניכם שלחן הוא שאמר דוד תערוך לפני שלחן נגד צוררי דשנת בשמן ראשי כוסי רויה** (תהלים כג).

2. I know that the correct pronunciation is *arachin,* but it is also true that in the Yeshiva world it is almost universally pronounced *erchin*. I have decided to throw pedantry to the winds and will use the terms interchangeably. It is just easier that way. Let us all be relaxed and get on with the more important aspects of the issues.

3. See Rambam, Hilchos *Erchin* VeCharomim 8:8: **אין ... מעריכים ... בזמן הזה** שאין שם מקדש בחטאינו לחזק את בדקו ... ואם ... העריך ... (ו)היו מעות ... ישליכם לים הגדול ...

All this means that theoretically the monetary obligation that is part of the ערכין vow could be undertaken even today, but the money would have to be destroyed.

Under such circumstances, of course, no one would ever shoulder this vow and there would be absolutely no occasion for the video crew to film anything. Nevertheless, as the essay makes clear, the values that inhere in the mitzvah of *erchin* are fundamental and timeless.

Sounds pretty attractive, does it not? "Saved from Gehinom," "Invited to the Ribono shel Olam's table" above all, "Considered as having oneself been brought as a sacrifice."[4] All this for having simply gone through the *erchin* process. So there has got to be something else that happened to me. I have changed. I have somehow been able to touch a level of sanctity. Little I has somehow grown into a bigger "I"!

It is time to stop theorizing and to start thinking hard. We do not have *erchin* today. But as the Rambam explained it (please look back to footnote 3), that seems to be because the financial part of the transaction would not have any useful application. But might it not be that if I tried hard to understand what the person who says ערכי עלי really means with that proclamation, I could duplicate that even today. Not, of course, in any formal sense, but when we are really trying to better ourselves, who cares about formality? Is it perhaps in my power, even in this benighted[5] age, even for me who till now has lived a pretty benighted life, to haul myself up by my frayed bootstraps and achieve some measure of … what? I dare not even think. Of what … of what … of what … of what?

You get the idea. Look at one of the headings in the third chapter: "Meet My Friend the Beis HaMikdash *Yid*." Do you know a Beis HaMikdash *Yid*? Would you like to? What could these words possibly convey? To understand what this is all about, you have to have a visa to the world of *erchin*. That visa can be picked up at the third chapter.

Let us move on to chapter 2. The title of that essay makes the apparently audacious claim that there *is* such a thing as Creative Judaism. Before we begin to make our argument in favor of this claim I want to present to you my main source for this assertion. It comes in the S'fas Emes on Chanukah for the year תרמ"א. (Page 214 in my edition of the Bereishis volume.)

> חנוכה ופורים הם הארות מרגלים. רק הג' רגלים המפורשים בתורה הם תורה שבכתב. ויש נגד זה ג"כ רגלים מתורה שבע"פ. והם אורות המקבלים כדמיון אור הלבנה שהיא מאור החמה כידוע. כן ע"י כוחן של בנ"י בקבלתם היו"ט כראוי. נשאר מכל יו"ט רשימה בכנס"י. ובכח זה הוציאה כנגדן רגלים אחרים. וחנוכה

4. Maybe even considered to be an עולה תמימה, as Yitzchak was.
5. Dictionary definition: Ignorant. It is usually meant to describe a high (or perhaps it should be "low") level of ignorance. "Forget it. He just doesn't get it!"

הארה מחג הסוכות. ופורים מחג השבועות. ומחג הפסח מקוים אנו להיות עוד כמ"ש כימי צאתך מארץ מצרים אראנו נפלאות.

> Chanukah and Purim are reflections of the light emanating from two of the three pilgrim festivals that are explicitly mandated by the Torah.[6] These two are to be considered "Torah" as are those three but in contrast to those that have the status of *Torah SheBichsav, Written Torah* these are *Torah SheBeAl Peh, Oral Torah*. They are comparable to the light reflections that reach us from the moon of which the source is the sun.
>
> In precisely the same way *klal Yisrael* was able to receive the light of the *"Torah SheBichsav* ordained festivals" with so much native understanding and appreciation *that this light became a part of them thus that from within themselves they were now able to produce their own Torah, Chanukah and Purim.*

I think that with this quote the case is made so that we can now get on with our introductory remarks.

We will be thinking about two areas in which *klal Yisrael* reached the highest level of consummate creativity: (a) the establishment of Chanukah and Purim, the two Yamim Tovim that had their germination in the Jewish heart rather than in the written Torah, and (b) the ordinances concerning *Eiruvin* and *Netilas Yadayim,* the products of no less a mind than that of Shlomo HaMelech himself.[7] Along the way you will meet up

6. In the course of this passage the S'fas Emes mentions that Chanukah "springs" as it were from Succos and Purim, from Shavuos. Pesach, the S'fas Emes asserts, will produce its own "oral law" festival at the coming of Moshi'ach.

The reasoning behind all this is of course interesting in the extreme but is not important to us in the present context.

7. At this point a word is in place concerning Jewish creativity. I understand that among our fellow Yidden, our brothers and sisters, there are those who, be the cause what may, were never exposed to Torah. Their Jewish hearts yearn for closer ties to the Ribono shel Olam, but they have no idea what might constitute a truly Jewish expression of their longing. Their ideas for an appropriate statement must needs draw upon foreign assumptions that invariably disappoint.

That is not the "creativity" with which we are dealing here. As I was thinking how to express what I want to say here, it struck me that a *mashal* might be best.

Here goes: When I was in my early teens, one of the books that we read in the non-Jewish school that I attended during parts of the war was *The Black Tulip* by Alexandre Dumas. The plot is not interesting for us, but it revolved to some extent about a valuable prize that had been offered to any horticulturist who could produce a tulip the petals of which would be entirely black.

with some interesting discussions. We will be spending a little time on prepositions, a subject for which you have surely been yearning since your last grammar lesson in school. But, as they say: "This too shall pass."[8]

But, getting to the "meat" of the discussion, you will find some very important aspects of the mitzvah of *Hakhel*. In a way this mitzvah has much in common with the *Arachin* that we discuss in the third chapter. As is the case with *Arachin*, it is not performed in our times but nevertheless, as will become evident in our discussion, it deals with some important Jewish values. In the *Hakhel* section we will also be thinking about *Shemitah* and Succos so all in all the chapter should turn out to be rewarding.

Simply for the shock value, I considered the following wording for introducing the two *Ahavas HaShem* essays. *Another mitzvah that we do not fulfill today is Kri'as Shema* ... Such an opening would have been in terribly bad taste — Baruch HaShem we all recite the Shema twice daily (or, counting the Shema that we recite when going to sleep, three times) — and the sentence would have been manifestly ridiculous. So why did I contemplate writing it?

Well, I already said that it would have been for shock value. Now, what is *that* supposed to mean? Let me explain. We all know that certain props in our daily lives are so ubiquitous that, in practice, they become "invisible." By this I mean that they are so obviously "there" that their presence simply does not register on our minds. Do you remember seeing the fork you used last night at supper? The first *parshah* of *Kri'as Shema* is, from earliest childhood, so firmly imprinted on our minds that, unless we really work on it, it becomes something that just happens, without at all leaving any significant mark upon us.

Here is my *mashal*. Nobody, but nobody, tried growing his tulip in a coal bin instead of in the earth. The challenge called for botanical wizardry, not for stupidity. If you go to the coal bin, you end up with a chunk of coal that happened to be lying around there.

והמבין יבין!

8. As an aside, I would suggest that you read even this part of the essay carefully. The preposition that will interest us is בשביל (as in בשביל תורה and בשביל ישראל in the beginning of Bereishis). If you read that part, you will realize how careful one must be in translating from one language to another. I do not know whether what I wrote there is correct, but if it is, that would mean that a number of translations of the targeted Rashi got it wrong. הלא דבר הוא!

Here is a confession. If before I started writing these essays, someone would have asked me for the precise message that the first *parshah* of *Kri'as Shema* is supposed to deliver, I would, quite frankly, have been stumped. That is not because I cannot read or understand the words but because their cohesion simply escapes me. Of course I would have been able to count up the various *mitzvos* that are mentioned but would have been hard put to explain what each of them is really doing there.

Would you like to try your hand?

If you can find the energy to struggle through these two essays, that problem will (or, at least I hope it will) no longer plague you. Taken together, it is a pretty long piece that, incidentally, allows us to make several interesting ports of call along the way. What, for example, is the function of the בכל לבבך ... ובכל נפשך ... ובכל מאודך phrase? Does it define the mitzvah in the sense that if you cannot muster such inspiration you have not fulfilled the mitzvah, or does it fill some other purpose? And so on, and on, and on.

Come on! Dive in! The *Arachin* chapter invited us to meet the "Beis HaMikdash *Yid*." What about meeting the "Shema *Yid*" — in your own heart?

For *dikduk* devotees, there is an exciting passage in the second of the two essays. Just check out the subheading of that chapter: "The Grammar of Loving the Ribono shel Olam ... *Kal* and *Pi'el* Where It Really Matters." (Now comes the really important question: Will this information attract more or fewer readers? I hope that the answer is "more" — not so much because I would like people to enjoy my essays but because there is no disgrace in understanding basic *dikduk*. Those of you in whom the word generates instant recoil will be the worse for it. Even sadder, it is likely that such a negative attitude will also damage your children.)

The highlights of the two chapters on *Ahavas HaShem* will be the quotes from the RaMChal that are offered at the end of the second essay. They can really make a difference in our recitation of the Shema.

I cannot really claim that the first chapter of this section, "Looking Through the Frosted Window," is actually on a par with the earlier essays as I have presented them in this introduction. If you insist on formal parity, I would have to come up with something like this: The four other chapters were concerned with

Jewish viewpoints that are meant to contribute to greater כבוד שמים. Well, coping "Jewishly," that is, correctly, with the dreads of chronic pain, can certainly be subsumed under that heading.

But that is not the truth. The truth is that many years ago when I wrote this essay, I got feedback from a number of readers who were kind enough to let me know that they had felt themselves helped by the ideas in that essay. This book seemed an ideal venue in which to bring about a resurrection, and here it is.

I am going to end this introduction right here. Originally I had intended to write a preamble, similar to the ones you have just now been reading, on each of the remaining essays. I have decided against it. For the first five essays I had been afraid that the rather forbidding content might discourage some of you from plunging in. It was important for me to make the case that really they are quite user-friendly and, would you know it, informative and therefore useful.[9] The rest of the essays that deal with more familiar material — though from perspectives that I hope you will find new and exciting — will anyway not threaten.

Thank you all for coming along on the trip. For me it proved to be a major challenge. There was much that I had to learn, much that I had to unlearn. I cannot begin to tell you how many *sheimos* bags I filled along the way. However, in those bags there are many undeveloped ideas that, with loving nurturing, might well blossom into — dare I say it? — another book. Who knows?

In the meantime I will bid you all farewell in the words of the wonderful couple whom, as reported in Succah 52a,[10] Abbaye overheard as they bid each other good-bye after having traveled together for a while:

אורחין רחיקא וצוותן בסימא

We are going to have to part ways because
From here on we need to travel different roads.
It is a shame that we have to split up.
The company that we kept up to here was very sweet.

9. I was toying with another adjective, "enjoyable," but could not quite summon up the courage. Still, there is nothing wrong with hoping.
10. Take my advice. Look up that Gemara. It is very interesting.

PART I

Reaching Higher: Finding New Meanings in Some Very Old Ideas

1.

Looking Through the Frosted Window

WHEN THINGS ARE HARD TO SEE AND UNDERSTAND

SOME REFLECTIONS UPON CHRONIC PAIN

Thank God I do not write from experience.

This will certainly tend to attenuate my message. A great thinker once said that no theologian should be allowed to put pen to paper until he has spent six months in the cancer ward of a children's hospital. We can borrow his thought and say with equal justification that anybody who has not gone through the purgatory of chronic pain cannot really have much of significance to say on the subject.

True — but not completely true. And this for two reasons. First, the wider sweep of vision that distance makes possible can provide a sense of context and perspective that cannot be attained by the sharper, more focused picture painted in such vivid colors by the brush of experience. Second — and more important — it seems to me that the soil in which the seeds of understanding, comfort, and coping can germinate must be laid, and tilled, long before crisis sets in. All of us must learn to think and feel like an *ehrlicher yid*. After that, there are simply those who are tested and those who are not.

And God tests only those who can grow through the testing. They are the strong ones who have earned God's trust. They get to find out what the rest of us will never truly know. How theoretical were the theories upon which they have built their lives? How did their poetry translate into prose? How *ehrlich* is their *ehrlichkeit*?

Let us start, then, undeterred by our sense of inadequacy — which in the right place and at the right time can have its uses — to try to discover the components of a thought world that could lend us strength in our time of weakness, hope when our minds tell us to despair, and love when we find it hard to love — or even to care.

An Eved Does Not Set His Own Agenda: Many of life's frustrations come about when the goals we have set elude us. We have worked out a strict learning schedule that will enable us to finish a given *masechta* in a reasonable time — and a *meshulach,* who needs our help, knocks at the door. We have set aside an evening for quality time with our children — and some communal responsibility, which will brook no excuses, intrudes.

We become angry, guilt-ridden — and ultimately diminished.

It need not be so — indeed, it ought not to be so.

An *Eved* does not set his own agenda.

We are here to do not what we perceive to be important, but what God, through the workings of *hashgachah,* reveals to us to be our task.

A *mashal* of Rabbi Yisrael Salanter (quoted in *Maasay LaMelech, Chafetz Chaim al HaTorah, Ki Sissa*) comes to mind:

A king sent an ambassador to another country to perform a given task, adjuring him that under no circumstances was he to make a wager with anyone. When the ambassador was ready to go home, he went to say good-bye to the neighboring king who thanked him for his good offices. However, he had one question: Why was he subjected to the insult of having a hunchback assigned as ambassador to his court? The diplomat was aghast at the accusation and vehemently denied that he was a hunchback. The king insisted and declared his willingness to bet a million dollars that the ambassador was indeed malformed. The latter removed his shirt, showed that his build was perfectly normal, pocketed the million dollars, and returned home fully expecting to be rewarded for having enriched the royal treasury by such a large amount of money.

The king who had sent him was furious. He had made a ten-million-dollar wager with his neighbor that the ambassador would never remove his shirt.

The *nimshal* is clear enough.

Obviously such an attitude to life does not absolve us from making decisions. Our paths are not always clear, and often an array of choices leaves us thoroughly confused about what God really wants from us. But sometimes there simply are no alternatives. Then we are, so to speak, off the hook. We know exactly what it is that we have to do, and we can focus our minds to do it right.

There is no room for frustration — there is every need for concentration.

There is a correct way of serving God through bearing pain. It may prevent us from following courses that we had carefully plotted, from fulfilling plans that had been thoughtfully and lovingly laid.

But — it turns out — these were our plans, not God's. He has something else in mind for us. Resolutely, keeping our shirts on, we must change direction.

We may not know where the new road leads. But that need not really matter. We do what we are called upon to do. Obedience to a fate that we cannot alter — and ought not to want to alter (Bava Kama 38a)[1] — may be its own reward.

Losing Battles and Winning Wars: It is hard to be submissive. It is doubly hard when we are wracked by agonies that we don't really — can't really — believe we deserve.

Acute suffering can sometimes generate corrosive morbidity, or, equally bad, misplaced, and ultimately destructive, belligerence. Both are essentially healthy reactions taken to unacceptable extremes. The two may also combine and cause a disintegration of the sufferer's resources at the very moment at which he stands most in need of them.

The sequence goes something like this: I am suffering. Suffering is the wage of sin. So I must have sinned. But I know my friends and neighbors; I don't seem to be much worse — and am perhaps much better — than they are. Therefore I must be wrong. I did not understand myself at all. I am somehow evil, and though I don't *seem* to be worse than anyone else, there just *must* be some dreadful malignancy lurking within my most innocent acts of omission or commission. God must hate me. Why should I go on living?

Or: I am suffering. Suffering is the wage of sin. I have sinned and deserve to be punished. But this seems to me to be out of all proportion. Look at so and so. He, too, has sinned and seems to be doing just fine. Why me? God must hate me for no good reason. So I will repay hatred with...

1. A daughter of R. Shmuel bar Yehudah died. Some students suggested to Ullah that they should go together to comfort him. He refused: "Why would I want to get involved with comforting the Babylonians? It becomes an exercise in blasphemy. For they say, 'What can we do!' The implication is that if they could change what God had willed, they would do so."

Thus the two appear in their separate manifestations.

The combination is easy enough to figure out: I must be wicked, but something tells me that I am not. So I feel rebellious. But then I really *am* wicked. So now I am a rebel and God hates me. But that is not fair. He made me rebel, so how can He blame me? But isn't questioning God's justice the very acme of wickedness? I have sunk too low. I have failed. But have I?

The truth is that both guilt and questioning have their legitimate place. If we understand this, we will be able to use both of these reactions positively and will not distort them into the caricatures delineated above.

First we visit guilt.

Suffering must lead to introspection. There is nothing wrong with that, and everything right. When we fall victim to misfortune, we are to examine our actions closely. The likelihood is that we will not come up empty-handed. If we did, we are to assume that our commitment to Torah learning was not what it should have been (Berachos 5a).[2]

So, as a first step, we are to trace our problems to our shortcomings. It cannot be otherwise in God's world. But it is the possibility of *not* coming up with an answer that is significant. Our Chazal seem to accept that even earnest and honest self-analysis may not yield an explanation that satisfies. Even the ultimate and unfailing explanation offered by the Sages — our less than perfect commitment to Torah learning — has not, after all, marked our conscience. If it had, we would have discovered it as we examined ourselves in the first place.

Can it be that occasionally we will lack the wherewithal to recognize the justice of our fate? Yes.

We cannot, in the end, be what we are not. And if our sense of fairness is not developed enough to plumb the exquisite calibrations of God's justice, then we will simply have to remain with a question.

If the concept of "suffering equals sin" resonates within us, if we can discover our transgressions and have our agonies guide us

2. When we are called upon to suffer, we should search carefully through our actions ... If he searched but could not find any wrongdoing, he should assume that [the suffering results] from an insufficient commitment to Torah study. If he cannot find even this imperfection, then let him be aware that his suffering belongs to the category of *yisurim shel ahavah*.

toward a pure contrition, so much the better. If not, that, too, is part of living. We do not have to understand everything.

And now the confusion. The nagging and merciless "Why?" and the "Why me?" and the "Why anybody?" And the large and brooding question mark that hangs suspended over so much of human experience. All the hunger, all the sores, broken limbs, and broken spirits, the screams and the taunts, the lashes and the screw, the myriads of the poor and the writhing, the disenfranchised and the disheartened — all, all refracted, magnified, and focused through the prism of my own intolerable pain.

Is it all right to question?

Yes!

That is the short answer that the long and complex saga of Iyov teaches us. Iyov struggled and fought and challenged and asked, and asked, and asked, and asked some more. In the end God said that he spoke well — better than the hapless friends who thought they had all the answers (Iyov 42:7).

So, it is all right to ask.

But can this be true? Can unadulterated faith and dogged challenge coexist? What of the uncomplaining acceptance of God's decrees. What of *Tziduk HaDin*? What of *HaTzur Tamim Po'olo*? Was Aharon not silent in the face of unbearable loss?

We have said that it is all right to question — not that it is the only way. There is Aharon who kept silent, and there is Iyov who did not. There is Nachum Ish Gamzu who reveled in the sheer horrors of his destitution (Taanis 21a),[3] and there is Habakkuk who demanded an explanation for the chaos that he observed and for which he could find no excuses (Habakkuk 1:2–3).

It is all right to question, all right even to challenge, when

3. It is told of Nachum Ish Gamzu that he was blind in both eyes and had lost both his arms and both his legs. His entire body was covered by leprosy.

He lay in a shaky bed, the legs of which were placed in bowls of water so that the ants might not climb all over him.

Once, the house in which he lay was unsafe, so his students wanted to move him first so that his safety would be assured, and only then to take out the furniture. But he said, "Children! Take out the furniture and only then move me. Once you take me out, the house might come down and the furniture will be destroyed. But I am convinced that as long as I am in the house, it will not collapse." They moved out the furniture and then carried him out. Immediately, the house fell down.

After he had explained to the students why these terrible sufferings had overtaken him, they cried out, "Alas, that we have to see you thus."

He responded, "Woe to me if you had not seen me thus."

question and challenge are rooted in *emunah*. "You o God Who are ground of my being, focus of my longings, the life that quickens me, the warmth that suffuses me, my Father, my King, my only real reality, why are You so incomprehensible? How can I serve an enigma, how can I love a contradiction? How can I find You when, upon every approach that I attempt to make, You seem to recede further and further into inscrutable essence that brooks no familiarity. I so desperately want to fear You, want to love You. Can you not make fear and love more possible?"

It is never all right to rebel.

We can sometimes lose a battle but win a war.

We might wish, when we are plagued by questions, that our faith could be stronger, more pure, less subject to the roilings that are presently leaving us no peace. The Aharon mode might suit us better than that which Iyov legitimized.

But Iyov, in the end, met his God and found his vindication.

No small matter — that!

A Single Wish: Most of us have wondered at one time or another what our choice might be if some benign genie would pop out of a bottle and grant us a single wish.

What would we like more than anything else in the world?

I know what I would choose.

I would like to learn the art of concentration, to have the ability to focus upon some subject that is of significance to me. Not to be as helpless as I am in the face of the myriad, banal, and inconsequential stimuli that insist upon crashing my earnestly erected — and pathetically ineffective — defenses.

What could I not accomplish — if I could just learn discipline?

Do not stray after your hearts and after your eyes — so that you might remember. There it is. We won't remember until we learn the art of single-minded intensity. Our minds, our best intentions, and — sadly — our potential for achieving greatness lie, like so many dried and dead leaves, along the meandering paths gouged out indiscriminately by our messy thinking.

Pain focuses the mind.

Would-be comforters are not allowed to begin speaking to the mourner until he opens the conversation (Mo'ed Katan 28b). His mind is consumed by his sorrow. He cannot think of anything — may not wish to if he could. It is his prerogative to decide whether he wishes to be distracted or, indeed, relieved.

The source of this halachic ruling is the story of Iyov. When the friends came to see if they could help him in his dreadful travail, they sat by him for seven days without uttering a word. For seven days — seven days! — they must have watched him, single-mindedly engrossed in the contemplation of the sheer enormity of his suffering.

Seven days.

When life gets serious, the useless, the frivolous, even the merely dispensable, lose their attraction. They can no longer deflect our thinking.

The big issues, the significant and the elevating, loom large and occupy center stage.

It does not take much to change.

Eliezer ben Durdaya had frittered away an entire life. The filth in which he had wallowed, the morass of lust in which every last spark of humanity must have become submerged, defy the imagination — and certainly the vocabulary — of normalcy.

And one single focused thought, one flash of insight that something might yet be salvageable, created the *Rabbi* Eliezer ben Durdaya, the paradigmatic *ba'al teshuvah* who taught that it takes just one second to build an entire world (Avodah Zarah 17a).[4]

Chronic pain must be a dreadful burden to bear. But, viewed as challenge and opportunity, it may just be the genie in the bottle. *Happy is the man whom God chastises* (Psalms 94:12).

Living Life Seriously: The tanna R. Eliezer was a fighter in the epic mode. He fought his father that he might learn Torah. He fought the dreadful pangs of starvation as, unnoticed and uncared-for, he sat among the thousands of Rabbi Yochanan ben Zakkai's students (Pirkei d'Rabbi Eliezer HaGadol 1). He fought his colleagues for what he perceived to be the truth in the

4. It was said that R. Eliezer ben Durdaya had made a point (before he became a *ba'al teshuvah*) of visiting every single prostitute in the world. On one occasion he heard that there was a prostitute ... in some far-flung place. Immediately he obtained the money needed to engage her services and crossed seven rivers in order to reach her.

When he was finally with her, she derided him. His actions put him beyond the pale. He would never be able to do *teshuvah*.

Shocked at what he had heard, he cried bitterly until he sobbed his heart out and died.

A heavenly voice cried out, "*Rabbi* Eliezer ben Durdaya will make his way into *Olam HaBa*."

stupendous struggle surrounding the *tanur achnai* (Bava Metzia 59b),[5] and he fought the dreadful loneliness and bitterness of the years of ostracism that he suffered as a result (Sanhedrin 68a).

In the end, he fought the debilitation of his final illness.

Four of his students visited R. Eliezer as he lay on his deathbed, writhing in pain. Among them was R. Akiva. All needed to find some suitable words. What does one say at such a time?

The other three made their decision. They would vie with one another in their efforts to express their sense of impending loss: "You have meant so much to us. More than the rain drops." "... more than the sun." "... more than our very parents."

Rabbi Akiva would have none of this.

With rough and rugged disregard for the niceties, paying very short shrift to the embarrassment his friends might feel at his cavalier dismissal of their approach to the problem, he was short, brutally short, and to the point.

5. The issue was the status of a certain oven in relation to the laws of *tum'ah* and *taharah*. R. Eliezer held that it was *tahor* while all his colleagues ruled that it was *tamei*.

In a stirring confrontation R. Eliezer, refusing to bow to the majority opinion, put his ideas to the test. If he was right, the river flowing nearby was to move from its bed — and it moved. A nearby tree was to jump to another location — and it immediately became uprooted. And finally, the very walls of the Beis HaMidrash were to come to his aid. Ominously, they began to fall inward until — in what must surely be one of the most dramatic moments in the history of halachic discourse and discord — R. Yehoshua called out to them to desist. They had no business to become involved.

Unimpressed, the Sages continued staunchly to maintain the validity of their position.

The walls stopped falling, in obedience to R. Yehoshua's exhortation. They did not straighten up, in deference to R. Eliezer.

As a final resort, R. Eliezer now called for divine intercession. Even in this, he was answered. A heavenly voice called out, "Why do you argue with R. Eliezer, whose ideas invariably accord with the halachah!"

Once more, R. Yehoshua took up the cudgels, this time, as it were, against God Himself. "The halachah does not reside in heaven. The very *Bas Kol* has no halachic standing. We have a Torah and in it is written that the majority opinion prevails!"

The Gemara goes on to relate that R. Noson met Elijah the prophet and asked him what God did at that moment. How did He view R. Yehoshua's defiance?

Elijah answered that God smiled and declared: "My children have got the better of Me!"

Eventually in view of R. Eliezer's continued intransigence, the Sages felt constrained to pronounce a *cherem* against him.

I have chosen to tell this story in some detail in order to show just how mightily R. Eliezer was willing to fight for the truth as he perceived it.

"Suffering is precious!"

Rabbi Eliezer asked his attendants to sit him up, the better to be able to concentrate upon Rabbi Akiva's thought.

"What authority," he wanted to know, "can you adduce for your contention?"

Rabbi Akiva picked his way through a series of complex scriptural passages. His point, he demonstrated, is solidly grounded in the sources and is based upon the cleansing and atoning properties of pain (Sanhedrin 100a).

There is an almost surreal atmosphere to this scene. We can picture the rabbi on his deathbed, attendants and perhaps family hovering over him, waiting with dread foreboding for the inevitable end. He ignores them all, ignores death itself, and enters upon a discussion that might as well have taken place on a quiet afternoon in the Beis HaMidrash. R. Akiva has made an interesting observation. R. Eliezer is intrigued and would like to know its provenance. R. Akiva has all the time in the world to elaborate.

No sense of crisis, none of looming death and bereavement. And — most remarkably — the other friends, for all the attention that R. Eliezer pays to them, might as well not have existed.

For their sake, we are hurt. Would common thoughtfulness not demand that their distress somehow register with R. Eliezer? For that matter, should R. Akiva have rejected their thinking so bluntly?

We wonder what was going on in R. Eliezer's mind while his former students were singing — and sighing — his praises. What would have been his reaction if R. Akiva, too, had simply added another description of just how much he had meant to them all?

Perhaps for those few moments he, too, thought that the expression of these sentiments constituted an appropriate farewell. One can, one supposes, do worse than end a productive life with a fond review of significant achievements, of important and meaningful relationships.

R. Akiva's unadorned aphorism may have shocked him, too, as it surely shocked those others whose sentiments it so passionately disavows.

Suddenly a new dimension is introduced. There is not much time left. If suffering is precious, then I need to know, and to know well and clearly, how to mine it to the fullest. Why is it precious? How can it serve me? How can these last moments that are left to me on earth be made to yield their bounty to the fullest?

It is too late now to allow those others to bask one last time in the love of his attention. That would surely have been the instinct of the great Rebbi who had longed for so many lonely years that just these students would return to him (Sanhedrin 68a).[6] It is too late now for anything at all other than to live for the time that was left to him — and to live seriously.

If R. Akiva would be able to provide a source for his contention — and if that source would guide him on his final road, then R. Eliezer needed, and needed desperately, to know of it.

R. Akiva explained: Suffering can atone. Suffering can galvanize change. Understood correctly and utilized appropriately, it can rebuild shattered lives.

The Gemara does not report R. Eliezer's reaction to what R. Akiva told him. But we may surmise that it lent him the fortitude to win another, perhaps the last of his great battles. For a man who had built his life around the dictum that our friend's dignity should matter to us as much as our own (Avos 2:9),[7] it must have come hard to ignore his other three visitors as thoroughly as he did.

6. When R. Eliezer became sick, R. Akiva and his colleagues came to visit him. ... They sat down at a distance of four cubits [because of the *cherem* that had been imposed and made it impossible for them to come closer].

He asked, "Why have you come?"

They answered, "To learn Torah."

He asked, "And where have you been till now?"

They answered, "We were too busy."

He said, "I would be surprised if any of you will die a natural death."

So R. Akiva asked, "What will be my fate?"

He answered, "Yours will be harder than any of the others."

R. Eliezer placed his arms over his heart and moaned, "Alas! My two arms are like two Torah scrolls that have remained unopened. I have learned much Torah and I have taught much Torah. I have learned much Torah but took no more from my teachers than a dog might lap up from the sea. I have taught much Torah but my students took no more from me than a dropper might draw from a bottle."

The Gemara then continues with a description of R. Eliezer's death. The final moment came when his students asked him a question concerning the laws of *tum'ah* and *taharah*. He succumbed with the word *tahor* on his lips.

7. This is the first of three maxims that, as is reported in Avos, R. Eliezer thought to be fundamental.

Significantly, in old age, R. Eliezer seems to have adjusted this very extreme demand to some extent.

Berachos 28b tells that when his students came to visit him during his sickness, they asked him to instruct them in the path that would lead them to *Olam HaBa*.

But it had to be done. There simply was no time.

That, too, in the throes of dying, became for him one of life's struggles.

Suffering is precious, too precious to waste.

In the Thick of the Fray: What do we do about life's challenges?

David's prayer that God probe the mettle of his loyalty by exposing him to temptation (Psalms 26:2) is frowned upon by the Sages (Sanhedrin 107a).[8] Indeed, in our daily morning service we ask God not to put us to the test (ואל תביאנו לידי נסיון).

But — as the late Rav Hutner observed — David's ill-advised prayer was not expunged from Psalms.

Apparently, then, the longing to flex one's muscles in the service of God is legitimate.

But, our daily *tefillah* tells us otherwise.

Let us see what happens.

I take out my Tehilim before *Shacharis* and, with feeling and fervor, join David in his prayer: בחנני ה' ונסני, *Challenge me, o HaShem, and put me to the test!* Then I open my siddur and pray — as earnestly — ואל תביאנו ... לידי נסיון, *Do not expose us ... to a test.*

Which do I mean?

Both, says Rav Hutner.

Each sentiment, taken alone, is *treif*. As they interplay with each other, a balance emerges that helps us cope with life's exigencies.

Of course one who loves God would want to demonstrate his loyalty by plunging into the thick of every fray. But that urge must be tempered by a sober awareness of what failure would mean. Of course, one who fears God trembles at the thought of

Once more he had three pieces of advice to proffer. Once more the first concerned the need to be considerate of others.

But this time he did not demand that another's dignity should matter as much to ourselves as our own. He asked only that we always take care not to offend against the respect due to another.

8. David had asked God why He identifies Himself as the "God of Abraham, Isaac, and Jacob" but not as the "God of David." God answers that whereas the Patriarchs had been tested and proved, David had not. Immediately David asked that he, too, should be exposed to a situation that would probe the mettle of his loyalty.

The story of Bas Sheva, in which David fell short of the standards expected of him, came about as a result of that request.

being seduced by the siren song of sin. What if he will prove to be too weak and uninspired? On its own, such cold and restrained calculation would drain the religious life of much of its music. Somehow, somewhere, there must be room to ignite a passion, to nourish a hope that perhaps temptation will come his way — and that he prove to be equal to its blandishment.

Thus does the symbiosis of the two attitudes function — affecting practice not at all. We do not seek to expose ourselves to battle — we are afraid of failure; but we will not shirk it when we are called — we crave the heady sense of service loyally performed.

Here's the challenge of dealing with life's challenges. When we are called, when *hashgachah* has placed us in the front lines, then the timid, אל תביאנו ... לידי נסיון becomes — for this context — inoperative, and the robust, exhilarating בחנני ה' ונסני may be engaged unimpeded.

Each dull, debilitating, draining throb of pain becomes a prod, urging us on to greatness. Each momentary sense of helplessness and hopelessness becomes a depressed spring, hoarding the energy that will propel us onward and upward.

Chovos HaLevavos (Ahavas HaShem 1) tells of a chasid who used to get up in the night and say:

> My God. You have starved me and left me naked, have made me dwell in the night's worst darkness, making me experience both Your might and Your greatness.
>
> Were You to burn me in fire it would only increase my love for You and the joy that I feel in You.

Quite clearly, pain, even chronic pain, can have its uses.

2.

Yes, There Is Such a Thing as "Creative Judaism"[1]

(NOW WHAT COULD THIS POSSIBLY MEAN?)

Once we have the Succah packed away we face a rather drab winter season ahead of us; Tu BiShvat hardly seems to count.[2] Baruch HaShem for Chanukah and Purim! Where would the winter months, be without them? Hey! Just a moment! Where would we *takke* be without them? How did *klal Yisrael* face the winter *before* Mordechai and Esther set us straight in Shushan, and *before*, many years later, the Chashmona'im pronounced their defiant "No!" to the aggressive Hellenistic juggernaut?

Here is what we are really asking. Does the "year" as handed to us by the Ribono shel Olam not seem lopsided in the extreme? Every one of our special days, Pesach, Shavuos, Rosh HaShanah and Yom Kippur, Succos and Shmini Atzeres, jostles for space between Nisan and Tishrei. From Marcheshvan to Nisan — nothing!

Why?

1. The term "Creative Judaism" carries some unfortunate associations in our often benighted society and we are going to have to distance ourselves from those. There are many good Jewish people who yearn for closeness to the Ribono shel Olam but have never been exposed to the Torah. With nowhere to turn for authentically Jewish inspiration they come up with artificial usages that help them not at all. (See Yeshaya 2:6, ובילדי נכרים יספיקו, *they find a modicum of satisfaction by adopting alien customs.*)

Here is a *mashal*: As a youngster attending a non-Jewish school during the war, I was given the task of reading Dumas' *The Black Tulip*. Central to the book's plot was an offer of a grand prize for a gardener who would be able to produce a tulip all of whose petals would be black. I do not really remember much of what the book was about, but I am quite sure that not a single contestant decided to try to grow his tulip in the coal-seam of a mine instead of in the earth. The challenge called for horticultural finesse, not for stupidity.

והמבין יבין.

2. But see *Our Cousins the Trees* also in this volume.

Back in the fifties there was a popular children's book called *A Hole is to Dig*. It was written by a kindergarten teacher who was amused by the way her little charges tended to define the everyday objects with which they came into contact. She jotted their ideas down and, Behold! A best-seller children's book was born. Here, somewhat late, is a contribution that I would have made:

A Space is to Fill.

I will argue that the empty winter months were just that: "empty", so that we, *klal Yisrael*, would be able to "fill" them with Yamim Tovim of our own. By leaving us that space, the Ribono shel Olam was hinting that he wanted us as partners in building the structure of the Jewish year.

Let me explain. We are going to be taking a bit of a detour but it is going to be worth our while. The ultimate purpose of all this is to uncover some aspects of Judaism of which we usually do not hear very much. It concerns our (*klal Yisrael's*) mandate to engage in creative Judaism. By the time that we get to the end of this essay you will have a better idea of what I mean with this strange idea.

Let us get going.

We will be studying a piece of the Maharal right at the beginning of the Gur Aryeh on the very first word in the Torah. You all will certainly recall that Rashi takes the ב in the word בראשית as standing for בשביל, thus, ב - ראשית = בשביל "ראשית" which, in turn, means that "heaven and earth" were created "בשביל" the Torah and Israel.

EXCURSUS

At this point we are going to have to enter the exciting world of prepositions. I can almost hear you groaning as the memories of endless excruciatingly boring grammar lessons come back to haunt you. That's O.K. I can sympathize. It takes boundless commitment and love on the part of the teacher to make the study of the "parts of speech" interesting and enjoyable. Maybe you just did not luck out. The truth, though, is that grammar can be a lot of fun and, as we shall very shortly discover, correct application of its arcane rules can almost literally move worlds.

So what is a preposition?

The *Chicago Manual of Style* offers: "A preposition is a word or phrase that links an object (a noun or noun equivalent) to another word in the sentence to show the relationship between them." Now clearly there are very many different kinds of relationships and we can therefore anticipate that there are many different prepositions. For prepositions that consist of a single word the Manual lists nineteen examples: *as, at, by, down, for, from* and the like. For reasons that will soon become clear, we will center upon what the Manual calls, *phrasal prepositions,* prepositions that consist of entire phrases. Examples are, *for the sake of, in accordance with, in addition to,* and the like.

Let us remember where we are heading. We are grappling with the Chazal that maintains that God created heaven and earth **בשביל** התורה שנקראת ראשית **ובשביל** ישראל שנקראו ראשית. According to our definition "בשביל" is clearly a preposition that relates the noun ראשית (standing for Torah and Yisrael) to ברא אלהים את השמים ואת הארץ. How are we to understand בשביל in this context?

* * *

With a certain degree of trepidation I decided to look at the offerings of the various English translations that were accessible to me. In a rare show of unanimity they all used "*for the sake of.*" The message appears to be that God created the world *for the sake of* Torah and Yisrael.

There are two reasons that persuade me to question this rendering. In the first place I do not really understand what might be meant by such a statement. Certainly בשביל can convey the idea "for the sake of" when the context is right. For example, when Berachos 58a reports that a grateful guest ought to compliment his host by saying כל מה שטרח לא טרח אלא **בשבילי**, that is precisely what he means. My host worked long and hard, for no other reason than that I should enjoy a tasty meal (that is, for "my sake"); he himself could have made do with much simpler fare. But, in what sense does the Torah benefit (the Torah's "sake") from the creation of "heaven and earth"? What can possibly be meant by asserting that heaven and earth were created "for the sake" of Torah?

Moreover, and this is my second point, It is very clear to me that the Maharal in Gur Aryeh and also in the Nesiv HaTorah[3] does not agree with this translation. Here is a quote from the relevant passage from the Gur Aryeh.

> אמנם עיקר סוד זה מה שנברא **בשביל** התורה הוא כי ראשית כל הבריאה היא התורה שהיתה נבראת קודם שנברא העולם אלפיים [שנה] (ב"ר ח, ב), ... **ומפני שהתורה היא ראשית הכל ממנה נשתלשל הכל, ובשביל זה בשבילה נברא הכל**, כמו האילן שהוא נטוע אינו גדל רק **בשביל** העיקר שהוא ראשיתו **ובשבילו גדל**,
> ומכל מקום **תכלית גידול שלו להוציא פירות**, ובשביל תכלית זה גדל וצמח, שאם אין הפרי שיצא בסוף לא היה גדל, וזה הוא שגורם גידול שלו,

[I am going to offer a paraphrase rather than a translation. I care very much that Maharal's thinking should come across clearly and the style of his writing simply does not lend itself to a smooth English translation.]

If, as is indeed the case, it is accurate to say that a tree develops בשביל its roots, and this because the roots appear before anything else and therefore the entire tree develops out of the potential that is contained in the roots, so too it can be said that heaven and earth developed בשביל the Torah that preceded everything else by two thousand years. The Torah is, so to speak, a kind of blueprint that determined the nature of the "heaven and earth" that God would create.

Nevertheless the *purpose* (תכלית) of the tree (for *whose sake* the tree was planted) is the fruit that will eventually grow on the tree. It is only in anticipation of this fruit that the tree was planted. There is no doubt that the fruit and nothing else is the *cause* of the tree — is that for whose *sake* the tree was planted.

Maharal makes it very clear that בשביל העיקר does not mean that it was for the *sake* of the roots that the tree was planted but that it was for the sake of the fruit. So "בשביל התורה" which he compares to בשביל העיקר cannot be translated as for the sake of the Torah. בשביל התורה as the Maharal understands it, can only

3. Here is a short excerpt from that passage:

ואם כן דברי תורה מחזקים ותומכים הכל עד שיש לעולם קיום, וכל זה מפני כי התורה היא סדר האדם באיזה מעשה יהיה נוהג ואיך יהיה מסודר במעשיו וזהו ענין התורה. וכמו שהתורה היא סדר האדם, **כך התורה היא סדר של העולם עד שהתורה היא סדר הכל**, רק כי סדר האדם הוא נגלה ומפורש בתורה, כי אי אפשר זולת זה כי על האדם מוטל לשמור את הסדר הראוי לו ולכך הדבר הזה נגלה במפורש לאדם, אבל סדר כל העולם כולו גם כן הוא בתורה **שאין התורה רק סדר מציאות העולם בכללו.** וזה שאמרו במדרש (ב"ר פ"א) שהיה מביט בתורה וברא את עולמו.

mean precisely what בשביל העיקר would mean in the *mashal* of the tree. As the tree develops "in accordance" with the needs (the "blueprint") contained in the roots, so too God created heaven and earth in accordance with the plans that the Torah lays down for the world.[4]

[Please do not be surprised that I am claiming such versatility for בשביל. My אבן שושן dictionary brings five disparate meanings with examples and obviously where there are five there can also be many more as people make use of this very handy little preposition.]

Here are the five:

1. למען: The well-beloved, "For the sake of ..." from Shabbos 2:5: המכבה את הנר ... בשביל החולה שיישן.
2. בגלל: "As a result of ..." from Rashi to Yeshayahu 2:6: עזבת את עמך בשביל עוונם.
3. בעבור: (Perhaps only in modern Hebrew) "For ..." נתקבל מכתב בשביל מר וכו'.
4. "To": from Rashi to Eicha Rabosi 2:10: ושלח בשביל סנהדרין ובאו לקראתו.
5. "So that": (Pesachim 7:*) שורפין אותו לפני הבירה בשביל ליהנות מעצי המערכה.

Very clearly there is what seems to be an almost unlimited range.]

It is time to turn to the בשביל ישראל clause. We recall from earlier in this essay that there can be as many meanings to a preposition as there are relationships between units. Accordingly we will not be surprised if, as we shall soon see, the meaning of the second בשביל is entirely different from that of the first. We argued that the first בשביל meant that the way the Ribono shel Olam created the world accorded with the value system of the Torah. The Torah determines how the world is to function. Clearly, without a lot of mental gymnastics involving a lot of huffing and puffing that is not going to fit comfortably with בשביל ישראל. We are going to have to come up with something new.

So what did Chazal have in mind when they said that the Ribono shel Olam created the world "בשביל ישראל"?

4. It is of interest to note that Daas Zekeinim MiBa'aley Hatosfos reads "ב"זכות התורה instead of בשביל התורה.

The Maharal in the Gur Aryeh on the first *pasuk* of the Torah will help.

> בשביל ישראל והתורה. בב"ר (א, ד). ויראה לומר מה שנברא העולם בשביל אלו ב' דברים, דכתיב (משלי טז, ד) "כל פעל ה' למענהו", רוצה לומר כל מה שנברא בעולם בשביל הקב"ה נברא ולכבודו נבראו (יומא לח.), "כל הנקרא בשמי לכבודי בראתיו" (ר' ישעיה מג, ז),
>
> ואין כבוד מן הנבראים אלא כאשר יקיימו את מצוותיו ועובדים אותו, ואין זה רק באומה הישראלית, ועליהם נאמר (שם שם, כא) "עם זו יצרתי לי תהלתי יספרו", שלכך יצרתי אותם כדי שיספרו תהלתי.

Here is a short paraphrase: Yeshayahu 43:7 makes very clear that the Ribono shel Olam created this world "for His sake".[5] That purpose will come to fruition through *klal Yisrael* (עם זו יצרתי לי תהלתי יספרו).[6]

Here are the implications: Yisrael, from the very beginning, held and holds the key to the full realization of God's dream. The בשביל in the phrase, בשביל ישראל שנקראו ראשית does not mean, "For Israel's sake". It means "To provide Israel with the necessities required for fulfilling its creative purpose — the propagation of כבוד שמים.

Now what?

Here is what we are going to do. We are going to spend a little while thinking about a truth that we all know but which most of us (including me until very recently) do not do much about. Here is that truth. Yidden are bound by all manner of *mitzvos*. Some are דאורייתא, that is, that they are more or less directly[7] derived from the Torah text, and some are דרבנן,[8] meaning that they

5. Things are going to get a tiny bit confusing here. When the Maharal uses the expression בשביל in the phrase רוצה לומר כל מה שנברא בעולם **בשביל** הקב"ה נברא he *takke* means "for His sake". But don't allow that to make you nervous. It is just a coincidence. As we get around to "בשביל ישראל" it will be crystal clear that that "בשביל" means something entirely different. Sorry about that.

6. Please absorb the implications of this short verse with great and serious *kavanah*! It may well be the most important sentence that you will ever, throughout your life, read. God created *klal Yisrael* for only one reason! That their life in this world, their actions and their attitude, will infuse our physical world with as much sanctity and awareness of the Ribono shel Olam as it is able to project while still remaining what it is — a physical world!

7. I use this expression because not all Torah *mitzvos* are spelled out directly in the text. Some are derived from the מדות שהתורה נדרשת בהן.

8. An example is the obligation to wash our hands (as specified in *Halachah*) before we eat bread. See Rambam *Hilchos Berachos* 6:1. See there, *Halachah* 2: [ש]זו מצות חכמים היא שנצטוינו בתורה לשמוע מהן.

were enacted by various rabbinic authorities. In practice both are binding and while there are some hierarchical differences between the two, these impinge only rarely on practical living.

Instead of bundling all d'Rabanan *mitzvos* together I would like to attempt some (by no means complete) categorization. Please understand that this classification is in no way a formal one. To the best of my knowledge no such differentiation between various levels is recorded anywhere. It is simply an informal attempt to make all of us aware that there are indeed gradations; something that can lead to some interesting insights as we shall try to demonstrate.

Representative of the first group, the one that is least groundbreaking, involves the taking of the ארבעה מינים, the *four species*, on Succos. In the Beis HaMikdash this was done on each of the seven days of the Yom Tov (ושמחתם לפני י' **שבעת ימים**) while beyond its boundaries the obligation was limited to the first day only (ולקחתם לכם **ביום הראשון**). After the Temple was destroyed R. Yochanan ben Zakkai ordained that henceforth the "seven day" performance of the mitzvah was to be universal זכר למקדש, as a memorial to the heady days of joy that animated the people while the Beis HaMikdash still stood in all its glory.

That is a *mitzvah d'Rabanan* that is easy enough for us to grasp. Nothing really new had to be established. The ארבע מינים were the same as had always been used; the change to seven days even outside the Beis HaMikdash was also not breaking really new ground. There was after all the precedent of the Beis HaMikdash where the seven day schedule had been standard. It made sense to try and commemorate, or perhaps even reenact, the joy that had been expressed on Succos in the wonderful "pre-churban" days. In short, this d'Rabanan conserves rather than innovating. The "חדוש" element seems to be simply a minor shift of already existing concepts.

I am inclined to list *d'Rabanans* such as מוקצה מחמת איסור as the next level. Here there is no doubt that Chazal created a category (מוקצה) that had not existed before. However, the idea of staying away from even the permitted in order to avoid the forbidden has clear sanction in Torah law, specifically in the *parshah* of *Nezirus*. *He who witnessed the disgrace of the Sotah should distance himself from wine by vowing to become a* Nazir (Berachos 63a and elsewhere) or, "Keep your distance" we say to the Nazir. "Take the longer route! Do not come anywhere near to the the vineyard!" (Shabbos 13a and elsewhere).

D'Rabanans such as these fit comfortably into the maxim taught by the אנשי כנסת הגדולה that we are to *build a fence around the Torah* (Avos 1:1).

From these two rather simple examples I would like to move on to two others[9] that seem to go far beyond what we have seen till now. I would like to consider Shlomo HaMelech's ordinances of נטילת ידים, ערובין and שניות (see note 9).

Here is a passage from Shabbos 14b.

> אמר רב יהודה אמר שמואל בשעה שתיקן שלמה עירובין ונטילת ידים יצתה בת קול ואמרה בני אם חכם לבך ישמח לבי גם אני (משלי כג:טו) ...
>
> R. Yehudah taught in Shmuel's name: When Shlomo HaMelech ordained the concepts of Eiruvin and Netilas Yadayim a heavenly voice came forth and said, "My son, if your heart has found wisdom, My heart too will be gladdened." (Mishley 23:15) ...

It sounds a little strange, does it not? There are hundreds of Rabbinic ordinances concerning all kinds of issues. Why is it that just these two (see note 9), promulgated by Shlomo HaMelech, merit such an enthusiastic heavenly endorsement?

Then there is the use of "גם" in the phrase, ישמח לבי **גם** אני? It is my impression that often גם implies a subordinate position. Let us take a phrase with which we are all familiar, **וגם** חרבונה זכור לטוב. The idea expressed in that phrase is that while only Mordechai deserves a full "ברוך" for his prime role in the Purim story a level of recognition to which Charvonah cannot aspire, he nevertheless deserves honorable mention, a kind of bronze medal. Clearly the use of "גם" in this context shows that Charvonah was no more than a bit-actor in the story of Israel's salvation.

Actually we do not have to wait for Purim. Right at the beginning of Chumash we have ותתן **גם** לאישה **עמה** ויאכל. That "עמה" leaves no doubt at all as to who is the main player in that dreadful

9. Things get a little confusing here. Shlomo HaMelech is really associated with *three* ordinances, *Eiruvin, Netilas Yadayim* and *Sheniyos*. There are occasions upon which only the first two, not the third, are mentioned. Tosafos (Eiruvin 21b) suggests that the *Sheniyos* ordinance may have been made later than the first two. In any case whatever we will be saying about the first two will be applicable also to the third.

drama. See Rashi there. *She shared the fruit with him so that he should not remain alive and marry another woman after Chavah will have died because of her transgression*. And Rashi does not leave it there. He continues: "וגם לרבות כל בהמה וחיה" *Even the animals were invited to enjoy the illicit feast*! After thinking about these Rashis we will be awake to the implications of Metzudos' language: אז ישמח לבי **גם** אני **כשמחת לבבך** הואיל ומידי באה לך החכמה. The Ribono shel Olam is telling Shlomo HaMelech that He will join him in *his* joy. Apparently the Ribono shel Olam's joy will be subordinate to that of Shlomo HaMelech (כשמחת לבבך). Now what can that possibly mean?

Now even if we admit that not every גם carries such a subordinate implication and that is certainly the case, it still does not explain the use of this term in our verse. What, as Metzudos explains it (הואיל ומידי באה לך החכמה), does it really add to anything?

I have some suggestions to make. They are my own in the sense that I could not find any *meforshim* who deal with these issues. These thoughts will have to stand or fall on their own merits.

Eiruvin 21b describes Shlomo HaMelech's innovations as follows:

> אמר עולא אמר רבי אליעזר בתחילה היתה תורה דומה לכפיפה שאין לה אזנים עד שבא שלמה ועשה לה אזנים.
>
> Ullah taught in R. Eliezer's name, "Before [Shlomo HaMelech promulgated his ordinances], the Torah could have been described as a heavy basket that was not outfitted with handles. Shlomo's accomplishment was that he fitted it with handles.

What could Ullah have meant with his metaphor? Let us postulate that he understands the efficacy of forbidding שניות because people would realize that if even a woman who is more distantly related to me than is the actual ערוה is forbidden, then certainly the ערוה herself would be forbidden, then how is this illustrated by the example of the כפיפה priding itself on its new handles? In what sense can it be said that the שניה is a "handle" for the ערוה?[10]

I discussed this question with several friends and colleagues and some of them tried, with the aid of many fiercely

10. Here is Rashi to Yevamos 21a: אזנים של קופה לאחוז בהן הקופה ומשתמרת שלא תפול, ה"נ ע"י שניות מתרחקין מן הערות.

gesticulating thumbs, to show that, indeed, a שניה would make a wonderful "handle" for a basket (!). The sad news is that they left me, and I think also themselves thoroughly unconvinced. But even if they were right, even if the metaphor were eminently apropos, it would not explain why a metaphor was needed in the first place. What does this one teach us that we could not have understood without it?

I want to take a moment to discuss the idea of making a *fence* around the Torah (ועשו סייג לתורה, Avos 1:1). The Vilna Gaon in his commentary to Pirkei Avos makes it his business to find Torah sources for the teachings that are recorded there in the various *Mishnayos*. For ועשו סייג לתורה he cites *pesukim* like ואל אשה בנדת טומאתה לא תקרב which besides forbidding actual intimacy with a נדה also prohibits קרבה, (from ק ר ב *to approach*) physical contact of any kind. He brings another example from the *halachos* governing *nezirus* that besides forbidding the drinking of wine prohibit even the drinking of any liquid in which grapes have been steeped (וכל משרת ענבים, BeMidbar 6:3).

It seems to me that שניות would not fall into the same category as the Gra's two examples. It is easy to see that קרבה to a particular woman might lead to intimacy *with her* or that a delicious grape juice might persuade one to have some wine. Wine, after all, is universally available and the chances for slip-ups are high. But how would intimacy with a woman who falls into the category of שניה entice the man into approaching a *different* woman, a woman, please note, of whom in the entire world there is only one?[11]

I wish to argue as follows: If making a סייג for the Torah consists of forbidding an otherwise permitted x because were x not to be proscribed it would likely *lead to a clearly barred y*, then, as we have just explained, שניות would not fall into the category of סייג. There seems to me to be no reason at all to assume that intimacy with a lesser ערוה should result in intimacy with the ערוה.

[My contention will be that, as Ullah explains it, Shlomo HaMelech's ordinances do not fall into the "סייג" category, at least to the extent that סייג is to be defined as x leading to y.

11. Let us take אם אמו as an example. Rashi at Yevamos 21a writes, אמו כתיבה בתורה וגזרו רבנן על אם אמו **כדי שלא יפגע באמו**. How likely would that be?

Moreover look at Sanhedrin 103b: כי הוא אמון בא על אמו ...אמרה לו אמו "כלום יש לך הנאה ממקום שיצאת ממנו?" אמר לה "כלום אני עושה אלא להכעיס את בוראי?"

Here an entirely different psychological impetus is involved as we shall see.]

Here is what I think that Ullah is teaching us:

It seems to me that it would be logical to assume that all the three new concepts that Shlomo HaMelech promulgated, Eiruvin to protect Kedushas Shabbos, Netilas Yadayim to protect the taharah of Terumah and שניות to protect the sanctity of marriage, would all be based upon the same theory.[12] That theory postulates that the more widespread the appreciation of the value of exalted living would spread among the people, the more conscientious would be their attachment to their own and their community's sacred standards. The requirement that an *Eiruv* would need to be erected where earlier none had been required, that a degree of spiritual uncleanliness would attach to our busy hands that would have to be removed before partaking of a meal, and that even a whiff of incestuous impropriety would henceforth stand in the way of what had earlier been a perfectly acceptable matrimonial relationship, would bring us all face to face with the beauty of self-control, the first rung on the long, steep ladder that ultimately leads to the world of the sacred.

Da'as HaKohol, communal sensitivity will make sure that the road to the real ערוה will remain blocked. Shlomo HaMelech had wrought a miracle. He had created a communal ambiance that would protect the ערוה from violation more efficiently than would a platoon of soldiers.[13]

Before Shlomo HaMelech had forbidden שניות the ערוה in a particular case would have been an isolated problem known to only a few people and easily overlooked. Once she had become a part of a large group of people, all disqualified by certain familial ties, not as close as hers but, under the new standards still

12. This although Rashi is careful in his language at Eiruvin 21b: ,ועשה לה אזנים **שתקן** עירובין וידים **וגזר** על השניות.

13. I cannot say with absolute certainty that what I have suggested is a paraphrase of what Rashi tells us at the bottom of Eiruvin 21b ד"ה ועשה לה אזנים. However, a phrase that Rashi uses, seemingly without being absolutely *forced* to do so, persuades me that we are at the very least, not very far apart.

Here is Rashi's wording: ... וע"י כך **אוחזין ישראל במצוות שנתרחקו מן העבירה** כדרך שנוח לאחוז בכלי וכו' I do believe that the language seems to back me up. What do you think?

significant, this entire cohort (the ערוה included) had become the "elephant" in the room that could not be ignored.

The cumbersome basket (the ערוה) had finally been endowed with handles (all the other people in that cohort). These handles would create a well-known and well-loved context that would enable the ערוה to be lifted on high for all to see. The wall of the sacred would be safe. It would not be breached.

Here, as I understand it, are the answers to the questions that I posed earlier in this essay. 1. Why were just these ordinances left to Shlomo HaMelech more than were the many other rabbinical ordinances that dot our Shulchan Aruch? 2. Why did these ordinances, more than any others, deserve the accolade of being endorsed by the heavenly voice? 3. Why the bothersome "גם" that seems to ascribe a "subordinate" role to the Ribono shel Olam in this matter.

The first question: Shlomo HaMelech's Involvement:

The thesis that we have worked out above, postulates that the three ordinances associated with Shlomo HaMelech work differently from the regular סייגים instituted by Chazal. The regular סייגים prohibit an in itself inoffensive x so that a forbidden y might not be compromised.[14] Shlomo HaMelech took a broader view. He dealt with the כלל rather than with the פרט. He instituted entirely new halachic concepts (an עירוב and נטילת ידים) that were designed to raise awareness of the sacred among the people thereby generating an ambiance within which abuses of the Torah's standards simply would not occur.

That is what Jewish kings are supposed to do and it was just Shlomo who was most particularly associated with this task.[15]

14. Remember from earlier in this essay the examples that the Vilna Gaon to Pirkei Avos offers for עשו סייג לתורה. One was the Torah's insistence that קרבה to an ערוה be avoided because it might lead to intimacy, and that the Nazir is forbidden to drink any kind of grape juice in order to make sure that his drinking would not progress towards drinking wine.

15. See Maharsha to Sotah 40b:

> ושם ישב דוד לפני ה' גו' והענין כי מקום המשכן והמקדש **הוא כסא ה'** כדכתיב **אוה למושב** וכו' **לו** ולמלכות בית דוד קרי הכתוב כסא ה' כמ"ש בד"ה **וישב שלמה על כסא ה'**:

The explanation for the fact that Dovid was allowed to sit in that part of the Mishkan that was later, once the Beis HaMikdash was to be built, to be designated as the Azarah derives from the fact that the Beis HaMikdash, as a whole, is the Ribono shel Olam's throne. This is based on Tehilim 132:13, כי בחר ה' **בציון** אוה **למושב** לו, *For HaShem chose Zion (the Temple), He craved for it as His throne.*

EXCURSUS

The task of this Excursus is to give a solid body to the claims that I have just made in the preceding paragraph. I have chosen to put this material into an Excursus in order to make life a little easier for you, dear Reader. I suggest that for the time being you skip this Excursus and move on with the rest of the essay. I am sure that you will feel less guilty for skipping a passage that, when all is said and done is "only" an Excursus and not a formal part of the essay.

The truth is that I am torn. Should I argue "pro" or "con" skipping? The information contained in this Excursus is, I believe, priceless. On no account should it be lost. On the other hand, there is the real danger that, if you read it now you will get caught up in its beguiling world and forget altogether about finishing the essay. After all the effort that you invested to get up to this point that would be a real shame.

Here is my suggestion: Skip it for now and get to the end of the essay so that you will have the satisfaction of having a דבר שלם under your belt. That done take a little break and then tackle the Excursus. You will not regret the time that you spend on it.

Once you have done all that you will really have a complete picture of the territory that we have covered in this essay.

Here goes:

I venture to propose that the mitzvah of *Hakhel,* to which we are introduced at Devarim 31:10-13, ought to be viewed as the most exalted Jewish experience ever. There is simply nothing that compares to it. Let us trace the details in the Rambam in the third *perek* of Hilchos Chagigah (Sefer Korbonos).

Here is part of *halachah* 1.

> מצות עשה להקהיל כל ישראל אנשים ונשים וטף בכל מוצאי שמיטה בעלותם לרגל ולקרות באזניהם מן התורה פרשיות שהן מזרזות אותן במצות ומחזקות ידיהם בדת האמת וכו'
>
> אימתי היו קורין במוצאי יום טוב הראשון של חג הסכות שהוא תחילת ימי חולו של מועד של שנה שמינית וכו'

We are commanded to gather all Israel, men, women and children during the year immediately following the

Moreover we find Shlomo HaMelech's throne designated as *HaShem's throne* (I Divrei HaYamim 29:23, וישב שלמה על כסא ה', *Shlomo took over the throne of HaShem).*

> *Shemitah* year, as the people come up for the pilgrim festival of Succos. We are to read to them from the Torah such sections as animate them to fulfill the commandments with alacrity and encourage them in their practice of the true faith …
>
> When is this reading to take place? After nightfall of the first day of Succos, that is at the very beginning of חול המועד …[16]

Let us pay careful attention to the timing of this observance. It is to be performed on the first day of Chol HaMo'ed Succos just a couple of weeks after we have made our final farewells to the *Shemitah* year that ended with Rosh HaShanah. Can a more holy moment in the Jewish experience be imagined? Remember that the Torah postulates an agrarian society tied by a thousand bonds to field and vineyard. The seventh year arrives, Hoes and shovels are stacked away; the fields lie fallow and silent. The entire economy goes, so to speak, into hibernation, not just for the winter months but for an entire year. From beginning to end the enterprise is manifestly ridiculous; it is an act of national suicide and is not to be taken seriously. From our enlightened twenty-first century perspective it can safely be relegated to one of the many, many slagheaps of history.

"True" or "not true"?

"True" of course! The whole exercise makes no sense.

Well it doesn't, does it?

So why does it?

As he does so often, the S'fas Emes is going to help us through this muddle. We will quote him a few lines down but before we get to him we need to get familiar with the background upon which he bases his thought. We will visit the last few lines of Tehilim 103 and see what the midrashim do with them.

16. I do not know whether the following has any merit. I offer it for your consideration.

In the course of this Excursus we will be learning about the extremes of sanctity that *klal Yisrael* will have reached *on Succos* immediately after the *Shemitah year.* We will be studying the Midrash that teaches us that during the Shemitah year even the many of us who are no more than simple proletarians rise to the level of the angels.

Perhaps חול המועד is particularly suited to this celebration. It too celebrates the ability of the prosaic weekday to rise to the occasion that permits us to meet (מועד from י ע ד, *to plan a meeting*) our God.

כ. ברכו ידוד מלאכיו גברי כח עשי דברו לשמע בקול דברו.
כא. ברכו ידוד כל צבאיו משרתיו עשי רצונו.

20. "You angels, mighty heroes who do His bidding,
Who are ever obedient to his bidding, bless HaShem."
21. "All His legions, His servants who do His will, bless HaShem."

The midrashim that we are about to quote will wonder why the *legions* mentioned in v. 21 are described as **כל** צבאיו while the *angels* addressed in v. 20 are not modified by that adjective.

In the meantime let us clear up who are the מלאכיו and who the צבאיו.

גבורי כח, רבי יצחק נפחא אמר אלו שומרי שביעית, בנוהג שבעולם אדם עושה מצוה ליום אחד לשבת אחד לחדש אחד שמא (לשאר) [לכל] ימות השנה ודין חמי חקליה ביירא כרמיה ביירא ושתיק יש לך גבור חיל גדול מזה?

R. Yitzchak the blacksmith taught: The description *mighty heroes* in v.20, refers to those who adhere conscientiously to the laws of Shemitah. [They are called *mighty heroes* because] people in general are prepared to invest great effort into the performance of a mitzvah for a day, a week or even a month. However being prepared to abstain for an entire year from any agricultural activity, is preposterous.

Nevertheless, these people have to watch their fields and vineyards lie fallow for an entire year without complaint. Could one imagine a mighty hero greater than these?

Now we turn to the midrash on the verse 21:

רבי תנחום בר חנילאי פתח (תהלים קג) ברכו ה' מלאכיו גבורי כח עושי דברו וגו' במה הכתוב מדבר אם בעליונים הכתוב מדבר והלא כבר נאמר ברכו ה' כל צבאיו הא אינו מדבר אלא בתחתונים. עליונים ע"י שהן יכולין לעמוד בתפקידיו של הקדוש ב"ה נאמרו ברכו ה' **כל** צבאיו אבל תחתונים ע"י שאינן יכולין לעמוד בתפקידיו של הקדוש ברוך הוא לכך נאמר ברכו ה' מלאכיו ולא כל מלאכיו.

R. Tanchum bar Chanilai opened the discussion of these verses as follows:

"You angels, mighty heroes who do His bidding,Who are ever obedient to His bidding, bless HaShem."

[He asked] Who are the *mighty heroes* mentioned here? They cannot be the denizens of the upper spheres (actual angels), since these are the referents of v. 21 (צבאיו). Therefore they must be humans, denizens of our physical world.

[This explains why the word "כל" appears in v. 21 (**כל** צבאיו) but not in v. 20 (the expression used is מלאכיו not **כל** מלאכיו). The denizens of the upper world (true angels) are angelic by nature and will always, under all circumstances, remain angelic. There are no exceptions. All of them are always an active part of the divine legions. However the מלאכיו of verse 21 are really human beings. They are not angels at all. So why does the TaNaCh refer to them as מלאכים? Because sometimes they do become very, very Mal'achim-like. We could call them "part-time angels.

Would you, dear Reader, want to know when? Read on. It is time to unpack the Sefas Emes that I promised earlier.

> ... כדאיתא במדרש "גבורי כח" בשומרי שביעית הכתוב מדבר. רואה שדהו בייר ושותק **ועי"ז יוצאין מהנהגה הטבעיות** וזוכין לשמיטה כמ"ש והיתה שבת הארץ לכם לאכלה כעין העליונים שניזונין מטמיון של מלך. ועליהם כתיב ברכו ה' מלאכיו כדאיתא במדרש **שאע"פ שהם בעולם הטבעי וזורעין ואוספים** מ"מ כשבא שמיטה ושובתין **נתלבשו בבחינת מלאכיו** וכו'

The Midrash teaches us that the term, גבורי כח in Tehilim 103 refers to those who adhere conscientiously to the laws of Shemitah. They are truly heroes for they must watch as their fields lie fallow and do not complain. This heroism *allows them to escape the cause and effect of a purely physical world* and to *enter a world in which the supernal rules supreme*. They "become" angels.

This is meant by the verse, והיתה שבת הארץ לכם לאכלה, which can be translated as *It will come about that the very resting of the land in the Shemitah year will itself generate a source of sustenance for you, for you will become like the real angels whose "food" comes from the "warehouse"* (טמיון) *of the king*. It is as a result of all this that the Jewish people are called מלאכים, *angels* in the Tehilim passage, for although they live in the physical world planting and reaping their fields, nevertheless when the Shemitah year arrives and they celebrate the earth's Sabbath, they array themselves in the garb of angels.

Let us get back to the timing of *Hakhel*. It is to take place almost immediately after the most recent Shemitah year has ended. But, note! *Almost* immediately, not immediately. We wait a couple of days until the Ribono shel Olam has taken us by the hand and led us into the Succah.

Close your eyes a moment and think what is happening. With the memory of the angelic trappings that adorned us throughout the recent Shemitah year still real, still very much alive, we now enter what for us is as close to the *Kodesh HaKodoshim*, the Holy of the Holies, as we can get. Surrounded, as it were, by the ענני כבוד, the *clouds of glory*, with only the flimsiest of roofs between us and the Ribono shel Olam, we, so to speak, touch the very heavens.

I imagine that by this time you will agree with me that the *Hakhel* ceremony may well be the highpoint of Jewish experience.

And it is the king who is the hero of הקהל. It is he who is charged with penetrating Jewish hearts with his readings. Let us peek over the Shem MiShmuel's shoulder as he explains the mitzvah of *Hakhel* in his commentary to VaYeilech.

דהנה יש להבין עיקר ענין הקריאה שהי׳ המלך קורא, למה? דמה חידש להם המלך בקריאתו התורה, הלא תורה שבכתב כתובה לכל?

אך הענין דהנה ברמב״ם ז״ל (פ״ג מהל׳ מלכים ה״ו) שמלך לבו הוא לב כל קהל ישראל, ע״כ. וזאת היתה הכוונה בקריאת התורה ע״י המלך, מחמת שלבו לב כל קהל ישראל יכנסו דבריו בלב כל העם בעומק לבם. וזוהי כוונת ירבעם שעשה עגלים ולא הניחם לבוא לירושלים, היינו שהי׳ חושש שאם יבואו לירושלים וישמעו הקריאה מרחבעם יכירו וידעו כי לו המלוכה כאשר דבריו יחדרו לתוך לבות בנ״י:

Here is a paraphrase of some of this section:

The author finds it difficult to understand what the purpose of *Hakhel* might be. The king offers no explanations at all of what he is reading. It is simply a matter of reading a Torah text that is anyway available to his whole audience. So nobody, or almost nobody, is hearing anything new.

So what is the point?

His solution lies in the Rambam (Melachim 3:6)... *the king's heart is the heart of the entire Jewish people and it must be protected from straying in inappropriate directions*. The hope is that since his heart "is" the heart of the entire Jewish people, we can expect that whatever he reads will penetrate deeply and meaningfully into the hearts of his listeners. Hearing these well-known and well-loved sentences from their king will usher them into a new world of Torah-sensitivity.

We can do no better than to end this, our celebration of the Jewish king, than to quote Rambam from Hilchos Chagigah 3:6.

אפילו חכמים גדולים שיודעים כל התורה כולה חייבין לשמוע בכוונה גדולה יתרה ומי שאינו יכול לשמוע מכוין לבו לקריאה זו שלא קבעה הכתוב אלא לחזק

דת האמת ויראה עצמו כאילו עתה נצטוה בה ומפי הגבורה שומעה שהמלך **שליח** הוא להשמיע דברי האל.

Even great scholars who know the entire Torah are obliged to listen with great and unparalleled attention ... The experience must give them the feeling that at this very moment they were hearing these words *from God*! This, because the king is acting as God's agent (שליח), charged with making *His* words known to the people.

* * *

We have now come to a point at which we are in a position to answer the questions that we asked concerning the three ordinances in which Shlomo HaMelech was involved.

Here is how I think that the answer to these profoundly significant questions should be worded..

The values represented by ערובין, נטילת ידים and שניות have much to contribute to Jewish living. Nevertheless the Ribono shel Olam gave us His Torah without them. Why? Because God was "seeking" the partnership of *klal Yisrael* in perfecting the world that he had willed out of the infinite nothingness that had preceded creation.

Way back, near the very beginning of this essay we began to hint at the desirability of this partnership. It lies implicit in the otherwise hopeless void of the Marcheshvan-Nisan emptiness. We determined there that "A space is to fill". Throughout the centuries during which that space lay empty, its availability challenged us. From where would our inspiration come? It is all very well to seek to be creative but only the Ribono shel Olam can create *ex nihilo.*

Let us listen to the S'fas Emes's (לחנוכה תרמ"א in the Bereishis volume) take on Chanukah and Purim.

חנוכה ופורים הם הארות מרגלים. רק הג' רגלים המפורשים בתורה הם תורה שבכתב. ויש נגד זה ג"כ רגלים מתורה שבע"פ. והם אורות המקבלים כדמיון אור הלבנה שהיא מאור החמה כידוע. כן ע"י כוחן של בנ"י בקבלתם היו"ט כראוי. נשאר מכל יו"ט רשימה בכנס"י. ובכח זה הוציאה כנגדן רגלים אחרים. וחנוכה הארה מחג הסוכות. ופורים מחג השבועות. ומחג הפסח מקוים אנו להיות עוד כמ"ש כימי צאתך מארץ מצרים אראנו נפלאות.

Here is a very, very important rendering of this very, very important passage.

Chanukah and Purim are reflections of the light emanating

from two of the three pilgrim festivals that are explicitly mandated by the Torah.[17] These two are to be considered "Torah" as are those three but in contrast to those that have the status of *Torah SheBichsav* these are *Torah SheBeAl Peh*. They are comparable to the light reflections that reach us from the moon of which the source is the sun.

In precisely the same way *klal Yisrael* was able to receive the light of the "*Torah SheBichsav* ordained festivals" with so much native understanding and appreciation that this light became a part of them thus that from within themselves they were now able to produce Chanukah and Purim.

S'fas Emes' powerful and clarion-clear language deserves better than this, my rather pitiful מנחת עני. But under the circumstances it will have to do. I am offering it because I believe it to be the key that will open up our understanding of Shlomo HaMelech's involvement in his three ordinances.

I will spell out what I mean by this.

If you have access to my book, *For Rashi's Thoughtful Students* you can discover (see particularly chapter 9) that the division between the upper and lower spheres that God established on the second day of creation[18] was not absolute. This is a huge *sugia* and can have applications on at least two levels. In the book that you are now reading you have the essay that deals with the splitting of the Yam Suf ("Water Walls at Yam Suf") in which I suggest for good and sufficient reasons that that miracle was an example of the עולמות העליונים so to speak crashing the barriers into our physical world. That is level #1. An example of the second level would be Purim and Chanukah as explained by the S'fas Emes that we have just now discussed, where humans (those who established these Yamim Tovim) reached up, as it were, and captured their inspiration from above.

At this point I am going to quote myself (with some changes and additions) from earlier in this essay.

17. In the course of this passage the S'fas Emes mentions that Chanukah "springs" as it were from Succos and Purim, from Shavuos. Pesach, the S'fas Emes asserts will produce its own "oral law" festival at the coming of Moshi'ach.

The reasoning behind all this is of course interesting in the extreme but is not important to us in the present context.

18. יהי רקיע בתוך המים

The thesis that we have worked out above, postulates that the three *takonos* associated with Shlomo HaMelech work differently from the regular סייגים instituted by Chazal. The regular סייגים prohibit an in itself inoffensive x so that a forbidden y might not be compromised.[19] Shlomo HaMelech took the larger view. His quarry was *Yidishkeit* rather than x's and y's. He, so to speak, reached up into the heavens and there, on the celestial book-shelves, found three brand-new *Masechtos, Eiruvin, Yadayim* and *"Sheniyos"*[20]. He checked them out, brought them down into our world and thereby enriched us with treasures that, over the centuries, have left us gasping at their beauty.

Here was partnership at its best. The Ribono shel Olam found what He had wanted. Shlomo HaMelech, the man, was human and eventually passed away. Shlomo HaMelech, the "idea" had discovered the infinity that lodges in the Jewish soul — the Bais HaMidrash — and became immortal.

Nothing would ever again be the same. And that is what Jewish kings are supposed to do. They are supposed to chair-lift us upwards towards the peaks.

What did the heavenly voice say?

Once more, I am going to quote myself from earlier in this essay. Here is a passage from Shabbos 14b.

אמר רב יהודה אמר שמואל בשעה שתיקן שלמה עירובין ונטילת ידים[21] יצתה בת קול ואמרה בני אם חכם לבך ישמח לבי גם אני (משלי כג:טו) ...

R. Yehudah taught in Shmuel's name: When Shlomo

19. Remember from earlier in this essay the examples that the Vilna Gaon to Pirkei Avos offers for עשו סייג לתורה. One was the Torah's insistence that קרבה to an ערוה be avoided because it might lead to intimacy, and that the Nazir is forbidden to drink any kind of grape juice in order to make sure that his drinking would not progress towards drinking wine.

20. There is, of course, no such thing as a formal *"Maseches" Sheniyos*. I took the liberty of "inventing" such a *"masechta"*, permitting myself a small literary hoax, trusting the readers to understand what I am doing. Theoretically there could have been such a *masechta Sheniyos* and as far as my little flight into the fancy of a heavenly library is concerned, there might as well have been. For our purposes Sheniyos fits right in there together with *Eiruvin* and *Yadayim*.

21. There is, of course, no such thing as a formal *"Maseches" Sheniyos*. I took the liberty of "inventing" such a *"masechta"*, permitting myself a small literary hoax, trusting the readers to understand what I am doing. Theoretically there could have been such a *masechta Sheniyos* and as far as my little flight into the fancy of a heavenly

HaMelech ordained the concepts of Eiruvin and Netilas Yadayim a heavenly voice came forth and said, "My son, if your heart has found wisdom, My heart too will be gladdened." (Mishley 23:15).[22]

It sounds a little strange, does it not? There are hundreds of Rabbinic ordinances concerning all kinds of issues. Why is it that just these two, promulgated by Shlomo HaMelech, merit such an enthusiastic heavenly endorsement?

We have been through a lot together in this very complicated essay. If at this point you are still with me I am going to assume that we are more or less on the same page in our thinking. I am going to put your patience at risk and hope that you will not be upset if the following is going to sound a little *drushy*. Well, maybe it will turn out to be *drush*, and, really, what's wrong with that? But maybe it will turn out to be *peshat*. I vote for plan B. I really think it *is* the *peshat*.

Do you want to join me? Let us analyze the possibilities together. O.K.?

How is the "אם" in אם חכם לבך to be understood? My אבן שושן dictionary has approximately fifteen different meanings for אם that cover a wide range. For example, there is of course the familiar *if* (אם אשכחך ירושלים), but there is also *Is it possible*? (האם תמנו לגוע). And so it goes, on and on. I suppose that *if* is the most likely, so let us assume that: *If your heart is wise*. Now, what is the question? Shlomo HaMelech has originated two *takonos*. Does that involve wisdom or not? I would guess that anyone who has ever labored over *Eiruvin* and/or *Yadayim* would assert that it requires a great deal of wisdom. So again, what is the question?

Can we solve this riddle?

Here is my take: A little earlier in this essay I argued that Shlomo HaMelech's *takonos* were essentially different from the usual סייג לתורה. They did not forbid an x in order to protect a y but, instead, expanded the Torah in a way that was designed to generate new sensitivity to sanctity among his subjects, thereby creating an ambiance designed to assure caring and therefore

library is concerned, there might as well have been. For our purposes Sheniyos fits right in there together with *Eiruvin* and *Yadayim*.

22. The Gemara also quotes another *pasuk* from Mishley. I have left it out because our interest in this essay focuses only on the first one.

thoughtful living, notching the practice of Judaism up to new levels of responsibly undertaken practice. There would be no reason to fear thoughtless trampling on the values that the Ribono shel Olam held dear.

That sounds very good, but is it true? Maybe after all we are reading more into Shlomo HaMelech's *takonos* than they were designed to bear. Maybe it is we who are inventing these exalted considerations because they sound right to us, but they never really entered Shlomo's mind. Maybe, after all, it was nothing more than an x/y סייג, more complicated and wide-ranging than most but still, essentially, "family"?

I want to argue that the doubts that I have now expressed could well support the "אם". "*If* you are really as wise as I think you are." "*If* you took the high path of beckoning your subjects to scale the peaks instead of simply legislating another סייג, then ..."

Then what? *Then that would make me very happy* (ישמח לבי גם אני). Then you would be deserving of this accolade.

If all this is true, then even the difficult "גם" would be less difficult. We wondered why the Ribono shel Olam's joy would be "subordinate" (וגם חרבונה וכו') to that of Shlomo. The main joy would certainly be right down here in our physical world. It is certainly here that the "Tikun" in "Takanah" would come into its own. But the עליונים too, like happy Mechutanim rejoicing in a perfect match would join in the Simchah.

You surely recall that the title of this chapter is "Creative Judaism". Moreover, I promised that by the time you got to the end of the essay you would understand what I meant by this term.

Pay-up time has now arrived.

What exactly do I mean by "Creative Judaism"?

Really, if you have followed along in this rather complicated essay, you will have recognized that this double-barreled[23] Yidishkeit, that joins "plain" Judaism to a degree of creativity, is really the *chidush* of Shlomo HaMelech in at least two of his famous three *takonos*.[24] When he ordained "עירובין" he did not

23. Dictionary meaning: In English speaking and some other Western countries, a *double-barrelled* name is a family name with two parts, which may or may not be joined with a hyphen.

24. Please see note 9 above.

simply forbid something that had previously been permitted. He established a concept that had never been known before. The details of this concept, the "Whats" the "Hows" the "Whys" and the "Whens" of עירובין, pretty much fill an entire, highly technical *Masechta*. The same goes for נטילת ידים.

If that is not "creative", what is?

There are many directions that you, my patient reader, could take in following up on this thought. At this point I will leave you to it and wish you all the best of *hatzlachah* in your quest for a partnership with the Ribono shel Olam. All your efforts will be very worthwhile.

3.
Arachin

A SHORT INTRODUCTION

The mitzvah of *Arachin* (or *Erchin,* see footnote 7 in this essay. Henceforth we will be using *Erchin*) is one of those that fell into disuse with the destruction of the Temple. None of us has ever witnessed this transaction and therefore most of us have very little idea of what it is all about. Herewith a short, non-technical survey of some of the nuts and bolts that are involved.

The root ע ר ך, which actually means *putting two things side by side to facilitate comparison* (see Rav Samson Raphael Hirsch to BeChukosai), ended up being used as *evaluation*. The following will seem strange to us but, as we will learn in the essay, it has a logic of its own. At the very end of Sefer VaYikra the Torah assigns a monetary value (*eirech,* the singular form of the plural *erchin*) to every human being. To us this "value" seems entirely arbitrary, but, once more it has a logic of its own. This "value" should not be confused with "market value" that is the amount that a willing buyer would be willing to pay to a willing seller. Market value would be determined by any number of qualities, properties or the like. Within the world of *Erchin* there are only two criteria that determine a person's *eirech*: gender and age. Depending upon whether the subject is male or female, at age *x* his (or her) *eirech* would be such and such an amount, at age *y* it would be different as specified in the Torah.

That is it. Now you know what an *eirech* is.

Now for the mitzvah aspect. In BeChukosai the Torah tells us that among the many vows that a person might make is one that results in his having to donate his (or her) *eirech* or the appropriate *eirech* of someone else, to the Beis HaMikdash.[1] The formal language used would be ערכי עלי (or, when donating someone else's *eirech* (in Rambam's view even that of a non-Jew) ערך פלוני עלי. This would translate as: "I accept an obligation upon myself (עלי)

1. Which is why this mitzvah cannot be performed in our times.

that will require me to give my *eirech* or if the person is pledging someone else's *eirech,* this person's (ערך פלוני) to the appropriate treasurer in the Beis HaMikdash."

With this information tucked away in your mind, you should be able to make your way through the essay.

Best of luck in your efforts. You will come across some interesting eye-openers along the way.

ARACHIN
MEET MY FRIEND THE "BEIS HAMIKDASH *YID*"

Believe me, my friend is worth meeting. He will touch your life in ways of which, as things stand now, you cannot even dream. You will begin by admiring him and end up by loving him. Eventually the determination to emulate him will fill your life. New worlds will open up for you and ... and ... and ... and you can guess at the rest.

However, if I am going to take you to meet him, we will need to do some groundwork.

Here goes.

Some of you may be aware that among the many volumes of the *Pachad Yitzchak,* the collections of the writings of the late great Rav Hutner, there is one volume devoted to his letters. Among those letters (#94) there is one that touches upon an issue that is going to occupy us in this essay. It is the question of a "double life" versus a "broadened life". Here is the background. A former student had returned from learning in Eretz Yisrael planning to enter upon a secular career. He expressed his discomfort at the thought that he would be leading a "double life". The Beis HaMidrash where he would be learning and the office in which he would be working seemed to him to be incompatible. Rav Hutner undertook to set his mind at rest. A multiplicity of dots will "double" only when you arrange them in a straight line. The more dots you add, the more will the product of your multiplication increase. If, however, you arrange your dots in a circle centered upon a single midpoint, the singularity of your original loop will not be altered; it will be enlarged (broadened) but will remain a single whole. Rav Hutner argued that if the midpoint of his interlocutor's life will be the Torah, he has nothing to fear from any "double life". Broadened, yes; doubled, no!

Clearly the letter assumes that a "double life" is not a blessing, and, within its particular context, I have no problem with that judgment. Still, I am going to argue that there are important exceptions; sometimes a "double life" is precisely what is required.

I am going to make this point by quoting a few excerpts from my book *Music Made in Heaven,* which attempts to understand something of Dovid HaMelech's turbulent life. We will discover that in certain ways Dovid did indeed live a "double life" and that there was nothing at all wrong with that. Once we have made that point convincingly we will be able to move on to the topic to which I want to devote this current essay; the study of Arachin, the mysterious vow with which Sefer VaYikra comes to an end. For those of you who possess *Music Made in Heaven* I will provide page numbers for the quotes.

> (Page 1) This book is about Sefer Tehilim. It is about Sefer Tehilim, even though Sefer Tehilim will hardly be mentioned. The Sefer that will be mentioned in almost every chapter and that will provide the many passages we will study in great depth is Sefer Shmuel. Now I know that this does not make much sense to you and it is hard to explain without going into the kind of detail that does not belong in a brief introductory chapter. I will give you just a short paragraph here, and for the rest I ask you to trust me that, as you make your way through *Music Made in Heaven,* everything will turn out alright.
>
> *My goal is to answer a question that seems to me to be very compelling. It is this. Why does Sefer Shmuel not quote any of the Tehilim that, as their introductory verse often testifies, were said in the context of events very carefully spelled out in Sefer Shmuel? Telling the story and leaving out the fact that it served Dovid as inspiration for one of his immortal compositions is giving a very truncated account. An incomplete picture lacks certain dimensions of truth. A truth that is not rounded off is a half-truth. How can Sefer Shmuel be satisfied with teaching us half-truths?*
>
> *I will propose my answer to this question in the final chapter of* MUSIC MADE IN HEAVEN. *It will be built around an assumption that I will make concerning the respective characters of Sefer Shmuel and Sefer Tehilim. Sefer Shmuel, in its own terms, will be shown to be complete and lacking nothing. I will*

> *argue that Sefer Shmuel and Sefer Tehilim* OCCUPY TWO ENTIRELY DIFFERENT WORLDS. *The points of reference of the one are not those of the other. A chapter of Tehilim in the narrative parts of Shmuel would be like a total stranger crashing a wedding — he simply does not belong.*
>
> It is in this sense that, as I said above, *Music Made in Heaven* is about Sefer Tehilim, although Sefer Tehilim is hardly mentioned there. We will reach certain conclusions about the nature of Sefer Shmuel. Once we have established that, we will suggest that, by its self-definition, Sefer Tehilim has no place there.

The two paragraphs that I have italiized tell the story that I have in mind, the story of the two incompatible worlds in each of which Dovid was a citizen in good standing. The question that I have asked in the first of these two paragraphs is a strong one. Why indeed does Sefer Shmuel ignore the fact that the events that it records stimulated Dovid's flights into the rarefied[2] world of ecstasy that is the natural home of his *Tehilos*? Once the unique character of Sefer Tehilim becomes clear to us, the answer will be self-evident.

There exists a wonderful book called *David King of Israel* by the late Dr. Henry Biberfeld in which, with supreme sensitivity, he introduces us to the personality of Sefer Tehilim. With permission from the family I reprinted the following quote from that book. It appears on page 47 of *Music Made in Heaven*. Please read it with understanding.

> (Page 47) King Dovid's biography as told in the historical books gives only the surface outline of his life. It is a one-dimensional story describing his journey along the stormy road of persecution and jealousy through the valleys of betrayal and treachery, to the soaring heights of regal achievement and love. But the story does not tell what went on below the surface; of the tempests and upheavals, of the visions of supreme bliss and harmony in Dovid's soul. Only rarely do indications of the existence of these hidden worlds flash into the action flow of the narrative. Like geysers

2. Dictionary meaning: Elevated in character or style; lofty.

bursting forth in sudden and explosive fury, indicating the tremendous forces constrained in subterranean secrecy, those brief episodes reveal the magnitude and power of the forces at work behind the events of Dovid's life.

Dovid's real life is recorded in the psalms. This is the true mirror of his being, reflecting every phase of his life. *If the historical books show the outward contours of his image, the psalms probe the deepest secrets. The psalms are his world, the world of the idea of God with all its variety. It is a world detached from and beyond the material sphere.* Hence allusions to actual events occur only rarely in psalms. The historical books provide the form to be filled in with idea and experience.

...

When the supreme "event" of the idea of God was perceived by Dovid, an experience was born of such singular force that it reverberates through the ages. The psalms are the record of that great union, when the impact of the omnipresence of God struck the responsive chords of Dovid's being. From the moment when "the spirit of God came upon Dovid" it never again left him entirely. It spread and grew in him until his whole person, soul and body, was suffused with it. Dovid's reactions to the erratics of life were no longer his own. *The divine in Dovid's thought, felt, spoke, and acted through him...*

In the psalms we find all that we look for in vain in the books describing Dovid's outward life. Triumphs and tragedies, periods of calm and of unrest, of supreme confidence and hopeless despair, mystic surrender and moral reflections, universal love and implacable wrath, find expression in the psalms. They have words like thunderbolts or the whisper of a breeze, raging fire or soothing rain, fragrant flowers or corrosive acid, spanning the whole range of human experience.

There we are. Shmuel the book of narrative and Psalms the book of the soul occupy two different worlds. They are incompatible with each other and Tehilim cannot find a welcome in Shmuel. And that need not disturb us at all.

We are now ready to leave these introductory musings and get on with the essay proper. We will enter the mysterious world of the Arachin and ready ourselves to meet up with the "Beis HaMikdash *Yid*". The reason for bringing the "doubled" world issue into the preceding section is as follows. We found that Dovid HaMelech's concurrent dwelling in both the Book of Shmuel and the Book of Tehilim did not really present any problems. These two books represent entirely different "worlds." As we plough through the intricacies of *Erchin* we will find that the person who is *ma'arich* himself also creates an entirely different "world" for his own use. You will find out that he, in fact, will turn out to be the real "Beis HaMikdash *Yid*!"

To make things official we will insert the complete title once more. Study the title carefully. Exciting experiences are awaiting us just around the corner.

Arachin
Meet My Friend the "Beis HaMikdash *Yid*"

Providentially, I am writing this on the Wednesday of *parshas* Tetzaveh and it is in this very *parshah* that Ramban writes some very daring words concerning the Ribono shel Olam's motivation for having us build the Mishkan in the desert and, so one assumes, the Beis HaMikdash once we entered Eretz Yisrael.

Here are his thoughts at Shemos 29:46:

יש בענין סוד גדול, כי כפי פשט הדבר השכינה בישראל צורך הדיוט ולא צורך גבוה, אבל הוא כענין שאמר הכתוב ישראל אשר בך אתפאר (ישעיה מט ג), ואמר יהושע ומה תעשה לשמך הגדול (יהושע ז ט), ופסוקים רבים באו כן, אוה למושב לו (תהלים קלב יג), פה אשב כי אויתיה (שם יד).

The following falls into the category of a great mystery. Certainly we would have supposed that the Divine Presence among us is there because we the people have a need for its proximity, not that Ribono shel Olam needs to be among us. But that is not true. It seems that it is the Ribono shel Olam Who needs us. There are many verses that express this thought: *He has desired it* (Tzion) *for His habitation* (Tehilim 132:13) or, (Tehilim 115:12) *Here I dwell because I have desired it.*

How are we to understand these cryptic ideas?

The late R. Simchah Zisel Broyde, Rosh Yeshivah of the Chevroner Yeshivah in Yerushalayim, in his *sefer,* שָׂם דֶּרֶךְ proposes the following explanation. I will offer the Hebrew together with my paraphrase because I am not completely certain that I have understood his solution correctly. This way you will be able to make your own judgment.

> ... ודבר פשוט הוא שאין להקב"ה כל צורך בעבודת האדם, "אם צדקת מה תתן לו, אם חטאת מה תפעל בו ..." וכמו שנתבאר, כל מהלך זה "שהעבודה צורך גבוה" הוא בחסדו הבלתי משוער של הבורא, שבמה שמתרצה לקבל מאתנו , יש הנאה והטבה מופלאים, [על דרך קבלת אדם חשוב שהיא נתינה והנאה לנותן.]

> It is of course perfectly obvious that the Ribono shel Olam has no needs of any kind; neither our righteousness nor our wickedness touches Him in any way. Still He set things up such that, by accepting Israel's service and their sacrifices He would make it appear as though they were His benefactors and He their beneficiary.
>
> By accepting their bounty (which, in reality He does not need in the slightest) He knew that He would make them happy — and that, in His unbounded goodness, was what He wanted most.
>
> There is a halachic model that is based on just such logic. One of the methods by which a man betroths a woman is by giving her something of value in "exchange" for her willingness to become his wife. That is the function of the ring that the *Chasan* gives the *Kallah* under the Chupah. To our intense surprise the Gemara asserts that the betrothal can, under specific circumstances, be equally valid where it is the woman who tenders the gift to the man. This would hold true if the *Chasan* is a man of unusual importance who under normal circumstances would never agree to accept a gift from anybody. His willingness to accept a gift from this lady is viewed as a great compliment to her and is worth money to the woman. It turns out that her giving is a "taking" and his taking is a "giving."
>
> Precisely this principle is at work when we bring sacrifices to the Ribono shel Olam. It is He who, as it were, is accepting gifts, but does so only in order that His acceptance turns into an act of giving us the pleasure which, in truth, is what motivates the entire transaction.

The Ramban that we have just quoted is at Shemos 29:46 where his challenge was to offer an explanation for the prefix ל in "לשכני" as it is used in the sentence, וידעו כי אני ה׳ אלהיהם אשר

הוצאתי אתם מארץ מצרים לשכני בתוכם ... He disagrees with Rashi who renders, *on condition that* ..., and prefers, *in order to attain My purpose* ... He does not, however explain what exactly happens as a result of the Ribono shel Olam being "שוכן" among us.

For that we turn to S'forno on the previous verse that speaks of God's intention to make His abode among us, ושכנתי בתוך בני ישראל והייתי להם לאלהים.

> *I will dwell among the Israelites* so that I will be able to accept their service with goodwill and hear their prayers.
>
> *Thus, I will be their God,* meaning that I will direct their affairs without any intermediary, such that they will not have to fear any heavenly portends. My proximity to them will guarantee that they will always outrank the heavens.

I suppose that we could sum up this section of our essay by affirming that the presence of the *Shechinah*[3] among us generates a certain intimacy between the Ribono shel Olam and ourselves that will be manifest in appropriate ways.

We are now ready to move on to the next section of our analysis.

It seems to me that we could usefully explore the question whether it is possible to improve upon the degree of intimacy that is attained by the Ribono shel Olam dwelling in our midst. For example, we might wonder whether if we were able to actually move *into* or almost into the Mishkan or the Beis HaMikdash, we would be positioning ourselves more advantageously.

We might consider David's prayer (Tehilim 27), אחת שאלתי מאת ידוד אותה אבקש שבתי בבית ידוד כל ימי חיי לחזות בנעם ידוד ולבקר בהיכלו, *I ask only this from HaShem, that, throughout my life, I might dwell in HaShem's house.* What, precisely, was he trying to accomplish? Then there is the childless wife, Chanah, later to become Shemuel HaNavi's mother, who vowed that if God would grant her a son she would make a gift of him to the Ribono shel Olam (Shemuel 1:11, ונתתיו לה'). By this, as verse 22 (וישב שם עד עולם) makes clear, she meant that he would dwell his entire life either in or near the Tabernacle.

For what was David praying? What was Chanah planning?

3. The noun "Shechinah" derives from the root ש כ ן from which both לשכני and ושכנתי are derived.

Although chronology would seem to demand that we think about Shemuel before David, we shall go to David first. I suspect that his problem will be the easier of the two to solve.

DAVID:

It appears to me[4] that David's choice of words, "שבתי בבית ה'," echoes Chanah's language "וישב שם עד עולם" so precisely, that it almost begs to be understood as a wish to emulate his Rebbi, Shmuel. Shmuel had "lived" his entire life "in" Shilo where at that time the Mishkan was standing, and David was praying that he too might merit such a life.

> [Please note the following. The statement that Shmuel lived his entire life in Shilo is manifestly not true. I Shmuel 7:17 makes clear that later in his life when he was traveling all over the land to judge the people he would always return to Ramasah because it was there that his home was situated (כי שם ביתו). So he did *not* live near the Mishkan.
>
> The Chasam Sofer (Teshuvos Chasam Sofer, Choshen Mishpat 9) tackles this question and his solution has enormous halachic ramifications. This present context is not the place to deal with the issues raised by that *teshuvah*. In this essay I will be suggesting a different possible solution based on the Maharal which I will reference shortly. I urge you, if at all possible, to study the Chasam Sofer's *teshuvah* carefully.]

Now it seems clear that David was not considering giving up the kingship. It is equally clear that most of the obligations that royalty imposed upon him could never be exercised while living "in" HaShem's house.

So what did he mean?

I believe that an answer can be found in Maharal's Gur Aryeh to Shemos 12:40 which teaches that Israel's "dwelling" (מושב) in Mitzrayim lasted four hundred and thirty years. How is this to cohere with our tradition that we spent only two hundred and ten years there? Here is a paraphrase of a short section of a long passage.

4. By this I mean that I have not seen this point in any *sefer*. Please make your own judgment.

We are all considered to "belong" to the place to which indeed we belong, that is our formal, permanent dwelling. "Home" is where I really "live", even if my business or other interests or circumstances force me to be absent for many years. Those absences are מקרה, *fortuitous happenings* that do not alter the essential facts. Once the Ribono shel Olam had told Avraham that his children (from Yitzchak's birth onwards) would, for four hundred years, be sojourners in a land in which they would be strangers, that land became their formal home for those four hundred years. The fact that it would be another one hundred and ninety years before they actually arrived there is not relevant. From Yitzchak's birth onwards, Mitzrayim was the place where we "were".

That given, things fall readily into place. David knew well that even if his kingly duties would not permit an actual move into the "Beis HaShem", he could still make it his formal "home". Even when in the midst of the wildest battle, far removed from any trace of sacred ground, the real "he" could, and therefore would, be savoring the sweetness of HaShem and the contemplation that finds its most ideal expression within the Temple boundaries. He may have had to leave the Temple confines behind, but they would not leave him.[5]

The introductory verse of many of the Tehilim makes clear that they were composed under the most dreadful circumstances. That surely proves that his prayer was fulfilled. His entire life would be lived as a "Beis HaMikdash *Yid*".

We started out by asking whether there were ways that could bring about a closer intimacy than that generated by the presence of the Ribono shel Olam in our midst. If we think of Dovid HaMelech as the נעים זמירות ישראל, *He who brought sweetness to Israel's songs* (II Shmuel 23:1), the answer is of course an emphatic "Yes!" Sweetness does not fall off trees. In my book, *Music Made in Heaven* I surmised that perhaps Dovid had learned the sweetness of his music from tunes that the north wind coaxed

5. I imagine that many of us have met people who learned in yeshiva when they were young but were then forced by circumstances to leave. They take pride in the fact that in spite of the geographical distance, they, in their practices and attitudes, always remained "Yeshivish". (*Ich bin alemol gebliben a "Yeshiva Man!"*)

from the harp that hung above his bed to wake him up at midnight (Berachos 3b). We cannot know what sounds he heard but, whatever they were, they had been composed in heaven. It seems likely to me that only one who calls the Beis HaMikdash "Home" would have the ear to pick up those unique harmonies.

Shmuel

The story of Chanah's barrenness and her eventual vindication when Shmuel was born to her is too well known to require rehearsing here. However, we should be concerned with the technical aspects of the vow she made to God. The vow is mentioned three times and it makes sense to examine what she promised and what she intended.

The first mention comes at I Shmuel 1:11. She finds herself at Shilo together with her husband and makes her way to the Tabernacle to offer up her tearful prayers.

> ותדר נדר ותאמר ה׳ צבאות אם ראה תראה בעני אמתך ונתתה לאמתך זרע אנשים ונתתיו לה׳ כל ימי חייו וכו׳.
>
> She made a vow and said, "HaShem, Master of Legions, if You take note of the suffering of Your maidservant and You remember me and do not forget Your maidservant, and give You maidservant male offspring, then I shall give him to HaShem all the days of his life ..."

At this point we do not know precisely what she has in mind. How does one "give" someone to God? For the purpose of this essay we will go with Mezudos who renders, *I will give him to HaShem in the sense that he will spend his entire life dedicated exclusively to the service of God.*

Time passes and a baby boy is born. When Elkanah, Chanah's husband, gets ready for one of his frequent pilgrimages to Shilo, Chanah tells him that she prefers to stay at home until the child is weaned. At that time (verse 22):

> והבאתיו ונראה את פני ה׳ וישב שם עד עולם.
>
> ... I will bring him (with me) and he will appear before God and shall remain there forever.

When the child is weaned she takes him to Shilo, informs Eli the Kohen Gadol that this is the child for whom several years earlier she had prayed. She then tells him of her plans for the child.

> אל הנער הזה התפללתי ויתן ידוד לי את שאלתי אשר שאלתי מעמו. וגם אנכי השאלתהו לידוד כל הימים אשר היה הוא שאול לידוד וישתחו שם לידוד.
>
> This is the child for whom I prayed, HaShem granted me the wish for which I had asked. Furthermore, I have "lent" him to HaShem forever. As long as he lives he is "lent" to HaShem …

The idea that a mother has the legal right to bind her child to the kind of life that is envisioned here troubles many commentators. We know of no similar commitments having ever been made in TaNaCh or anywhere else and what we know of the laws governing *nedarim* and *nezirus* seems to offer no help.[6]

I have a theory that I wish to offer here. To the best of my knowledge there are no sources that would either confirm or deny it. True that it is the result of some research that I have done but the finished product comes, as far as I know, only from inside my own head. In this rather complex essay I am asking a lot from you readers; it is in no way easy reading, so I feel justified in asking one more fairly modest favor. Do not assume that my suggestion is the correct explanation. There should be quite a few amber lights flashing around you, advising, no, actually warning, to exercise caution. So, please, please, be cautious. On the other hand I would beg you not to dismiss it out of hand. A lot of fairly hard work and much love went into this project. If at least some of you would find it in your hearts and minds to agree that this might be going in the right direction, that would make me very happy.

Here goes.

6. For an excellent source and discussion of the various opinions, I recommend *Nachalas Shimon* by my good friend, Rabbi Shimon Krasner, Volume 1 of Shmuel 1, Chapter 3, page 42. In order to keep things as simple as possible we will be following Responsum 9 in Teshuvos Chasam Sofer on Choshen Mishpat. He suggests that Chanah might have had this extra-halachic privilege concerning Shmuel, since his birth had come about only as a result of her prayers. We will be referencing this Chasam Sofer later on in this essay.

THE MYSTERIOUS WORLD OF THE *ARACHIN*

Following immediately upon the grim and depressing *Tochachah* in BeChukosai, tucked away at the very end of Sefer VaYikra, we have a *parshah* that poses problems to a lot of people. I will quote a couple of verses together with a paraphrase, and, once that is done, we will be able to take our time discussing what we have read.

וידבר ה׳ אל משה לאמר.
דבר אל בני ישראל ואמרת עליהם איש כי יפלא נדר בערכך נפשות לה׳.
והיה ערכך הזכר מבן עשרים שנה ומעלה ועד בן ששים שנה והיה ערכך חמשים שקל כסף בשקל הקדש.
ואם נקבה היא והיה ערכך שלשים שקל.
ואם מבן חמש שנים ועד בן עשרים שנה והיה ערכך הזכר עשרים שקלים ולנקבה עשרה שקלים.
ואם מבן חדש ועד בן חמש שנים והיה ערכך הזכר חמשה שקלים כסף ולנקבה ערכך שלשת שקלים כסף.
ואם מבן ששים שנה ומעלה אם זכר והיה ערכך חמשה עשר שקל ולנקבה עשרה שקלים.

The Ribono shel Olam spoke to Moshe:

"Tell the Benei Yisrael that when a man chooses to express a vow that has as its object his 'soul value,' that is to be given to HaShem.

If this "value" is to be for a male between the ages of twenty and sixty, then that 'value' is determined at fifty *shekel.*

If it is to be the 'value' of a female of that age, then that 'value' is determined at thirty *shekel.*

If the age [that is being 'valued'] is between five years and twenty years ... then for a male ... and for a female ...

If the age of the person is between one month and five years then the value for a male ... and the value for a female ...

If the age of the person is sixty years and over then for a male ... and for a female ...

Let us first deal with this "tucked away" business. On the face of it this is a *parshah* like any other. What is it doing in this out-of-the-way place?

R. Samson Raphael Hirsch whose Torah commentary really leaves hardly any stone unturned, addresses even this rather out-of-the-way question. He takes off from the fact that the verse that brings the *Tochachah* — and really the whole of Sefer

VaYikra — to a close, reads אלה החקים והמשפטים והתרות אשר נתן ה׳ בינו ובין בני ישראל בהר סיני ביד משה. That is a fitting *finale* to VaYikra, the *book that contains most of* the basic and binding laws that govern us. The positioning of Arachin[7] indicates clearly that it is not a part of that set. Certainly the fulfillment of the minutia that constitute the details of this procedure will fall under the rubric, "mitzvah". But it is in no way binding to undertake anything of the sort. *Erchin* will always come about through the unprompted urges of the heart.

Here is what R. Samson Raphael Hirsch has to say on this matter:

> The Jewish priestly code does not attach special value to Sanctuary donations, and does not see in them special piety, especially pleasing to God ... The Sanctuary of the Kohanim sees its mission not in gaining possessions but in gaining hearts and souls ...

So *Erchin* makes its modest *debut* only after the Chukim, Mishpatim, and Toros have had their day. In making these vows part of our thought and our life, we will be consulting not the Jewish law-books but the yearning Jewish soul.

As *parshios* in the Torah go, this one is particularly difficult to understand even at the surface level. The words themselves are markedly uncooperative. Most of them we can translate (more or less) but once we have an at least serviceable English equivalent, we still have no sense at all what they really mean in the given context.

What, for example, can ערכך נפשות really mean? I suppose that נפש is the easier of the two, although it too has a number of different meanings. Here is a partial list from a reasonably responsible dictionary: *soul, life, person, living, being, blood, desire* and so on. A little further along, that same dictionary writes: *As the essential of man [it] stands for man himself.* It offers אל תבוא **נפשי**, *let me not be involved* (Bereishis 49:6), or, תמות נפשי מות ישרים, *let me die a righteous death* (BeMidbar 23:10) as examples.

7. That is the correct way of pronouncing the word. Since, speaking of these laws and even of the tractate that bears their name, the entire world more or less uses the incorrect "*Erchin*," we will not "separate ourselves from the Tzibbur". We will throw pedantry to the wind and use "*Erchin*".

For ערך we will quote a snippet from R. Samson Raphael Hirsch's commentary:

> The basic meaning of ע ר ך is "to place things that belong together next to each other". By extension it also means, "to place things side by side for the sake of comparison", as in, אין ערוך אליך (Tehilim 40:6). Thus ערך also means, "to describe the value or significance of an object" ...

The Rav has been discussing the verbal form. Of course the word appears also as a noun; for example, לא ידע אנוש ערכה (Iyov 28:17). When we use the word *Erech* or the plural, *Erchin*, we have that meaning in mind.

What exactly is the "soul value" with which we met up earlier in our rendering of the *Erchin* passage? I do not believe that you will find it in any dictionary, so the challenge of ascribing meaning to this strange expression is aimed solely at us.

It is important to get the following straight. We normally associate the concept of value with a market price. How much would an interested buyer pay a willing seller for this unit? In our situation this definition can have no meaning. Market prices obviously fluctuate by what might be called "accidental" variables. How skillful is this slave? What brand is this car? How urgent is the buyer's need for this commodity? And so on. From the truncated offering of the *parshah* of *Erchin* that we offered above, it is clear that the *only* variables that affect the amount of each *erech* are gender and age. Besides these two, nothing, absolutely *nothing,* can influence the amount to be paid to the Beis HaMikdash. Nothing even vaguely connected with demand or quality or any other concept that plays a role in the market makes any difference.

So "value" is not market value.[8]

8. It so happens that *Erchin* have a nonidentical twin called *Damim.* This latter concept is one that accords absolutely with the market value with which we are familiar. It shares with *Erchin* the fact that it can be used for making a donation to the Beis HaMikdash. We can vow, *"Dami alay,"* "I vow to donate my *market value*," as readily as I can vow, *"Erchi alay"*, "I vow to donate my *Erech*." Both amounts would normally be channeled to *Bedek HaBayis,* the fund from which building upkeep and the like would be drawn (Rambam, Hilchos *Erchin* 1:10).

In this essay there is no need for me to attempt to understand the rational why age should influence the amounts and why in each age cohort women come in at a lesser rate than men. That is of course a very interesting issue and will become even

So, what is it?

We will not reach a satisfying conclusion unless we spell out the problem in all its complexity. Let us isolate as many aspects of this rather mysterious religious gesture as we can.

We begin with the knowledge that "value" is somehow involved since the word ערך, as we learned earlier from R. Samson Raphael Hirsch, carries that meaning. Now I am not confusing "value" with "price". I know that even in English we can speak of a "valuable" experience even when we know that its "value" will never, and perhaps can never, be converted into cash. But still it must involve a certain "someone" who has gained something meaningful. Who is a winner when we attach an arbitrary "value" of fifty *shekalim* to any and every male who, by no effort or choice of his own, has made it into the cohort of "twenty-to-sixty-year-olds"? The entire concept seems to be totally without any meaningful meaning.

Then there is the matter of motivation. What would persuade our thirty-five-year-old friend from the previous paragraph to undertake a vow of "*Erchi Alay*"? Absolutely nothing seems to have changed for himself of for anyone else, except that he now has an obligation to dig into his wallet and hand over fifty *shekalim* for *Bedek HaBayis* to the Temple Treasurer. But, if that is all there is, why go through the whole charade? If, for whatever reason, he wishes to donate fifty *shekalim*, why not just do so? Why weigh down his generous gift with an, in practical terms totally meaningless, "*Erech*" designation?

Clearly we are missing something very fundamental here. We are going to have to discover a certain something that *does* in fact happen, that *can* be valued and that will turn out to be very, very fundamental to authentic Jewish attitudes.

As in so many other areas of Torah, the Chazon Ish will take us by the hand and lead us firmly and convincingly to where we need to get. We will study two excerpts from his writings on *Erchin*; the first, a one-line definition of the meaning of the word, the other a short paragraph that disabuses us from some erroneous assumptions that we have made.

more interesting as we develop a theory that would explain what precisely a person has in mind when he vows to donate an *Erech* to the Beis HaMikdash. I strongly recommend that if that track of the matter at hand interests you particularly that you read up on R. Samson Raphael Hirsch's ideas in the Chumash.

First, then, the definition:

ענין הערך בלה"ק הוא **ערך כבוד הדבר ומציאותו** ולא ערך נגד חליפין ודמים.

The "value" of which the Hebrew ערך *speaks concerns*
The dignity and very existence of the subject;
It does not have "value" relative to
Exchanges or payments in mind.

Please, dear Reader, excuse my exuberance. I am practically dancing. Those among you who have become at least a little acquainted with the Chazon Ish through his voluminous writings, in all the various *genres* in which they appear, will understand me when I say that, had he only written this one sentence, we would still have come to "know" him pretty well. The equivalent of this simple statement comes alive in every sentence in every one of the heavy, infinitely challenging, volumes that he has bequeathed to us.

Here is the message:

SIMPLY "BEING" CARRIES ITS OWN DIGNITY
AND THAT DIGNITY HAS VALUE.
EVERY HUMAN IRRESPECTIVE OF ABILITY,
INTELLECT, OR OTHER "ACCIDENTAL" QUALITIES,
IRRESPECTIVE EVEN OF YIDDISHKEIT OR OTHERWISE,
IS EQUAL TO EVERY OTHER HUMAN BEING AT
THAT FUNDAMENTAL LEVEL.

IN THE WORLD OF HUMANITY WITH WHICH IT DEALS,
"ERCHIN" IS THE GREAT LEVELER.

Now, let us turn to the promised paragraph. It is mind-boggling in its implications.

ונראה דענין הערכין שאינו חייב מדין נדר את הסך הקצוב, אלא שהוא נתפש במצות הערכין, וכענין התפסת נזירות, ומתחייב במצות התורה בתשלומי הערכין, וכו' ואינו עובר בלאו דבל יחל, דהוי כהתנה שלא יהא נתפס בנדר, וכו'.

In this paragraph the Chazon Ish is teaching us that the assumptions that I made earlier were simply not true. I had thought that "*Erchi Alay*" was simply a way in which to make a donation to the *Bedek HaBayis* treasury. I asked that if that were the case, why not make the donation straight to the treasury? Why dress it up in what appears to be a meaningless costume which, in practical terms, seems to imply nothing at all? Later I discovered that the Chazon Ish also traveled that route. He too had originally thought that *Erchin* had no meaningful halachic body to it. He went so far as to write, ולפי האמור מצות הערכין אינו אלא כענין מצות בן סורר למ"ד לא היה ולא עתיד להיות, שאינו אלא למצות לימוד הפרשה וחוקתיה. That, of course, is an enormously powerful negative judgment; and the Chazon Ish drew what was for his towering and unwavering attachment to truth, the necessary conclusion. He labels that approach as a "דוחק" and forthwith proceeds to stand the entire *Erchin sugia* on its head and to explain its halachic components in a radically new fashion.

The paragraph that I have just quoted opens his revised explanation of how *Erchin* works.

Here is a paraphrase of this stupendous paragraph. In order to make these very technical few sentences more readily understandable, some background material will be provided.

[Please consult the somewhat truncated quote of the *parshah* of *Erchin* in BeChukosai that I offered earlier in this essay. Here is how we translated the second *pasuk*. "*Tell the Benei Yisrael that when a man chooses to express a vow that has as its object his 'soul value,' that is to be given to HaShem.*" The paragraph that we are about to paraphrase will demonstrate that, in Chazon Ish's view, our translation is incorrect. This is because in my translation I postulated that the object with which the vow occupies itself is the actual "soul value" of the נערך. It is, in short, a vow to give a certain amount of money to the Temple treasury. Based on this erroneous translation I wondered what the purpose of this *parshah* might be. If his objective is to donate a certain amount of money to *Bedek HaBayis* why does he not simply say so?]

The Chazon Ish argues that the vow is not at all centered upon the money that will eventually have to be handed to the Temple treasurer. The vow that a person undertakes when he says "*Erchi Alay*" is analogous to the vow with which one swears to become a *Nazir*. Now we all know that a *Nazir* is forbidden to drink wine. But that is not what his vow is about. "I accept *Nezirus* upon myself" does not, in any way, mean, "I undertake not to drink wine." That prohibition binds not because he vowed to abstain from wine. He did not. He vows only to become a *Nazir*. The minute that he enters that state, his vow has been fulfilled. He is now forbidden to drink wine, not because he vowed to abstain from wine but because a *Nazir* is forbidden to drink wine. If he were to drink wine once the *Nezirus* has "taken hold" of him, he has not transgressed his vow. That was satisfied by the simple fact that he has become a *Nazir.* When he drinks wine he has transgressed the prohibitions that result from his *Nazir* status.

The money that is to be paid to the Temple treasury is exactly analogous to the Nazir's wine. The vow that he undertakes when he declares "*Erchi Alay*" means that he submits himself to the status of *Erchin.* That status now "takes hold" of him. Just as "*Nezirus*" (not the vow) prohibits wine, so the state of being "taken hold of" by the *Erchin* status obliges him to pay out a certain amount of money. That obligation does not derive from the vow. It derives from the *Erchin* status that, generated by his vow, has "taken hold" of him.

The Chazon Ish has taken us a giant step forward. But he has not explained what is meant by the status that the *Erchin* vow confers upon us. Here the "*Nazir*" analogy pretty much breaks down. We know that the Torah (BeMidbar 6:5) pronounces that one who becomes a *Nazir,* "קדוש יהיה," has become enveloped by a certain type of sanctity. Does anything analogous happen to a person who vows "*Erchi Alay*"?

It turns out that, indeed, there may well be. Here is a quote from *Shiltei HaGiborim* to Avodah Zarah 13a:

> גם האומר "ערכי עלי" מקדיש שפיר כלי ידוע דהיינו גופו ועצמו שהוא מקדישו, אלא שהוא פודהו אח"כ מיד הקדש בדמי ערכו.

Similar statements can be found in the Beis Yosef and the Shulchan Aruch HaRav to Orech Chaim 306. The idea is stated most dramatically by the Alshich to BeChukosai:

> כי על כן אמר ערכי עלי למען תחול קדושה על עצמו מעין כל דבר שהוקדש ונפדה שלא יבצר מלחול בו קדושה מהכין לו הכנה להנהיג עצמו בקדושה כאומר בלבו "איני אשר הייתי עד כה כי עתה הוקדשתי לשמים ונתתי ערכי לה'."

Now, needless to say, we have absolutely no right to state with any certainty that it was this idea-construct that the Chazon Ish had in mind when he wrote of an "*Erchin* status" that "takes hold" of the person who takes an *Erchin* vow. Still, since eminently respectable sources do apparently subscribe to these ideas, it seems reasonable to accept them at the very least as a hypotheses.

Still, we are not quite home yet. As far as I have been able to trace things, I have not found anyone who defines the sanctity that is generated by an *Erchin* vow. Once more, the *Nazir* analogy seems to let us down. While associating *Nezirus* with the admirable character trait of פרישות, *separateness*, is probably much too superficial, it still gives us a general area that is certainly broad and welcoming enough to serve. We have a healthy sense of what is probably to some degree involved. There are people who are פרושים without being *Nezirim* so we have a good idea of what might be entailed. If we were to say that a *Nazir* is one who has raised the *Avodah* of *Perishus* to a formalized and halachically defined state, we would probably not have strayed too far from the truth.

But humans simply do not ever become *hekdesh*.[9] So even if we were to grant that *Erchi Alay* would somehow generate a certain *kedushah* that needs to be redeemed (נפדה) for money, we have nothing analogous that could somehow guide us to an understanding of what practical manifestation that *kedushah* would take.[10]

It is time to return to the first of the two quotes from the Chazon Ish that we cited earlier. He defined the value that is described by the term ע ר ך as relating to כבוד הדבר ומציאותו. We found that, as far as people are concerned, it relates to the factor of humanness that is common to every single human being who lives now or who ever lived on earth.[11]

9. I am using "hekdesh" to describe a sanctity that derives from being in some way tied to, or owned by, the Beis HaMikdash. *Nezirus* and *Kehunah* of course belong to an entirely different order of *kedushah*.

10. I suppose that if we were to take the Alshich at his words, להנהיג עצמו בקדושה, to describe some form of special piety, this would serve. But how would such sanctity be subject to פדיון?

11. The time has come to expand a little bit upon the connectedness between ע ר ך and humanness. Please note that I use "humanness" instead of "humanity" because the latter term has come to be associated more with acting in a "humane" manner, being caring and sympathetic toward another's problems. The former term has the

Perhaps, at this point you, dear Reader, are beginning to see where I am heading. Remember that our study of the *Erchin* concept was stimulated by our interest in Chanah's vow that if she were to be blessed with a son, she would "give" him to HaShem with all that this implied. Among the commentators available to me, nobody seemed quite sure from where Chanah's right to

advantage of being focused and clear. It means only one thing: *the state of being human* and it is that which is engaging our interest in the present context.

So "humanness" it is and that explains the first of two issues that I would like to tackle in this note. What logic is there in expressing the value of a given unit with only the two variables of gender and age having any voice in the amount to be determined? How can it be that the many, many qualities that interest us in all other contexts — intellect, abilities, charm, beauty, dexterity and the like — have nothing to say?

The answer becomes clear when we are focused upon simple humanness. Gender and age are the two constituent elements of humanness at its most basic. We all are either male or female and, at whatever point in a life we are interested in a particular person, he is at a particular point (read, age) that exists along the time line of his life. That is humanness unqualified and unadorned; all else is commentary, by which I mean that all other qualities are gifts (or disadvantages) that are added on to the basic unit.

That should make things pretty clear.

The second issue that I want to tackle here is much more earthshaking. It deals with the Torah's attitude to simple, unadorned humanness. Does it have any meaningful חשיבות? How does the Torah judge the significance of "life" in isolation?

I think that we can best come to some meaningful conclusion by considering the עבד כנעני.

Most of you readers will have come across the concept, שלשים של עבד. It means that if my ox killed your עבד כנעני I will be fined thirty *shekalim* which I will have to pay to the master. The *Meshech Chochmah* suggests that this amount is not arbitrary. It corresponds to the *Erech* of a woman during the peak years (between twenty and sixty) of her life. That the assessment of the עבד כנעני should be based on the female *Erech* rather than that of the male makes sense. Since the victim is an עבד כנעני who is obliged in only those *mitzvos* in which women are included, it could be said that the master lost a "female" unit and it is that which determines the amount.

Nevertheless, the *Meshech Chochmah* stresses, if someone were to be מעריך a living עבד כנעני, who, let us postulate is between the ages of twenty and sixty, he would owe the Temple treasury the full fifty *shekalim* which any other man in this cohort would command.

I assume that the explanation for this apparent inconsistency is as follows. If we are thinking of שלשים של עבד, we are considering the עבד in his relationship to his owner. Within that relationship, and *only* within that relationship, the עבד has a status that is equal to that of a woman. However when our perspective lies completely outside this relationship (even though that relationship is real since at that point he is still an עבד), he is a human being in all the glory that inheres in that status, and the Torah assigns him a standing that does not fall even a mite short of that of the greatest Gadol HaDor.

Life, as life, without any trimmings, seems holy indeed.

There is much room for thought here.

make such a vow derived. In footnote 6 we cited Chasam Sofer's suggestion that this case was unique. Shmuel had been born only as a result of her prayers. This gave her some measure of authority over his life and she had the right to determine how that life should be lived.

Basing myself on a very much expanded version of the Chasam Sofer's logic, I have a different suggestion to make.

Let us get back to "humanness", really to "life" at its irreducible essence. But there is a problem here. "Being" must "be" somewhere; must take place somewhere. Life requires a space, really a context. The twosome of gender and age should perhaps really be a threesome where the original two must be augmented by, must make room for, a third partner: location.

Now, that does not seem to be so difficult. We all live on Earth, it constitutes our world, it is where we feel at home. Problem solved.

Well, not quite. What if there are two worlds, each with welcoming open arms? At that point things become a little complicated. In which of these am I a citizen? Where do I belong?

Does anything of this mean anything from a practical point of view?

The truth is that for us, living in twenty-first-century Pikesville, there really is no problem. Whether we like it or not, we are all "down to Earth".

Chanah's world was different. There really was a choice.

There was a choice because there *was* a Mishkan. Shilo quite literally *was* a different, really a competing, world.

How so?

Here is how. The ceiling of Moshe Rabbeinu's Mishkan was made of two large curtains that were connected to each other by turquoise[12] loops (לולאות) that ran along the edges where they met. Golden hooks (קרסים) were inserted into these loops, thus effectively making the two large curtains into one that was sufficiently large to cover the entire Mishkan.

Shabbos 99a teaches that if one were to stand beneath the point at which the two curtains were connected and look upward the golden hooks in their turquoise loops looked like stars in the sky.

12. A bluish color.

Is this significant? Why would this be recorded in the Gemara? Maharal believes that it is very significant indeed. Here is a quote from his *Chidushei Aggados* to Shabbos.

נראין לולאות המשכן כו׳. דבר זה בארנו במקום אחר משום שמעשה משכן דכתיב (ויקרא ט׳) ויהי ביום השמיני, הויה בפני עצמה דומה אל הוית עולם,[13] **והויה זאת של משכן למעלה מן הויות העולם** כי לכך כתיב במשכן ביום השמיני שהוא למעלה ממעשה בראשית שהיה בשבעת ימים וכלל אמרו ז״ל במדרש (במד״ר פי״ב) שקול מעשה משכן כמו מעשה שמים וארץ כתיב הכא ויהי ביום השמיני וכתיב התם ויהי ערב ויהי בוקר. **כלל הדבר מעשה משכן הויה בפני עצמה למעלה מהויית מעשה בראשית מתיחס לו דומה לו כמו שבארנו בפרשת שמיני, וזה מה שאמרנו כאן נראים לולאות במשכן ככוכבים ברקיע, ר״ל כי דומים מעשה משכן אל מעשה שמים וארץ.**

It turns out that the Mishkan is indeed a "world" unto itself under its own canopy of stars. This world may well offer an alternative to that other beautiful world of which most of us consider ourselves as citizens in good standing.[14]

13. Maharal has written that he has explained these concepts elsewhere. My search program has not been able to find anything even remotely similar anywhere in the Maharal. In addition, the terms that Maharal uses such as הוית העולם do not seem to occur anywhere in the Midrashim. The apparently verbatim quote from the Midrash: שקול מעשה משכן כמו מעשה שמים וארץ כתיב הכא ויהי ביום השמיני וכתיב התם ויהי ערב ויהי בוקר also does not seem to exist.

Instead, starting, it is true, with the word שקול, we have:

ד״א את המשכן שהוא שקול כנגד העולם שקרוי אוהל כשם שמשכן קרוי אוהל כיצד כתיב בראשית ברא אלהים וגו׳ וכתיב (תהלים ק״ד) נוטה שמים כיריעה ובמשכן כתיב ועשית יריעות עזים לאוהל על המשכן וגו׳ כתיב בשני (בראשית א) יהי רקיע ויהי מבדיל וגו׳ ובמשכן כתיב והבדילה הפרוכת לכם בשלישי יקוו המים מתחת השמים ובמשכן ועשית כיור נחושת וכנו נחושת לרחצה וגו׳ ברביעי יהי מאורות ברקיע השמים ובמשכן ועשית מנורת זהב טהור וגו׳ בחמישי ועוף יעופף על הארץ וגו׳ ובמשכן והיו הכרובים פורשי כנפים בששי נברא אדם ובמשכן ואתה הקרב אליך את אהרן אחיך בשביעי כתיב (שם ב) ויכולו השמים וגו׳ ובמשכן ותכל כל עבודת משכן וגו׳ בבריאת עולם כתיב ויברך אלהים ובמשכן ויברך אותם בשביעי ויכל אלהים ובמשכן ויהי ביום כלות משה בשביעי ויקדש אותו ובמשכן ויקדש אותו הוי את המשכן (מדרש רבה במדבר 31:21).

14. I think that we are going to have to do a little housekeeping over here. I believe that my perception of the implications of the term מחנה שכינה is correct, but this gives rise to a problem. Here is a quote from the Rambam in his presentation of the mitzvah of מורא מקדש, the obligation to stand in awe of the Mishkan and the various subsequent בתי מקדש. This obligation is expressed in various activities that are forbidden in these holy confines. It is for example prohibited to go in wearing shoes, or just in order to take a stroll or to use the precincts as a shortcut and so on. Here is the Rambam's introduction to these laws.

מצות עשה ליראה מן המקדש ... ולא מן המקדש אתה ירא אלא ממי שצוה על יראתו.

It is an obligation to stand in awe of the Mikdash. But be aware that it is not the building, as building, that demands your respect. It is He Who demanded this behavior Who is to be respected. (Beis HaBechirah 7:1)

3. *Arachin*

I think that we have come to a point at which we may suggest a solution to the riddle of Chanah's vow. We recall that we mentioned that commentators struggle with this question. We cited Chasam Sofer who suggests that the fact that Shmuel owed his very life to her prayer gave her disposal rights over the form that that life was to take.

I have some thoughts that I would like to share with you concerning this answer. It is clear that the Chasam Sofer sets out from a premise that Chanah's vow was unique. Such an undertaking had probably never been made before and was unlikely to occur ever again. It seems to me that the tenor of the story as it is told belies this assumption. Neither Eli nor Elkanah expresses the slightest surprise at Chanah's plans. If this had been a *chidush* that Chanah had only now thought up, it seems to me that we

Now the Rambam is perfectly justified in using the language that he does. His ruling is based on Yevamos 6b, which reads: מורא האמורה במקדש לא ממקדש אתה מתיירא **אלא ממי שהזהיר על המקדש**. However, that is precisely my problem. Why say that we are to stand in awe of Him who ordained these standards? Why not say, "Stand in awe of Him Who lives in this house"? That, it seems to me, would be much more appropriate.

I have not come across anybody who deals with this question and for all I know there may be an abundance of excellent answers. In asking it I think that I am influenced by the Rashi to Bereishis 28:16 where Yaakov, upon waking up in the morning after his dream of the angels on the ladder, excuses himself for having gone to sleep in such a holy place. The *pasuk* says, ואנכי לא ידעתי, to which Rashi remarks, שאם ידעתי לא ישנתי במקום קדוש כזה. It seems to me that במקום קדוש כזה sounds more like the reasoning that I suggested than that which the Gemara assigns.

For what it is worth, here is my suggestion. Yoma 54a teaches that when everybody came to Yerushalayim on the Yamim Tovim, the *Poroches* was lifted up so that people were able to see the Keruvim in the Kodesh HaKodoshim in each other's embrace as man and wife. The idea was to inspire them with the message, ראו חבתכם לפני המקום. In many areas this warm and loving relationship between the Keruvim standing respectively for the Ribono shel Olam and *klal Yisrael* played a highly significant role. It occurred to me that if this was to be the spirit that was meant to permeate these מקומות הקדושים, then, at the same time to demand a bearing that implies a feeling of awe and formality would be out of place. Apparently when we enter the Beis HaMikdash, we are to feel an overwhelming love for the Ribono shel Olam. Perhaps it would be a little too difficult to have Him inspire awe in that very same "persona". Better to reserve that feeling for the Ribono shel Olam in His role as lawgiver rather than in His role as a loving husband.

[For the sake of transparency, I should note that in *perek* 15 of Hilchos Ishus, where Rambam describes how husband and wife ought to relate to each other, he suggests that the wife should regard her husband with מורא. I am sure that there is much that could be said on this point but this note is not the place. However I feel on safe ground to suggest that this desirable מורא would be less timely on some occasions than on others.]

would somehow have been apprised of this by the way that the story is told. As it is, we certainly get the impression that it made no ripples at all.

I want to suggest that what Chanah did may indeed have been common practice and, standing on its own, would not have elicited any particular reaction. I suggest that if, as Chasam Sofer suggests, the fact that Chanah's prayer had been instrumental in bringing about Shmuel's birth gave her disposal rights over the life that she had made possible, then that right ought to be vested in every father and every mother who had literally joined to create the physical existence of their child.

It seems to me further that this right has a solid halachic foundation in the *parshah* of *Erchin* as we have analyzed and explained it in this essay. I think it possible that we have hit upon a reasonable solution to the problem that plagued us so much earlier in this essay: What precisely is the nature of the sanctity that, to use Chazon Ish's expression, "takes hold" of the one upon whom the vow of *Erchin* has been pronounced. Could it not be that this sanctity is expressed by looking upon oneself as a "Beis HaMikdash *Yid*," one whose permanent "address," as we explained that term earlier when we were discussing Dovid HaMelech, is in the holy precincts, the ethos of whose life, his dreams and ambitions, his thought and his delights, are all anchored firmly there?

Here we come to a couple of paragraphs that deserve amply to be italicized and given a font size all of their own. This has been a complicated read and after all that I can hardly expect you to remember how we started this essay. Let me jog your memory. We quoted the late great Rav Hutner from one of his letters that seemed to decry the idea of living in a "doubled" world. A "broadened, single" world was fine; a "doubled" world lay beyond the pale.

We suggested that there may be situations in which even a "doubled" world might be acceptable. Think it over and I am sure that you will agree with me that we have discovered that situation.

Think it over. Perhaps we have something here.

We suggested that David's prayer may well have been the expression of a wish that he might attain the life that Chanah had mapped out for his Rebbi, Shmuel. We suggested that Chanah had found the license for her vow in the *parshah* of *Erchin*. We had thought that *Erchin* deals with an ambition to live out one's humanness as a "Beis HaMikdash *Yid*."

Up to this point I really cannot see anything particularly problematic in this chain.

Can we stretch the chain any further back? Does the "*Erchin*" system have any basis for its *chidush* that there exists an order of *kedushah* that, for want of a better name we have called the "Beis HaMikdash *Yid*"?

I believe that there exists such a source.

Hashgachah has decreed that I am writing this section on the Wednesday evening preceding *parshas* Pikudei. On Shabbos we are going to bid the Mishkan farewell. It has been a long four weeks to be engaged in a *sugia* that really seems very much to be a הילכתא למשיחא. What is it all really intended to mean to us?

The thought that crossed my mind was that in the forty years that constituted the crucible in which we were formed into God's people, ready to enter Eretz Yisrael, we could all have been described as living "בבית השם".

Here is a brief explanation of what I mean.

We all know that where and with whom people pitched their tents in the wilderness was by no means haphazard. The shortest and therefore the best way in which we can deal with this topic is to quote Rambam, Bais HaBechirah 7:11:

> שלש מחנות היו במדבר מחנה ישראל והוא ארבע מחנות ומחנה לויה שנאמר בה וסביב למשכן יחנו ומחנה שכינה והוא מפתח חצר אהל מועד ולפנים וכנגדן לדורות מפתח ירושלים עד הר הבית כמחנה ישראל ומפתח הר הבית עד פתח העזרה שהוא שער ניקנור כמחנה לויה ומפתח העזרה ולפנים מחנה שכינה וכו'.

The *halachah* assigns different levels of sanctity to each of these three "encampments." These are best expressed in the lack of tolerance that each of them has for certain levels of *tum'ah*. The details need not detain us here, but for our purpose it is crucial to understand that even the *Machaneh Yisrael* (later to be represented by Yerushalayim), the least demanding, required that anybody afflicted by *tzara'as* had to leave its precincts.

Very clearly the Mishkan, and later, the Beis HaMikdash in Yerushalayim, did not exist in isolation, its sanctity spread beyond its own confines (מחנה שכינה) to the Har HaBayis (מחנה לויה), and even further to encompass the whole of Yerushalayim (מחנה ישראל).

The difference between our lives as these were lived in the Wilderness and those that we experienced later, once we had entered Eretz Yisrael, was that in the Wilderness nobody, but really *nobody*, lived completely outside the "Mishkan Complex" as that is defined in its broadest meaning. Later, unless you lived in Yerushalayim, you were in no sense בבית השם; but in the Wilderness the entire encampment, all the way to its farthest reaches, was, at the very least, מחנה ישראל, and would certainly have qualified as בבית השם.[15]

If we are correct in our suggestion that the *Erchin* concept really harks back to the encampment in the Midbar, and spreads out to encompass Chanah's dream for her beloved child and David' prayer for a fulfilled life, then we realize that the *parshios* of the Mishkan are not at all הילכתא למשיחא. They are, on the contrary, positioned at the very center of Jewish living. A good *yid* is a "Beis HaMikdash *Yid*."

Perhaps it is appropriate to finish this essay on that note. Even today in the long and dreadful *galus* in which we are enmeshed we can, and therefore should, join Dovid Melech Yisrael in his entreaty that echoes in our hearts across the ages:

אחת שאלתי מאת ה׳ אותה אבקש
שבתי בבית ה׳ כל ימי חיי
לחזות בנעם ה׳ ולבקר בהיכלו

P.S. Whoever heard of a P.S. to an essay? Letters are one thing, essays, another. But, you know what? Throughout the arduous hours that I spent researching and writing this essay, I kind of felt that I was in a dialogue with you, the reader. I felt myself hiking along rough terrain, largely unexplored, grappling with ideas that in many ways were completely new to me. I needed to feel that you were right there, following along, critically it is true, but also friendly and encouraging. I needed to feel your support over the especially tough spots.

So, in a way, this is a letter as much as it is an essay.

Do you agree with me in the conclusions that I have reached in

15. Please note that קדשים קלים could be eaten throughout Yerushalayim, though not beyond. It seems obvious that the מחנה ישראל can, at least in certain senses, be considered בית ה׳.

my understanding of *Erchin*? I have, of course, no idea — unless you let loose with one of those missives which, I suppose, every writer must sooner or later expect. But the mere fact that you came along for the ride marks you as a fellow explorer. Let me wish you "Happy hunting" as you embark upon your own adventures.

Here is a thought with which I would like to leave you, I hope only temporarily. I feel that I have not taken the *Erchin* parts of this essay far enough. I am particularly intrigued by the fact that I can be *ma'arich* not only myself (declaring myself as a "Beis HaMikdash *Yid*" with all that that standing implies), but also another — and even a non-Jew (concerning neither of whom I have any rights to declare them to be anything at all). When I do that, the *Eirech* that I will have to pay for him is not one mite less that the *Eirech* of the greatest Gaon and Tzadik who is in the same age-bracket. What are the implications?

My intuition tells me that this truth can open many doors. (Do you remember that earlier in this essay I referred to *Erchin* as the great "Leveler"?) At this point I cannot tell you where those doors will lead. I sense the beginnings of another essay stirring within me.

Let us get together again, perhaps sometime soon! (But not, I am afraid, in this book.)

4.

Rambam on Ahavas HaShem

FEELING FONDNESS FOR THE RIBONO SHEL OLAM[1]

We are setting out on an exciting, rewarding, and, more importantly, a very necessary project.[2] I want to get the ball rolling by sharing a simple little diagram with you, one that will give us a sense of just how fundamental this matter really is. This diagram will illustrate my perception[3] of the way the first five *mitzvos* in the Rambam's Sefer HaMitzvos relate to each other and how as a group, they relate to the other *mitzvos.*

Here goes.

1. It seems to me that the root word א ה ב is particularly problematic since it covers a range running all the way from feeling fondness for the Ribono shel Olam, to a preferred recipe for preparing steaks (Bereishis 27:4 and 9).

Years ago when language had not yet become totally הפקר, the British used to pride themselves on the fact that they had two words, *love* and *like,* which helped them to avoid such anomalies. If a youngster declared that he "loved" ice cream, he was reprimanded. You can "like" the stuff; never love it! I have not found any explanation why *lashon hakodesh* should have tolerated such a relaxed attitude to such a fundamental concept.

I have decided to forgo the "l" word throughout this essay. We all know that not so long ago this word was usable in polite company and could have served perfectly well for our purposes. Unfortunately, in our benighted generation, it has become so disgusting, so encrusted in licentiousness and ugliness, that I feel it to have become inappropriate as a descriptive term for *ahavas HaShem.* So for better or worse, you are going to have to get used to *fondness.* I do not consider it to be particularly apropos as an English rendering for the laden Hebrew אהבה, but unless and until I come up with something better, that is what it is going to be.

2. It is also pretty complicated. You are going to have to buckle down seriously, but, after all, it is for challenges such as this that we are in the business of learning the Ribono shel Olam's Torah.

3. I use the expression "my perception" because as far as I know, nobody, including Rambam himself, takes these five *mitzvos* as a group, or actually two groups, a twosome and a threesome. Nevertheless, I believe that, as I shall now explain, they do belong together. Please see text for my thinking.

3	2	1
[2] להאמין היחוד וזו נקראת גם כן מצוותקבלת עול מלכות שמים		[1] להאמין שיש בורא עולם
[5] לעבדו	[4] להאמין יראתו ולהפחד ממנו	[3] לאהוב את ה'

Here is the explanation of the diagram. The first two *mitzvos* are, I think, unique. Alone among all the 613 *mitzvos*, they *define* the Ribono shel Olam for our benefit. He is both Creator and King. The next three *mitzvos* inform us of how we, as His handiwork (Creator) and subjects (King), are to relate to Him: We are to be fond of Him; to stand in awe of Him and to serve Him. Accordingly we would not be wrong in asserting that these five *mitzvos* are, in a sense, an introduction to the rest of Sefer HaMitzvos. The remaining 608 *mitzvos* give us directions concerning what we have to do, or refrain from doing, in order to establish and perpetuate the desired relationship (made up of Fondness, Awe, and Service).

Once we have diagramed these five *mitzvos* as we have, we may as well continue the system and apply the same thought process to *mitzvos* 3, 4, and 5. I would suggest that 3 and 4 relate to 5 as cause relates to effect. If I am "fond" of the Ribono shel Olam and "stand in awe" of Him, the need to serve Him follows automatically. Life, as it were, has been defined for me.

If all this theorizing can be accepted, and I see little reason for quibbling, then it turns out that, in Rambam's view, the very first obligation that binds a Jew once he has accepted the Ribono shel Olam as Creator and King is to be fond of Him.[4]

4. I do not know what criteria influenced the Rambam in determining the sequence in which he lists the *mitzvos* in Sefer HaMitzvos. However, the fact remains that in the *Yad*, in Yesodei HaTorah 2:1 and 2, he also deals with *ahavah* and *yir'ah* and his treatment is consistent with Sefer HaMitzvos. *Ahavah* comes before *yir'ah*.

The language in Yesodei HaTorah gives us a hint for why this might be so. In the *ahavah* section he writes, **מיד** הוא אוהב ומשבח ... while in the *yir'ah* section he writes, **וכשמחשב בדברים האלה** עצמן מיד.... The implication is that psychologically *ahavah* tends to kick in before *yir'ah* does. To me this seems intuitively puzzling but then I do not know what is involved.,

If we could put the Rambam's certainly carefully chosen language aside, I would have assumed that he simply felt that the *ahavah* relationship is inherently more significant than that of *yir'ah*. However, once more, I do not know the exact source for such an assumption. See Hilchos Teshuvah 10:1.

That makes a correct and healthy understanding of this mitzvah very important. Let us begin!

THE RAMBAM'S TREATMENT OF THE MITZVAH OF *AHAVAS HASHEM*

Before we start on the actual *sugia*, I want to tell you of the plan I have for this essay. Instead of simply sharing certain insights with you, I want to take you along on the trail that led me to them. I thought that you might find it interesting to join me in a little "Yeshivishe" research. Let us see what we can do with the available sources.

I hope that you will find this to be a stimulating exercise.

Obviously the ultimate definition of the *ahavah* for the Ribono shel Olam that is required of us must be solidly based in Chazal. Unfounded and ungrounded philosophic speculations are disallowed.

And here we stumble across a major problem. It seems to have been the custom of even our greatest teachers to have been less than totally precise in transcribing from earlier authorities. They seem to have been interested in the general sense of the quote rather than the exact terms that the originators actually used. We have this information from the great Ga'on, R. Chaim Heller in his *Petach Davar* to the second edition of his Sefer HaMitzvos.[5]

Here is a short quote from a very detailed presentation:

> וידוע דגם לאו בכל מקום שנמצא שינוי בלשון המובא בספרי הראשונים מכפי שהוא בתלמודינו, שיש להוציא מזה ולומר דגירסא אחרת היתה להם ז"ל. **דבאמת כוונו רק להביא את הענין ומשמעותו ולא להעתיק הלשון בדיוק**. וכה"ג כבר כתבו הראשונים ז"ל שדרך הש"ס לקצר הפסוקים לערבם ולהוסיף בהם וגם במשניות ובריתות כך היא דרכם של האמוראים וכו'.

Now, it happens that a very important source for our subject comes from the Sifri[6] to VaEschanan. It also happens that there

5. There is a tradition passed on by the late Ga'on, R. Yechezkel Abramski (see *Mitzvas HaMelech*, p. 20) and mentioned also in the Frankel Sefer HaMitzvos, p. 4) that when the Chafetz Chaim saw R. Heller's superbly annotated Sefer HaMitzvos he said that henceforth all previous editions of the Sefer HaMitzvos have the character of a ספר שאינו מוגה.

6. Please be aware that there exists a group of midrashim that are collectively known as *midrashei halachah*. In contrast to most other midrashim that deal mainly with aggadic material, these are devoted to interpreting the halachic parts of the Torah. We do not possess a *midrash halachah* to *sefer* Bereishis. The one that deals

are seemingly significant differences in wording among different recensions. That is going to make life a little harder for us. For reasons that should become clear as we go along, we will, for the purpose of this essay, stick with the Rambam's reading of the Sifri.

5	4
ספרי (פינקלשטין הארוווטץ)	ספר המצוות (העליר, מהדורה חדשה)
והיו הדברים האלה אשר אנכי מצוך היום על לבבך **למה נאמר**? לפי שהוא אומר ואהבת את ה' אלהיך בכל לבבך איני יודע באיזה צד אוהבים את **הקב"ה** ת"ל והיו הדברים האלה אשר אנכי מצוך היום על לבבך שמתוך כך **אתה מכיר את הקב"ה ומדבק בדרכיו.**	המצוה השלישית היא שצוונו לאהבו יתעלה, וזה שנתבונן ונשכיל מצותיו ופעולותיו עד שנשיגהו ונתענג בהשגתו תכלית התענוג וזאת היא האהבה המחויבת. ולשון ספרי, לפי שנאמר ואהבת את ה' אלהיך **איני יודע כיצד אוהב (חסרה מלת "אדם" המופיעה ב#6)** את המקום, תלמוד לומר והיו הדברים האלו אשר אנכי מצוך היום על לבבך שמתוך כך אתה מכיר את **מי שאמר והיה העולם.** כבר בארו לך כי בהשתכלות תתאמת לך ההשגה ותגיע **התענוג ותבוא האהבה בהכרח.**

7	6
משנה תורה, יסודי התורה 2:2	ספר החנוך
והיאך היא הדרך לאהבתו ויראתו בשעה שיתבונן האדם במעשיו וברואיו הנפלאים הגדולים ויראה מהן חכמתו שאין לה ערך ולא קץ מיד הוא אוהב ומשבח ומפאר ומתאוה תאוה גדולה לידע השם הגדול כמו שאמר דוד צמאה נפשי לאלהים לאל חי ... ולפי הדברים האלו אני מבאר כללים גדולים ממעשה רבון העולמים כדי שיהיו פתח למבין לאהוב את השם כמו שאמרו חכמים בענין אהבה שמתוך כך אתה מכיר את מי שאמר והיה העולם:	...וענין האהבה שנחשוב בפעולותיו ובפקודיו עד שנשיגהו כפי יכלתנו ונתענג בהשגתו בתכלית העונג וזאת היא האהבה המחויבת. ולשון ספרי לפי שנאמר ואהבת **איני יודע כיצד** אוהב **אדם את המקום** ת"ל והיו הדברים האלה אשר אנכי מצוך היום על לבבך שמתוך כך אתה מכיר את **מי שאמר והיה העולם.** כלומר שעם התבוננות בתורה **תתישב האהבה בלב בהכרח ...**

The Sifri is quoted in nos. 4, 5, and 6. We will consider those three first.

with *sefer* Shemos is called Mechilta. The one to VaYikra is called Sifro and the one to BaMidbar and Devarim is called Sifri (or Sifrei), actually the plural form of Sifro, called thus because it interprets two of the five books of the Torah. The Shema in which the mitzvah of *ahavah* is contained is in VaEschanan (*sefer* Devarim) and is therefore elucidated in the Sifri.

POSING THE QUESTIONS:

1. Number 4 poses a problem: **איני יודע כיצד וכו'**; number 5 simply makes a query: **למה נאמר וכו'**.
2. Number 4 has: איני יודע כיצד אוהב את **המקום**. Number 5 has **הקב"ה** instead of המקום.
3. As they offer their solutions, both numbers. 4 and 5 are consistent with the way that they posed the problem.[7] Number 4 has, ... אתה מכיר את **מי שאמר והיה העולם** while number 5 has אתה מכיר את **הקב"ה** ומדבק בדרכיו.
4. Number 6 has the same wording as number 4 except that it adds the word "אדם" in the phrase: כיצד אוהב [אדם] את המקום

SLEUTHING AND BEGINNING TO RECOGNIZE THE SIGNIFICANCE OF THE CHANGES

A careful reading of the two versions of the Sifri will show that each is internally consistent[8] but differs radically from the other in the way each presents the Sifri. We will begin with number 4 borrowing the addition of "אדם" from number 6.

לפי שנאמר ואהבת ... איני יודע כיצד אוהב אדם את המקום?
ת"ל והיו הדברים האלה אשר אנכי מצוך היום על לבבך שמתוך כך אתה מכיר את מי שאמר והיה העולם.

7. The Sifri is the equivalent of someone who goes to the information desk at the airport and asks help in filling out a form. He is unfamiliar with the topic and would appreciate some guidance.

The Rambam's reading depicts the fellow who comes rushing up to the information desk and starts yelling: "There must be some mistake. I know my way around here and there is no way that this flight can leave from that gate. That particular berth does not have the facilities for that size plane. Putting that plane at that gate is an impossible *shiduch*."

Meaning: God, Who is the מקומו של עולם, or, as the Rambam calls Him later, מי שאמר והיה העולם, Who stands *outside* the universe and its puny values and ideas, cannot possibly be accommodated inside the human heart where fondness must have its home. There simply is no room for Him!

The difference between the Sifri reading (number 5) and the Rambam (number 4) will be in what the clerk at the Information Desk has to do. In number 5 he will, unperturbed, be filling out the well-known lines on the form. It is all in a day's work. In number 4 he will take the fellow into the office and show him the blueprint of the miraculous machine that has recently been installed at the disputed gate. It has the ability to generate limitless EXPANSION. You just have to know which button to press. There will be no problem at all.

8. Please see footnote 7. "מקום" goes with "מי שאמר והיה העולם" and הקב"ה goes with "הקב"ה".

4. *Rambam on Ahavas HaShem*

The question asked in the first line of the Sifri can be translated as: "How can 'אדם' be fond of 'מקום'?" Once we get our translations straight, we will recognize that a real problem is being articulated.

Our first task will be to try to understand the name "מקום" when used to describe the Ribono shel Olam.

The most specific place is Bereishis Rabba 68:9.

> מפני מה מכנין שמו של הקב"ה וקוראין אותו מקום? שהוא מקומו של עולם ואין עולמו מקומו מן מה דכתיב (שמות לג) הנה מקום אתי הוי הקב"ה מקומו של עולם ואין עולמו מקומו.
>
> Why is מקום, the base meaning of which is *place,* used as a name for the Ribono shel Olam? It is to draw our attention to the fact that He (stands completely) outside the universe and is in no way a part of it (*extramundane*). He is the "place" that makes the existence of the world possible but is Himself in no way dependent upon it. The universe is entirely subordinate to Him and thus cannot be said to be His "place" (*intramundane*). It in no way limits Him.

Earlier we worded the question that number 4 (particularly with the Chinuch's addition of "אדם") asks: How can "אדם" be fond of "מקום"? The wording could not be more apposite. Adam was created from *adamah,* the lowliest part of our physical world. What possible connection, let alone fondness, can there be between him and the מקומו של עולם, One Who in no conceivable way can be said to have any commonality with the world of which man is a part?[9]

It now falls to us to understand the Sifri's answer.

9. In the first volume of the Frankel Mishneh Torah [not the Sefer HaMitzvos] in the section named ספר הליקוטים, at the bottom of the first column on page רלד, we have the following citation from R. Shlomo Eiger:

> והיאך היא הדרך לאהבתו ויראתו: ר"ל והלא אין אהבה כ"א מצד ההדמות או הטבעות או יחסות, גם אחר שמהותו יתברך נעלם תכלית ההעלם איך יצויר לאהוב מה שאינו מכיר כלל? וע"ז כתב בשעה שיתבונן, ר"ל שהיא מ"מ אפשרי השגה מצד פעולותיו וכל יותר שיתבונן בגדלותם יותר יאבהו. גם כיון שהכל פעולותיו הנה שפיר יש אהבה מחמת קבול תועלת ממנו ית'.

It was gratifying for me to see that my own researches had led me to the same interpretation of the Sifri's question as the one suggested by the great R. Shlomo Eiger. Within I will suggest a different way of understanding the Sifri's answer.

It seems to me that it is of particular interest that in the Mishneh Torah (Yesodei HaTorah 2:2) the Rambam begins his analysis of *yir'ah* and *ahavah* with the same question that the Sifri, as he quotes it, seems to be asking: והאיך היא הדרך לאהבתו ויראתו.

We stated earlier that in this essay we are going to follow Rambam's reading (number 4) of the Sifri. Up to this point we have used the other reading (number 5) as a foil to draw attention to the radically different wording that Rambam adopted. By this time all of us realize how profoundly altered the message of Chazal is once we speak of אדם/מקום instead of simply using הקב"ה throughout. We are now ready to drop number 5 from consideration and stick to the Rambam.

In his reading the Sifri counsels that if we wish to feel fondness for the Ribono shel Olam, we should read and of course live by the second part of *parshas kri'as Shema* שמתוך כך מכיר אתה את מי שאמר והיה העולם.

Let us look at the Sifri (according to Rambam's reading) once more.

1. מצוה השלישית היא שצוונו לאהבו יתעלה, וזה שנתבונן ונשכיל מצותיו ופעולותיו עד שנשיגהו ונתענג בהשגתו תכלית התענוג וזאת היא האהבה המחויבת.
2. ולשון ספרי, לפי שנאמר ואהבת את ה' אלהיך איני יודע כיצד אוהב (חסרה מלת "אדם" המופיעה ב#6) את המקום, תלמוד לומר והיו הדברים האלו אשר אנכי מצוך היום על לבבך שמתוך כך אתה מכיר את מי שאמר והיה העולם.
3. כבר בארו לך כי בהשתכלות תתאמת לך ההשגה ותגיע התענוג ותבוא האהבה בהכרח.

Please note that numbers 1 and 3 (in this listing) are the language of the Rambam. Between them the Rambam quotes the Sifri. Note further that, at least superficially, there appears to be a divergence between what Rambam says in number 1 and what he says in number 3. In number 1 he maps out a system that seems to lead to fulfillment of the *ahavah* requirement: 1 נתבונן, 2 נשכיל, 3 עד שנשיגהו, 4 ונתענג ... תכלית התענוג. He stops there. He appears to demand nothing else from us and ends with a statement that seems to sum it all up: **וזאת** היא האהבה המחויבת.

Now it is clear that the "...וזאת" refers to the entire four-stage process that we discovered in the previous paragraph. The Rambam is telling us the following: "It is true that I have stopped with the achievement of תענוג and have not mentioned anything about attaining *ahavah*. Please do not let that frustrate you. I know precisely what I am doing and, moreover, if you take a moment to look below at number 3 you will see that I end with the words ותבוא האהבה בהכרח. The point is that I do not believe that *ahavah* can be commanded. You either feel it or you do not.

If the Torah nevertheless *commands* me to feel fondness for God, it must be that there is a process that when conscientiously followed will inevitably lead to the feeling of *ahavah* and it is only that *process*, not the end result, that can be called a mitzvah.[10] The term "מחוייבת" can be applied only to the various steps of the process. The *fulfillment* of the mitzvah, the actual fondness that we are expected to feel, cannot be ordered. Having done all that we are called upon to *do*, we must rely on a successful outcome: ותבוא האהבה בהכרח.[11]

And now, entering into the last lap of our complex and exhausting chase, we come to the final sprint: the unavoidable and therefore doubly daunting "HOW!?" question. How does the latter half of the *parshah* lead us to fondness of the Ribono shel Olam? The Sifri promised us, ותבוא האהבה בהכרח; the Mishneh Torah promised us, **מיד** הוא אוהב .... Will they deliver? Can they deliver? Many of us have learned at least some Torah; of those, many can claim to have learned conscientiously and some even with heroic commitment. How many of them would assert that *as a result of their studies* their fondness of the Ribono shel Olam increased?

Here is my proposed solution. I want to suggest that the Sifri's answer to the insistently demanding *keitzad* is not limited to the *pasuk* that it actually quotes: תלמוד לומר והיו הדברים האלו אשר אנכי מצוך היום על לבבך, but that this verse is no more than the introduction to a longer passage that takes us to the very end of the first *parshah* of *kri'as Shema*.[12] [13] The Torah's prescription for attaining

10. אהבה **מחויבת**.

11. In that sense the mitzvah of *ahavah* can be compared to the mitzvah of Talmud Torah that also appears in the first *parshah* of *kri'as Shema*. Certainly the Torah's goal in commanding us to learn Torah is that we should know what it wishes to teach us — והיו הדברים האלה ... על לבבך. Still the mitzvah in its formal sense, what we are called upon to *do*, is the *studying* of Torah, not *knowing* it. The language of the Rambam in Sefer HaMitzvos, Positive Commands 7, is: ללמוד חכמת התורה וללמדה.

12. See Succos 34b where the Gemara works out that the *lulav*, *hadasim*, and *aravos* belong in one bundle while the *esrog* is to be held separately. This is based upon the fact that there is no *vav* joining the *esrog* to the *lulav* (פרי עץ הדר כפת תמרים) but that the other three *minim* have *vavs* combining them (כפת תמרים וענף עץ עבות **ו**ערבי נחל). In the first *parshah* of *kri'as Shema* all the *mitzvos* are combined by *vavim* (**ו**שננתם, **ו**דברת, **ו**קשרתם and so on). I do not know the *sugios* well enough to be able to say that the issues are exactly parallel, but it seems to me that certainly on the surface there appears to be a reasonable assumption that the comparison ought to carry some weight.

13. In English writing we would have added an ellipsis (...) to indicate that what has been said is not the whole story. I do not know when the ubiquitous וכו', which is used so frequently in later Hebrew, came into being.

ahavas HaShem is not limited to the simple act of learning as we understand that word. Rather it recommends a total immersion in the world of Torah, making it the main focus of our relationship with and the education of, our children (ושננתם לבניך), the consuming interest of our own intellectual activity (ודברת בם ...), the motivating energy of our physical activities (תפילין של יד), the source of our dignity, even of our majesty, as human beings created in the image of God (תפילין של ראש), and, finally, the determiner of the spirit that is to pervade our home (מזוזה).[14]

Please take a look at footnote 14. I can really imagine that someone who takes the "Torah leap" recommended in this passage, can indeed change his entire being. He may achieve a level of spirituality that his soul[15] will reach the point at which it will be able to flower into a true fondness for the Ribono shel Olam.

If you doubt this, let me introduce you to a *Yid* who knew this secret. Here is a quote from letter 3 in the first volume of the קובץ אגרות חזון איש.

14. Perhaps here we have a key to understanding stories told of some of our *gedolim* that I for one never really believed. For example, I read that the Ragochover Gaon continued learning uninterruptedly even while sitting shivah for a beloved family member. As an "אנוס" who was simply unable to break loose, he felt himself unbound by the halachic strictures that forbade this activity during times of mourning. My problem was that I felt sure that a person of the Ragochover's standing would learn totally לשם שמים, because that was what the Ribono shel Olam expected from His *Yidden*. What would be the point of learning when the Ribono shel Olam expressly forbade it?

Again I have come across stories of *gedolim* who, for whatever the reason, were unable to be anesthetized during required surgery. It is told that they asked their surgeon to wait until they (the patients) were involved in thinking through some particularly difficult *sugia*. After that the cutting could begin. Nothing would be felt.

Perhaps there really are such people — *ehrliche Yidden* in a big way.

Would that not be wonderful?

15. It is extremely important that you read the current essay in tandem with its partner, *"More on Ahavas HaShem"* which also appears in this volume. These two essays had originally been one, but in a moment of sanity I realized that a piece of that size would be way too unwieldy and would repel readers rather than attract them.

The reason for my exhorting you to read the two essays in tandem is that although the bodies of the two essays are not at all similar, their conclusions, while using different terminology, are essentially the same. In the current essay I have defined the Sifri's solution to Rav Eiger's question in terms of a total immersion in Torah values, thus attaining a level of spirituality that allows for a meaningful relationship with the Ribono shel Olam, whereas in that other essay I explained it in terms of RaMChal's ideas concerning the relationship of our souls to our bodies.

A reading of the two essays together will yield a more rounded picture than either of them could have yielded on its own.

... הלא אמרו אין דברי תורה מתקיימים אלא במי שממית עצמו עליה. המיתה שבכאן היא הנטיה מפשוטו של החיים לעומקו של החיים,לתוך תוכו של החיים. כל שהאדם מרבה בשבירת המדות מרבה חיים כי שבירת המדות היא הריגת החיים השטחיים ומיתה של היצר הממלא כל הגוף. הוא החיים המוליך בדרכה של תורה. מדות המושחתות רבות הנה והם עצמן ובשרו של האדם והממית אחת מהן המית את עצמו ומקצת עצמו ככל עצמו. ואמנם מיתה זו תחיה בעליה ודברי תורה מתקיימים בידו.

Chazal have taught us that the way to make the Torah that we have learned a permanent part of ourselves is to "die" for it. That death is the metamorphosis from superficial living (which now belongs to the past and is no more) to essential living, to the very soul of life. The more we wage war against our undisciplined, unschooled selves, the more we are born anew... That is so because ridding ourselves of undisciplined characteristics means ridding ourselves of a life that has no reality. There are many ugly character traits that really define us. Doing away with even one of them makes a real difference. ... To some extent we have died and in that death lies life....

Do you get the point?

And in letter 153 in that same volume:

... בהיותי שבור ורצוץ כל הימים ולא זכיתי לשום עונג מתענוגי החיים נוסף לכאבי הגוף ושבירתו כל הימים. הענג היחידי הוא לי לעשות רצון קוני ואין לי צער יותר גמור מכשלון בעון.

My entire life I have been crushed by debilitating problems besides the fact that I am in constant pain and severe discomfort. Only one joy lightens my burdens and that is when I know that I am fulfilling God's will and there is no pain greater than the awareness that I have somehow sinned.

And that brings us to a point at which we will finally be able to call it a day and round off our musings about *ahavas HaShem*. There is one last step that we ought to take. The Rambam has left us a wonderful gift and we would be ingrates if we would not take full advantage of it.

There are two *pesukim* in the Torah that on the surface are very similar to each other.

ואהבת את ה' אלהיך (דברים 6:5)

ואהבת לרעך כמוך (ויקרא 19:18)

We are to be fond of the Ribono shel Olam and we are to be fond of our fellows. To what extent do the two identical verbs mean the same thing?[16]

The Rambam appears to drop us a clear hint that some significant matters are at stake here. The mitzvah of *ahavas HaShem* appears in Yesodei HaTorah 2:2. The mitzvah of *ahavas rei'a* appears in Dei'os 6:3.

Here is some background information that will help us to understand the significance of these placements. Toward the end of the Moreh Nevuchim, the Rambam maps out what appears to be the intended structure of the Mishneh Torah that he is planning to write. Broadly speaking, much of what he writes there actually anticipates what we know today as the end result of that planning, although there are details concerning which he changed his mind along the path to fruition. These divergences need not trouble us in the present context.

Here is a quote of the two sections that will get us where we need to go.

> ראיתי לחלק ה'מצוות' לפי זאת הכונה אל ארבעה עשר כללים:
>
> הכלל הראשון כולל המצוות אשר הם דעות שרשיות[17], והם אשר ספרנום ב"הלכות יסודי התורה" ...
>
> הכלל השלישי כולל המצוות התלויות בתיקון המידות, והם אשר ספרנום ב"הלכות דעות".

We have reached a point at which the Rambam's placement of *ahavas HaShem* and *ahavas rei'a* respectively conveys a great deal to us concerning the nature of these two *mitzvos*. *Ahavas HaShem* is not a matter of *tikkun hamidos*, of *being nice*. It defines the very essence (דעות שרשיות) of the Ribono shel Olam's attitude toward mankind, the peak and glory of His creations.

16. Ramban to the VaYikra passage points to the differences between the prepositions. In the case of the Ribono shel Olam we have "את" whereas relative to our fellow we have "... ל". Ramban examines the disparate meanings but the differences that he discovers do not, as far as I can see, impact upon our interest here.

17. Ramban to the VaYikra passage points to the differences between the prepositions. In the case of the Ribono shel Olam we have "את" whereas relative to our fellow we have "... ל". Ramban examines the disparate meanings but the differences that he discovers do not, as far as I can see, impact upon our interest here.

4. *Rambam on Ahavas HaShem*

HE WANTS A RELATIONSHIP WITH US![18] [19]

ואהבת את ה' אלהיך

This indeed is a דעה שרשית! The Rambam was absolutely right in putting *ahavas HaShem* in Yesodei HaTorah and *ahavas Rei'im* in Dei'os. By doing so he clarified absolutely the character of the mitzvah of *ahavas HaShem.*

THE STRUCTURE OF THE FIRST *PARSHAH OF KRI'AS SHEMA*

I suppose that this essay is pretty much finished. Still, as a kind of postscript, a final farewell, I would like to spell out what, in light of all that we have learned together, seems to me to be the structure and meaning of the first *parshah* of *kri'as Shema* as Rambam might have understood it. My suggestion will be based upon what I have been able to glean from those portions of the Rambam (taken from the Moreh Nevuchim, the Sefer HaMitzvos, and the Mishneh Torah) that I have come across. It may not be correct. Please be aware of that as you follow along.

I will begin with quoting the Rambam in the first three *halachos* of Hilchos Yesodei HaTorah. Everything will follow from what the Rambam teaches us there.

יסוד היסודות ועמוד החכמות לידע שיש שם מצוי ראשון והוא ממציא כל נמצא וכל הנמצאים משמים וארץ ומה שביניהם לא נמצאו אלא מאמתת המצאו:
ואם יעלה על הדעת שהוא אינו מצוי אין דבר אחר יכול להמצאות:
ואם יעלה על הדעת שאין כל הנמצאים מלבדו מצויים הוא לבדו יהיה מצוי

18. At this point some of you might want to recall the deeply moving *piyut* from our Yom Kippur *machzor*: .... אשר אימתך ... ורצית שבח. It is hard to fathom why the Ribono shel Olam is so fond of us even in the face of repeated failures. And yet ... and yet ורצית שבח ...! As we have often noted: *Es iz gut tzu zein a Yid!*

19. Here is a Midrash from Bereishis Rabba 10:1:

> שוקיו עמודי שש וגו' (שיר השירים 5:15) שוקיו זה העולם שנשתוקק הקב"ה לבראתו כמה דתימא ועלי תשוקתו ומנין שכן הוא אומר שנאמר (בראשית ב) ויכלו השמים והארץ וגו' אין ויכלו אלא לשון תאוה שנאמר (תהלים 84) נכספה וגם כלתה נפשי וגו'

> (Describing the shepherd who plays such a major role in Shir HaShirim) *His thighs* (שוקיו deriving from ש ק ק, *to crave*) hint at *Olam HaZeh,* a world that the Ribono shel Olam craved to bring about ... as is written, ויכולו השמים והארץ, *Heaven and earth were completed.* God apparently longs for heaven and earth to come into being.

> Clearly the Ribono shel Olam wants to establish a relationship with us!

ולא יבטל הוא לבטולם שכל הנמצאים צריכין לו והוא ברוך הוא אינו צריך להם ולא לאחד מהם לפיכך אין אמתתו כאמתת אחד מהם:

> The most basic of all our assumptions is the knowledge that there exists an original Being Who, Himself, is the originator of all existence. Nothing that does not derive from the immutable fact of His existence can exist in either heaven or earth or what lies between them.
>
> If it were possible to postulate that this original Being would not exist, then absolutely nothing else would or could exist.
>
> Further, if we could imagine that nothing other than He were in existence, His being would not in any way be prejudiced. His existence is in no way dependent upon anything outside Himself. All creatures need Him but He needs neither them nor any single one of them.
>
> The truth of His existence is *sui generis*. In its absolute independence it is in no way comparable to any other truth.

Welcome to שמע ישראל ה' אלהינו ה' אחד. Now clearly the Being of Whom the Rambam speaks has no imaginable commonality with any other creature we have ever come across. So, knowing nothing at all about Him, there is still one thing that we know clearly beyond all doubt. There can obviously be no talk of any real relationship between Him and us or between us and Him. Nothing of the sort can even be imagined.

Except, of course, that, as we all know very well, the very next *pasuk* demands unambiguously that we develop a fondness for the Ribono shel Olam that, in intensity, exceeds anything that we could possibly imagine; **בכל** לבבך **ובכל** נפשך **ובכל** מאודך.

Does that make sense?

Well, that is really the problem that engaged R. Shlomo Eiger as I quoted him in footnote 9. Please take the time to glance back there for a moment. It is important that you have it clear in your mind in order to understand the first of the points that I wish to make now. It is this:

The connection between שמע ישראל ... ה' אחד and ואהבת ... had always escaped me. By what logic does the second verse follow upon the first? How does the fact that the Ribono shel Olam is the sole Creator of the entire cosmos lead to the conclusion that we ought to feel fondness for Him?

Is not the contrary true? Is not the lack of even the slightest commonality between us (Us? Doesn't "us" itself imply some form of cohesion?) exclude the possibility of any warmth of feeling?

That question is, in fact, the answer! The conjunctive adverb (the *vav* in ואהבת) in this case is not "therefore" but "in spite of...." The meaning of the juxtaposition between "שמע" and "**ואהבת**" is not, "I am the Creator of the world, *therefore* be fond of Me" but, "It is true that I am the Creator of the world, but, *in spite of that, against all intuitive certainty*, I want you to be fond of Me."[20]

And now we have that same question indicated in the Torah: We say שמע; we say **ואהבת** and we are perplexed: How, o God, are we expected to be fond of You of Whom we lack the slightest familiarity? The Sifri, echoed by Rambam, teaches us that it is the third section of the first *parshah* of *kri'as Shema* that will give us the answer to this impossibly difficult question. The possibility of feeling an unlimited fondness for the Ribono shel Olam is grounded in the "death" of which the passage in the Chazon Ish that we quoted earlier speak, a "death" that is really "life" in its most perfect form. Here it is once more:

> ... הלא אמרו אין דברי תורה מתקיימים אלא במי שממית עצמו עליה. המיתה שבכאן היא הנטיה מפשוטו של החיים לעומקו של החיים, לתוך תוכו של החיים. כל שהאדם מרבה בשבירת המדות מרבה חיים כי שבירת המדות היא הריגת החיים השטחיים ומיתה של היצר הממלא כל הגוף. הוא החיים המוליך בדרכה של תורה. מדות המושחתות רבות הנה והם עצמן ובשרו של האדם והממית אחת מהן המית את עצמו ומקצת עצמו ככל עצמו. ואמנם מיתה זו תחיה בעליה ודברי תורה מתקיימים בידו.

The great Chazon Ish knew of what he spoke. He understood the "life-nurturing" "death" that he describes. He was anticipated by the Rabbeinu Yonah in the second *sha'ar* of the *Sha'arei Teshuvah* 17.

> וכמה קשה המות למי שלא הפריד תאות העולם מנפשו עד אשר יפרידנה המות! ואמרו רבותינו זכרונם לברכה במסכת דרך ארץ, **רצונך שלא תמות? מות עד שלא תמות!** באור הענין, הרוצה שיהיה לו יום המות לחיי עד, ידבר אל לבו, אחרי אשר סופו לעזוב את האדמה ולהניח חפצי הגוף ובאחריתו ישטמם ויטשם,

20. The וי"ו at the beginning of a word does not serve only to imply some measure of commonality (this *and* that). It can also indicate a "but" or a "yet."

Take, for example, Tehilim 96:5, כי כל אלהי העמים אלילים וה' שמים עשה, *For the deities worshipped by the nations are no more than idols,* BUT *the Ribono shel Olam (actually) created the heavens.* Or Yeshayahu 51:13, ותפחד תמיד כל היום מפני חמת המציק ... ואיה חמת המציק, *And you live all day in constant dread because of the rage of an oppressor, yet (why would you dread him) of what account is the rage of the oppressor?*

יעזבם בחייו ולא ישתמש באדמה רק לעבודת הבורא יתעלה, ואז יהיה לו יום המות לחיים שאין להם הפסק.

Death strikes hard for one who never stopped indulging his taste for luxuries during his lifetime. It will be a difficult parting. Our sages taught this idea in *maseches Derech Eretz* when they declared, *"Do you wish never to die? Then die before your death!"* With this they meant to express that actual death can be a ticket to eternal life if only we prepare ourselves ahead of time. It is a matter of admitting to ourselves that the moment will come to all of us at which we have to bid farewell to all those physical pleasures that were so important to us, and that, moreover, we will come to look back at them with hatred and disgust. A healthy awareness of this truth will persuade us that it were best to break our dependence upon these attractions while we are still strong and active, and make use of what the earth has to offer only inasmuch as these contribute to serving God. If we manage that, then our death will indeed usher us into eternal life.

I feel that we have arrived at the point that we had hoped to reach. We have discovered that the first *parshah* of *kri'as Shema* is not an unfocused jumble of various *mitzvos* but a cohesive and coherent statement concerning the most basic principle of Judaism. The Ribono shel Olam is sole Creator and therefore the sole King of our world. Kingship, if it is not to be an egotistical tyranny, requires a positive relationship between the ruler and the ruled. The Ribono shel Olam insists that this self-understood relationship must, primarily, be one of intense fondness. But, on the second day of Creation the Ribono shel Olam had created a *rakiya*, an *expanse*, designed to separate the *mayim ha'elyonim* from the *mayim hatachtonim*. How can fondness be established over an unbridgeable distance? How can it crash the barrier?

The Shema hands us the Ribono shel Olam's answer to that conundrum: You cannot crash the barrier but you can eliminate it by turning our "nether" world into a satellite of the "upper" one. Total immersion in the world of the Torah will get you there.

מי כעמך ישראל גוי אחד בארץ

P.S. When you learned these last couple of paragraphs you probably heaved a sigh of relief. It has not been an easy trip and it is nice to know that we have finally arrived, safe, sound, and, above all, informed. The time certainly has come to find a new *sugia,* a new challenge, to conquer fresh worlds.

Certainly the last thing you need is a complicated postscript.

Well, the fact is that we all need it, as you will see in a moment. But since I want to remain friends with all of you, I will limit this section to a brief outline that will identify the issue that has popped up but will leave the deep thinking that it surely ought to set into motion to each of you on his or her own. I suggest that you take it just as far as it will take you. It is a big, a very big, *sugia.*

The *sugia* that I have in mind is called ברוך שם כבוד מלכותו לעולם ועד. The fact is that up to this point I have not dealt with it at all, though I probably should have.

As everybody knows, this sentence has been inserted into our *kri'as Shema* after the introductory verse, שמע ישראל. Why was it inserted and what is its function? I have dealt with this issue in detail in a book called *A Machzor Companion,* which was published by Mesorah Publications (ArtScroll) in 1993 and discusses the *tefillos* of Rosh HaShanah and Yom Kippur.[21]

Here very briefly is the issue. It seems from all the commentators that are or were available to me that ברוך שם is a statement of קבלת עול מלכות שמים just as is שמע ישראל. The difference between them lies in the fact that while שמע ישראל is exhortative (it is telling others what to do: !שמע, Listen!), ברוך שם is an actual expression of belief entertained by the person who is saying it. Accordingly, it seems to be a higher level of קבלת מלכות than is the Shema.

My feeling is that this may make a real difference in how we take the *vav* in ואהבת. I argued earlier in this essay that it should be taken as a question (*and this in spite of the fact* ...; see above). Perhaps, though, after such a heartfelt and deeply experienced קבלת עול, this rather unusual interpretation of the conjunctive *vav* may no longer be required. Perhaps we can all go back happily to the "and" to which we are used and no harm done.

What do you think?

Good luck in your contemplation of this significant issue.

21. I do not know whether they still have it available, but I did check Amazon and they seem to have eighteen copies. You can find the article in the Yom Kippur section of the book on page 143. If you cannot get ahold of a copy but would like to discuss the issue, by all means give me a call at (410) 484-7396 and I will be happy to talk things over.

5.

More on Ahavas HaShem

THE GRAMMAR OF LOVING THE RIBONO SHEL OLAM
WHERE YOU ARE GOING TO WISH THAT YOU HAD PAID MORE ATTENTION WHEN YOU LEARNED THE *BINYANIM* BACK IN SCHOOL
KAL AND *PI'EL* WHERE IT REALLY MATTERS

Recently I have been making myself a nuisance to my friends. Coming out of nowhere, I have been asking them whether they love the Ribono shel Olam. Interestingly enough, among a relatively large pool of respondents, I got only one unequivocal "Yes!" The rest usually obliged with an embarrassed half-smile together with a protestation: "I certainly try," or the like. None, including even our single hero, was really able to define what such "love" might involve. Everybody seems to find it difficult to define the requirements for fulfilling the mitzvah of *ahavas HaShem.*

And that is understandable. Here is one reason among many. When we struggle to understand the precise meaning of a given word, we can usually find some help by examining the various contexts in which it appears. We *close* mouths and doors and deals and arguments and come away with a very clear sense of what is meant in each case. We speak legitimately about loving our parents and our spouses, each in their own way. We love swimming, the spring and/or the fall, and Beethoven's piano concerto, and in each of these very disparate experiences we do not mean the same thing — and know it. And that is as it should be. There is no reason why simple ambiguities should hold any terror for reasonably intelligent people.

But "loving" the Ribono shel Olam is not a simple ambiguity. He is, of course, uniquely unique. What other love can throw any light upon the way to love Him!?[1]

1. The root א ה ב has unusual versatility as we will demonstrate a couple of pages further along. It functions within a huge trajectory.

This matter seems to me to be a singularly important issue. Coming, as it does, immediately after the Shema declaration, the mitzvah of *ahavas HaShem* is positioned such that its unique significance is obvious.

Clearly, we can use a lot of help.

I came across the Chinuch on the mitzvah of *ahavah*. I will quote a section just in order to underline the sheer enormity of this mitzvah as he understands it.

> דיני המצוה: שראוי לו לאדם שישים **כל מחשבתו וכל מגמתו** אחר אהבת ה׳, ויעריך בלבו תמיד כי כל מה שהוא בעולם מעושר ובנים וכבוד הכל כאין וכאפס ותוהו כנגד אהבתו ברוך הוא, וייגע תמיד **כל היום** בבקשת החכמה למען ישיג ידיעה בו. סוף כל דבר יעשה כל יכלתו להרגיל **מחשבות לבו כל היום באמונתו ויחודו** עד שלא יהי **רגע אחד** ביום ובלילה בהקיצו שלא יהא זוכר אהבת אדוניו בכל יום.
>
> והענין על דרך משל שיהא נזכר באהבת השם תמיד כזכרון החושק תכלית החשק בחשוקתו היום שישיג להביאה אל ביתו.

I would be remiss if I did not share the following problem with you. This passage leaves me absolutely unenlightened. The Chinuch seems to take for granted that his readers will understand why someone who would like to love the Ribono shel Olam would spend his entire day on apparently intellectual (בבקשת החכמה and similar expressions) pursuits. How would all this knowledge generate love? Or, if we want to base our question upon our earlier ruminations, what *kind* of love would be enhanced by the knowledge that the Chinuch is describing?

But let us leave that aside and concentrate on the sheer enormity of the Chinuch's expectations. Are there any takers? Can we even imagine a life in which *every second* is used in the service of *ahavah*?

Here are my plans for the rest of this essay. It will consist of three major portions. The first will be devoted to an in-depth study of the Rambam's presentation of the various facets of the mitzvah

The British used to pride themselves on the fact that they had two words, *love* and *like*, which brought some discipline to their language. If a youngster declared that he "loved" ice cream, he was reprimanded. You can "like" the stuff; never love it! I have not found any explanation why *lashon hakodesh* (the absolute standard for absolute precision in language, see Ran at the beginning of Nedarim) should have tolerated such a relaxed attitude to such a fundamental concept.

of *ahavas HaShem*. The second will demonstrate the important role that grammar will play in establishing various categories of this *ahavah*. Once we have gained some clarity in this rather complicated *sugia*, we will be ready to tackle the section that, to my mind, will constitute the very soul of this essay. I would hope that it will help us toward moving closer to a respectable fulfillment of this most fundamental mitzvah.

I dare to hope that if you stick with me through some very complicated passages, you will, in the end, not regret it.

THE RAMBAM'S TREATMENT OF THE MITZVAH OF *AHAVAS HASHEM*

We begin with Mitzvah 3 of the מצוות עשה in the Sefer HaMitzvos. I have divided the passage into six paragraphs. This division is nothing more than a matter of convenience. It will simplify the referencing of the various topics. It has no source outside my own mind.

1. המצוה השלישית היא שצוונו לאהבו יתעלה, **וזה** שנתבונן ונשכיל מצותיו ופעולותיו עד שנשיגהו ונתענג בהשגתו תכלית התענוג, **וזאת** היא האהבה המחויבת.
2. ולשון ספרי, לפי שנאמר ואהבת את ה' אלהיך איני יודע כיצד אוהב את המקום, תלמוד לומר והיו הדברים האלו אשר אנכי מצוך היום על לבבך שמתוך כך אתה מכיר את מי שאמר והיה העולם.
3. הנה כבר בארו לך כי בהשתכלות תתאמת לך ההשגה ויגיע התענוג ותבוא התענוג בהכרח.
4. וכבר אמרו שמצוה זו כוללת גם כן שנדרוש ונקרא האנשים כולם לעבודתו יתעלה ולהאמין בו.
5. וזה כי כשתאהב אדם תשים לבך עליו ותשבחהו ותבקש האנשים לאהוב אותו. וזה על צד המשל כן כשתאהב הא-ל באמת כמה שהגיעה לך מהשגת אמיתתו הנה אתה בלא ספק תדרוש ותקרא הכופרים והסכלים לידיעת האמת אשר ידעת אותה.
6. ולשון ספרי, ואהבת את ה' וכו' אהבהו על הבריות כאברהם אביך שנאמר ואת הנפש אשר עשה בחרן.

PARAGRAPHS 1–3: TEXTUAL ANALYSIS

In paragraph 1 we are told that it is a mitzvah to relate to the Ribono shel Olam in a way that is described by the root word א ה ב. This word can have many different gradations. It may be applied to many different points along a very large trajectory.

Here, for example, is the famous Rambam from the tenth *perek* in Hilchos Teshuvah.

... וכיצד היא האהבה הראויה הוא שיאהב את ה' אהבה גדולה יתירה עזה מאוד עד שתהא נפשו קשורה באהבת ה' ונמצא שוגה בה תמיד כאלו חולה חולי האהבה שאין דעתו פנויה מאהבת אותה אשה והוא שוגה[2] בה תמיד בין בשבתו בין בקומו בין בשעה שהוא אוכל ושותה יתר מזה תהיה אהבת ה' בלב אוהביו שוגים בה תמיד כמו שצונו בכל לבבך ובכל נפשך והוא ששלמה אמר דרך משל כי חולת אהבה אני וכל שיר השירים משל הוא לענין זה.

The concept can hardly be more inspiring.

On the other end of the spectrum we have Rivkah telling Yaakov to bring two tender goats so that she could prepare a dish for Yitzchak, כאשר אהב. That use of א ה ב is clearly in a completely different league. Now, these are obviously extremes, but surely there must be limitless gradations in between. Thus, when Rambam uses the expression, שצונו לאהבו יתברך (paragraph 1) to define the third mitzvah, he is not telling us very much. There seems to be no way in which to pin down what degree or indeed what kind of love is meant.

I believe that with the next sentence, Rambam is attempting to solve this problem. **וזה** שנתבונן ונשכיל מצותיו ופעולותיו עד שנשיגהו ונתענג בהשגתו תכלית התענוג, **וזאת** היא האהבה המחויבת. In Rambam's mind, the mitzvah of *ahavah* as it refers to the Ribono shel Olam has its own, perhaps unique, definition. The "אהבה המחויבת" is not a feeling but an action. We are to seek out the delight (תכלית התענוג) (mentioned here in paragraph 1 and again in paragraph 3) that results from gaining as much understanding of the Ribono shel Olam as is given us to comprehend. That is all that we can *do*. As for the rest, love must follow its own nature on its own.

The Rambam has made himself very clear: *ta'anug* = *ahavah*. Apparently, the greater the *ta'anug*, the more comprehensive will be the love that results. The Rambam has given us at the very least a hint for gauging the degree of our love. It is not much. But it is something.[3]

Paragraphs 2 and 3 give documentary legitimacy to what the Rambam has taught in paragraph 1.

2. Of course, at this stage we do not know *how* Torah study helps us toward *ahavah*. We will deal with this in the third section of this essay.

3. Of course, at this stage we do not know *how* Torah study helps us toward *ahavah*. We will deal with this in the third section of this essay.

PARAGRAPHS 1–3: CONTENT ANALYSIS

If we are going to be interested in finding out Rambam's ideas about the mitzvah of *ahavas HaShem,* we will have to visit both Hilchos Yesodei HaTorah, chapter 2, and Teshuvah, chapter 10.

Here are the passages. First Yesodei HaTorah 2:1 and 2.

האל הנכבד והנורא הזה מצוה לאהבו וליראה אותו שנאמר ואהבת את ה' אלהיך ונאמר את ה' אלהיך תירא.

והיאך היא הדרך לאהבתו ויראתו? בשעה שיתבונן האדם במעשיו וברואיו הנפלאים הגדולים ויראה מהן חכמתו שאין לה ערך ולא קץ מיד הוא אוהב ומשבח ומפאר ומתאוה תאוה גדולה לידע השם הגדול כמו שאמר דוד צמאה נפשי לאלהים לאל חי וכשמחשב בדברים האלו עצמן מיד הוא נרתע לאחוריו ויפחד ויודע שהוא בריה קטנה שפלה אפלה עומדת בדעת קלה מעוטה לפני תמים דעות כמו שאמר דוד כי אראה שמיך מעשה אצבעותיך מה אנוש כי תזכרנו ולפי הדברים האלו אני מבאר כללים גדולים ממעשה רבון העולמים כדי שיהיו פתח למבין לאהוב את השם כמו שאמרו חכמים בענין אהבה שמתוך כך אתה מכיר את מי שאמר והיה העולם.

Then we turn to Teshuvah 10:1 and 3.

אל יאמר אדם הריני עושה מצות התורה ועוסק בחכמתה כדי שאקבל כל הברכות הכתובות בה או כדי שאזכה לחיי העולם הבא ואפרוש מן העבירות שהזהירה תורה מהן כדי שאנצל מן הקללות הכתובות בתורה או כדי שלא אכרת מחיי העולם הבא אין ראוי לעבוד את ה' על הדרך הזה שהעובד על דרך זה הוא עובד מיראה ואינה מעלת הנביאים ולא מעלת החכמים ואין עובדים ה' על דרך זה אלא עמי הארץ והנשים והקטנים שמחנכין אותן לעבוד מיראה עד שתרבה דעתן ויעבדו מאהבה....

וכיצד היא האהבה הראויה הוא שיאהב את ה' אהבה גדולה יתירה עזה מאוד עד שתהא נפשו קשורה באהבת ה' ונמצא שוגה בה תמיד כאלו חולה חולי האהבה שאין דעתו פנויה מאהבת אותה אשה והוא שוגה בה תמיד בין בשבתו בין בקומו בין בשעה שהוא אוכל ושותה יתר מזה תהיה אהבת ה' בלב אוהביו שוגים בה תמיד כמו שצונו בכל לבבך ובכל נפשך והוא ששלמה אמר דרך משל כי חולת אהבה אני וכל שיר השירים משל הוא לענין זה.

The time has come to wonder about this arrangement. Why did the Rambam find it appropriate to divide his *ahavah* material between two sets of *halachos,* Yesodei HaTorah and Teshuvah?

PARAGRAPHS 1–3: HOW DOES AN ANALYSIS OF THE אהבה הראויה (*TESHUVAH* 10:3) LAND UP IN HILCHOS TESHUVAH?

That is the wrong question to ask. A glance at chapters 8 and 9 in Hilchos Teshuvah yields that chapter 10 follows very logically from these two. Our question needs to aim at the entire threesome. Why does this entire section belong here?

Here is what I mean.

The Rambam's treatment of the details and nature of *teshuvah*, as actual *repentance*, ends with the seventh *perek* of Hilchos Teshuvah. Chapter 8 begins with the words, הטובה הצפונה לצדיקים היא חיי העולם הבא והיא החיים שאין מות עמהן והטובה שאין עמה רעה הוא שכתוב בתורה למען ייטב לך והארכת ימים מפי השמועה למדו למען ייטב לך לעולם שכולו טוב והארכת ימים לעולם שכולו ארוך וזהו הוא העולם הבא. Thereafter, chapters 8 and 9 are entirely taken up by the issues of eternal and temporal reward and punishment. Our famous chapter 10 begins with the words, אל יאמר אדם הריני עושה מצות התורה ועוסק בחכמתה כדי שאקבל כל הברכות הכתובות בה או כדי שאזכה לחיי העולם הבא ואפרוש מן העבירות שהזהירה תורה מהן כדי שאנצל מן הקללות הכתובות בתורה או כדי שלא אכרת מחיי העולם הבא. It then goes on to extol the advantages to being motivated to serve God out of *ahavah* rather than out of fear. That is clearly a perfect fit with the earlier two chapters.

We could, of course, now try to understand why the Rambam chose Hilchos Teshuvah as the host for these three *perakim*. We won't. That is not our subject in this essay. It is time to rejoin Rambam at his desk and try to figure out why he chose Hilchos Teshuvah for his disquisition on the ideal *ahavah* (10:3) rather than including it in Hilchos Yesodei HaTorah, where he introduces us to *ahavah* as one of the 613 *mitzvos*.

RAMBAM'S DILEMMA AND HOW HE SOLVED IT

It turns out that the Rambam had perfectly legitimate reasons for dealing with *ahavas HaShem* in two different locations. From the point of view of its being a regular מצות עשה, its place is certainly in Yesodei HaTorah.[4] Then, for good and no doubt satisfying reasons, the Rambam felt that the place for his discussion of temporal and eternal rewards ought to be presented as a part of Hilchos Teshuvah. Within such a context *ahavah* as a motivating factor for serving the Ribono shel Olam (the subject of the tenth *perek*) is of course germane.

So far everything is clear. However, the Rambam obviously had

4. In an earlier version of this essay, I included a careful analysis of Sefer HaMada in general and Hilchos Yesodei HaTorah in particular. I decided to let that go since things are complicated enough as it is. Just for now, please trust me when I say that Hilchos Yesodei HaTorah are the natural home for *ahavah* as a mitzvah. This assertion is based upon Rambam's assertion in the third *chelek* of the Moreh Nevuchim that the Sefer HaMada is to be devoted to השקפות יסודיות.

things to say about *ahavas HaShem* that went way beyond the bare bones of its mitzvah status or the mere fact that as a motivating factor it is to be preferred to *yir'ah*. Remember Teshuvah 10:3, וכיצד היא האהבה הראויה וכו'. There is no doubt in my mind that he could have attached these ideas to the mitzvah element in Yesodei HaTorah as readily as he was able to inject it into his subject matter in the tenth *perek* of Teshuvah. Rambam was faced with a dilemma. Where does this celebration of *ahavah* most naturally belong?

My thinking is thus: (There is no suggestion here at all of anything definitive. Please take these ideas in the spirit in which they are offered; think them over and decide for yourselves.)

The Rambam's treatment of the subject leaves us with some questions. The first of these is raised by paragraph 4: כבר אמרו שמצוה זו **כוללת** גם כן שנדרוש ונקרא האנשים כולם לעבודתו יתעלה ולהאמין בו. What exactly is the weight of "כוללת" in this context? Does the Rambam mean that persuading people to worship the Ribono shel Olam is an actual and formal part of the base mitzvah, לאהבו יתעלה? Does it mean that if we do not engage in such activities we are actually מבטל a מצוות עשה? If that is what the Rambam means, then the fact that there is not even a hint to this obligation in Yesodei HaTorah 2:2, where the mitzvah element is discussed, seems truly shocking. Why not mention this aspect of the halachah together with its parent mitzvah?

If we are to conclude that it is not a formally binding mitzvah, then in what sense is it "נכלל"?

If we are to form an opinion on this issue, it would probably help to know what Chazal Rambam is referencing when he uses "וכבר אמרו." Who said what, and where did he say it?

Of course the first candidate would be the Sifri that Rambam quotes in paragraph 6 אהבהו על הבריות. There is, however, also Abbaye in Yoma 86a in the following passage. We will see in a few moments that this formulation appears to have had an enormous influence on the Rambam's thinking. Here it is.

> אביי אמר כדתניא ואהבת את ה' אלהיך שיהא שם שמים מתאהב על ידך שיהא קורא ושונה ומשמש תלמידי חכמים ויהא משאו ומתנו בנחת עם הבריות מה הבריות אומרות עליו אשרי אביו שלמדו תורה אשרי רבו שלמדו תורה אוי להם לבריות שלא למדו תורה פלוני שלמדו תורה ראו כמה נאים דרכיו כמה מתוקנים מעשיו עליו הכתוב אומר ויאמר לי עבדי אתה ישראל אשר בך אתפאר.
>
> אבל מי שקורא ושונה ומשמש תלמידי חכמים ואין משאו ומתנו באמונה ואין דבורו בנחת עם הבריות מה הבריות אומרות עליו אוי לו לפלוני שלמד תורה אוי לו לאביו שלמדו תורה אוי לו לרבו שלמדו תורה פלוני שלמד תורה

ראו כמה מקולקלין מעשיו וכמה מכוערין דרכיו ועליו הכתוב אומר באמר להם עם ה' אלה ומארצו יצאו.

So where do these quotes leave us? It seems to me that, at least for the Rambam, it created a kind of quandary. Although it seems clear from Abbaye's opening words, ואהבת את ה' אלהיך שיהא שם שמים מתאהב על ידך, that his source is in the mitzvah of *ahavah,* the Rambam actually codifies it in Yesodei HaTorah 5:11 where it appears *under the rubric of the mitzvah of kiddush HaShem*! Here is the quote.

> ויש דברים אחרים שהן בכלל חילול השם והוא שיעשה אותם אדם גדול בתורה ומפורסם בחסידות דברים שהבריות מרננים אחריו בשבילם ואע"פ שאינן עבירות הרי זה חילל את השם כגון שלקח ואינו נותן דמי המקח לאלתר והוא שיש לו ונמצאו המוכרים תובעין והוא מקיפן או שירבה בשחוק או באכילה ושתיה אצל עמי הארץ וביניהן או שדבורו עם הבריות אינו בנחת ואינו מקבלן בסבר פנים יפות אלא בעל קטטה וכעס וכיוצא בדברים האלו הכל לפי גדלו של חכם צריך שידקדק על עצמו ויעשה לפנים משורת הדין.
>
> וכן אם דקדק החכם על עצמו והיה דבורו בנחת עם הבריות ודעתו מעורבת עמהם ומקבלם בסבר פנים יפות ונעלב מהם ואינו עולבם מכבד להן ואפילו למקילין לו ונושא ונותן באמונה ולא ירבה בארוחות עמי הארץ וישיבתן ולא יראה תמיד אלא עוסק בתורה עטוף בציצית מוכתר בתפילין ועושה בכל מעשיו לפנים משורת הדין והוא שלא יתרחק הרבה ולא ישתומם עד שימצאו הכל מקלסין אותו ואוהבים אותו ומתאוים למעשיו הרי זה קידש את ה' ועליו הכתוב אומר ויאמר לי עבדי אתה ישראל אשר בך אתפאר.

Now how does *that* come about? If Abbaye offers his homily as deriving from the word ואהבת, why would the Rambam organize it under *kiddush HaShem*?[5]

From a purely technical standpoint, I imagine that we could explain the Rambam's decision to classify the issue on the *kiddush HaShem/chillul HaShem* continuum by the fact that Abbaye in contrast to the Sifri presents his thesis as an either-or matter: if you act in this manner it is great, but if you act differently, it is terrible. Within the context of the מצות עשה of *ahavah,* that would not be true. Someone who does not perform actions that would demonstrate his love for the Ribono shel Olam would still not be described as a sinner. Still, whatever merit this argument might possess, that would still not deal with the difficulty that we have raised. Abbaye makes it clear that he is expanding the meaning of ואהבת.

As long as we are trying to understand Rambam's ideas on

5. See Frankel Rambam, Sefer HaMaftei'ach, page שעד.

ahavas HaShem, there is another matter that can lay claim to our attention. What, in his view, is the function or weight of the words, בכל לבבך ובכל נפשך ובכל מאדך? The fact that the Rambam does not cite these requirements in either Yesodei HaTorah 2:2 or in the Sefer HaMitzvos seems to indicate that he does not view them as *defining* the range of the mitzvah aspect of ואהבת.[6]

So what exactly is the function of these requirements?

Now Rambam *does* reference these requirements in two other locations. One in Yesodei HaTorah 5:7.

> ומנין שאפילו במקום סכנת נפשות אין עוברין על אחת משלש עבירות אלו שנאמר ואהבת את ה' אלהיך בכל לבבך ובכל נפשך ובכל מאודך אפילו הוא נוטל את נפשך.

The other is in Berachos 10:3 where Rambam deals with the obligation to make the *berachah, Baruch Dayan HaEmes* when one is confronted with bad news. He writes

> וחייב אדם לברך על הרעה בטוב נפש כדרך שמברך על הטובה בשמחה שנאמר ואהבת את יי' אלהיך וגו' ובכל מאדך ובכלל אהבה היתירה שנצטוינו בה שאפילו בעת שייצר לו יודה וישבח בשמחה.

What are we to conclude from these two omissions from the Sefer HaMitzvos and Yesodei HaTorah 2:2 and two commissions at Yesodei HaTorah 5:7 and Berachos 10:3?

At this point, I think that we can safely say that the בכל לבבך clause does *not define* the basic mitzvah of *ahavas HaShem*. If our love of the Ribono shel Olam does not rise to the heights implied by these phrases, we will nevertheless have fulfilled the command at some level. However, they *do* expand the *practical* range of the mitzvah. They inform us that in certain circumstances we may be called upon to lay down our lives for the love of the Ribono shel Olam and that we are to feel that love even in situations in which our world appears to be crashing down upon us.

Now we come to a big question. Earlier in this essay we quoted the Rambam from Teshuvah, chapter 10. Here it is once more:

6. By this I mean that there is no equivalence between the בכל נפשך requirement and, let us say, the fact that succah walls have to be a minimum of ten *tefachim* in height. It is not true to say that just as sitting in a succah that does not comply with the requisite measurements disqualifies your action; you have not fulfilled the mitzvah, so too, if your *ahavah* of the Ribono shel Olam does not engage כל נפשך, you have not fulfilled the mitzvah of *ahavah*. Rambam's omission of any mention of these requirements at the two relevant locations makes clear that this is not the case.

... וכיצד היא האהבה הראויה הוא שיאהב את ה' אהבה גדולה יתירה עזה מאוד עד שתהא נפשו קשורה באהבת ה' ונמצא שוגה בה תמיד כאלו חולה חולי האהבה שאין דעתו פנויה מאהבת אותה אשה והוא שוגה בה תמיד בין בשבתו בין בקומו בין בשעה שהוא אוכל ושותה יתר מזה תהיה אהבת ה' בלב אוהביו שוגים בה תמיד **כמו שצונו בכל לבבך ובכל נפשך** והוא ששלמה אמר דרך משל כי חולת אהבה אני וכל שיר השירים משל הוא לענין זה.

From the words that we have bolded, it appears that בכל לבבך ובכל נפשך describes the kind of love to which the Rambam gives such lyric expression in this paragraph. Do the two *ahavahs* that we have just now discovered as deriving from those words, the one that prompts us to lay down our lives in defense of our basic beliefs and the other one that enables us to be filled with joy even when we are called upon to recite *Dayan HaEmes,* rise to the level of almost intoxicated *ahavah* that so excites the Rambam in Hilchos Teshuvah? Are we really persuaded that anyone capable of *mesiras nefesh* must have attained a level of love that, as in a physical infatuation שאין דעתו פנויה מאהבת אותה אשה touches upon the irrational, **שוגה** בו תמיד, and leaves him no peace, בין בשבתו בין בקומו בין בשעה כשהוא אוכל ושותה?

I do not really think so. Let us listen to the Rambam at the end of the fifth of the eight *perakim* where he describes people who have reached the exalted level of כל מעשיך יהיו לשם שמים.

ודע שהדרגה הזו היא דרגה גבוהה מאד וקשה, **ולא ישיגוה אלא מעטים** ואחרי הכשרה רבה מאד, ואם יזדמן מציאות אדם שאלה הם תאריו **איני חושב שהוא פחות מהנביאים**, כלומר שמפעיל כל כחות נפשו ועושה מטרתם ה' יתעלה בלבד, ולא יעשה פעולה גדולה או קטנה ולא יבטא שום מלה אלא אם אותה פעולה או אותה המלה מביאה לידי מעלה או לדבר המביא לידי מעלה ... וזה הוא מה שדורש[7] יתעלה ממנו **שתהא זו מטרתינו באמרו ואהבת את ה' אלהיך בכל לבבך ובכל נפשך**, כלומר בכל חלקי נפשך, שתשים תכלית כל חלק מהם תכלית אחת והיא לאהבה את ה' אלהיך...

I suspect that most of the myriads of *ehrliche Yidden,* who, throughout our bloodstained history have willingly and happily laid down their lives *al kiddush HaShem,* would have been the

7. I never thought that I would ever regret not knowing Arabic. I copied this passage from the Kapach edition, which uses ד ר ש. The אבן תבון translation printed in the Vilna Shas uses ב ק ש. My instinct tells me that there is a vast difference between the two expressions, ב ק ש being much the softer of the two. In light of the suggestion that I am about to make, that בכל לבבך has two possible meanings, one expressed in *halachah,* the other presented as a (nonbinding) ideal, it would be absolutely crucial to have access to the precise meaning of the word that the Rambam used here.

first to deny membership in the very exclusive club described by the Rambam.

Very clearly there seem to be a number of levels at which the phrase בכל לבבך ... speaks to us.

Let us try to get a little clarity.

I think that we will get where we need to get by way of the Sifri and Abbaye's teaching from Yoma 86a that we quoted earlier in this essay.

Here is the Sifri once more:

ד"א ואהבת את ה' אלהיך **אהבהו** על הבריות ...

Here is a part of Abbaye's teaching once more:

אביי אמר כדתניא ואהבת את ה' אלהיך שיהא שם שמים **מתאהב** על ידך שיהא קורא ושונה ומשמש תלמידי חכמים ויהא משאו ומתנו בנחת עם הבריות מה הבריות אומרות עליו אשרי אביו שלמדו תורה אשרי רבו שלמדו תורה אוי להם לבריות שלא למדו תורה פלוני שלמדו תורה ראו כמה נאים דרכיו כמה מתוקנים מעשיו עליו הכתוב אומר ויאמר לי עבדי אתה ישראל אשר בך אתפאר.

The Sifri and Abbaye are of course saying the same thing. The word ואהבת can apparently be made to yield that not only are we ourselves to love the Ribono shel Olam, we are also expected to get others to love Him. They use different verbal forms to express this idea; the Sifri uses **אהבהו** על הבריות while Abbaye uses שיהא שם שמים **מתאהב** על הבריות, but at the end they mean the same thing.

The problem is that the wording that the Torah uses, וְאָהַבְתָּ, simply does not convey this meaning. אָהַבְתָּ is the second person, past tense of א ה ב, *to love* in the normal active voice, *binyan kal*. In the sentence that we are discussing the וי"ו המהפכת that precedes אהבת changes the tense to the future. The word means simply, *you are to love* and nothing else. Where do the Sifri and Abbaye find the right to read into this word what it does not say?

I believe that there is a simple answer to this question.

Let us remember that the Torah text came to us without vowels. We read the text as we do only because that is our *tradition — mesorah* — all the way back to Moshe Rabbeinu. As it stands, the reading might just as well have been וְאִהַבְתָּ with a *chirik* instead of a *kamatz* under the א. That would have switched the voice from *kal* to *pi'el, the intense voice.*

There is no doubt in my mind that the Sifri and Abbaye had this reading in mind when they suggested what they did.[8]

What does that mean? What possible justification could there be for using a nonexistent reading as the source for an important lesson? Let me explain. This morning we were saying the *Hoshanos* in shul. All of us surely remember the phrase, וְהוּצֵאתִי אֶתְכֶם נָקוּב וְהוּצֵאתִי אִתְּכֶם, to teach us that the Ribono shel Olam is "with" us in our *galus*. Now there is no doubt at all that the *mesorah* demands וְהוֹצֵאתִי אֶתְכֶם. Nevertheless, since the other reading is *possible*, that, too, has the status of being able to communicate something of importance to us.

You may recall the Rashi at the beginning of Bereishis making use of this system. He began his commentary with the famous, אין המקרא הזה אומר אלא דרשני. The word בראשית must be understood as ב-ראשית, that is, בשביל ישראל שנקראו ראשית ... and so on. The Rashi goes on to say that if, after all that, we still insist upon some *peshat* meaning, we will have to read the letters ב ר א not as בָּרָא but as בְּרֹא. What can Rashi possibly mean? The *mesorah* demands בָּרָא? Once more we see that the Torah text is designed to communicate with us at every possible level. If the word could technically be read in a certain way, then even if, for *kri'as HaTorah* purposes, that reading would be unacceptable, it nevertheless is there to tell us something.

Sifri and Abbaye, each in his own way, claims that the possible אִהַבְתָּ has something important to teach us.[9]

We must, however, think about the weight of that "something." Does it, deriving as it does from a non-halachic reading, rise to the level of *halachah* or does it hover in some less defined עצה טובה place? Let us remember that neither of the two examples that I cited earlier (הוּצֵאתִי for הוֹצֵאתִי, בְּרֹא for בָּרָא) has any halachic repercussions.

The time has come to wind things down. We have asked a

8. The *pi'el* voice is a perfectly respectable expression for the root word א ה ב. The expression מאהבי occurs several times in TaNaCh (see, for example, Hoshe'a 2:7) and, the "מ" in front of the root word in the present tense is one of the characteristics of this voice. Think of למד, *to learn*, in the *kal*, and מלמד, *to teach* (= *learn intensely*) in the *pi'el*. Therefore, although there is no אִהֵב in the Torah, there is no reason at all to reject this suggestion. The form does occur in the *piyutim*.

9. For our purposes we need not now analyze the different verb forms that they use. It is enough for us to know that each of them is reaching the same conclusion by his chosen route.

great many questions and offered very few answers. But answers are what we need. I think that we have touched on all the information that we will require to straighten everything out. To keep things simple I will present my thesis without listing the questions once more. If you have come along this far in this difficult essay you probably remember them as well as I do.

The final introduction to the great dénouement[10] is the following short discussion of the *pi'el* "voice," or, as Hebrew grammarians call it, the *binyan* that we know as *pi'el*.

The uses of most of the other *binyanim, voices,* are familiar to us from English in which they are also used, although not in exactly the same way. We have active and passive, causative and reflexive, and so on. To the best of my knowledge, the *pi'el* has no equivalent in English. Its function is to intensify the verb. For example, אני שובר, which is the correct form for *kal*, means *I break*; אני משבר, which is the correct form for the *pi'el*, means *I smash*. It will be in this awareness of the difference between the *kal* and the *pi'el* that our understanding of the difference between the *kal* וְאָהַבְתָּ and the intensive *pi'el* וְאִהַבְתָּ (possible but non-halachic) will be grounded.

THE DÉNOUEMENT

The solutions that I am about to suggest are based upon the assumption that what is learned from the non-halachic וְאִהַבְתָּ, while certainly legitimate, does not rise to the level of a formal mitzvah. In a paradox that we will now explain, it is both more and less than the *halachah* that is derived from the formal וְאָהַבְתָּ.

It is less, in the sense that whatever is derived from the non-halachic וְאִהַבְתָּ is not halachically binding. It is more in that it vastly expands the range of what might be included at a non-halachic level in this mitzvah. The question that we asked earlier in this essay, why the Rambam does not mention paragraph 4 of the Sefer HaMitzvos, וכבר אמרו שמצוה זו כוללת גם כן שנדרוש ונקרא האנשים כולם לעבודתו יתעלה ולהאמין בו, in Yesodei HaTorah where the mitzvah is discussed, is now answered. This expansion of the formal command to love, the idea that we ought to draw others into the circle of those who attain closeness to the Ribono shel

10. *Dénouement* is a French word meaning "unknotting" that has been adopted into English. It is used to describe a situation in which, in the end, all problems are solved and everything turns out all right.

Olam, is certainly a meritorious act that is recommended on the basis of the intensified *pi'el* form of the וְאִהַבְתָּ reading. But it is not obligatory and therefore has no place in the Yad where the Rambam is concerned with formal obligations.

However, the Rambam found a halachic home for the Sifri's and Abbaye's teaching. The *pi'el* form of וְאִהַבְתָּ alerted him to the concept that true love would surely express itself in attempts to help others to those insights that kindled his own enthusiasm. Could those attempts not be considered to be acts of *kiddush HaShem*? Add to that the fact that Abbaye taught his lesson on an either-or continuum; good behavior sanctifies/bad behavior disgraces, and the Rambam's treatment becomes a natural. The *eitzah tovah* that is hidden but implied under the rubric of *ahavah* metamorphoses into a mitzvah under the rubric of *kiddush HaShem*.

Now that we are slowly getting used to the idea that there is an entire area of *ahavas HaShem* that falls outside of its mitzvah character, we can begin to tackle Rambam's apparently bifurcated treatment of *ahavah* by moving his lyrical celebration of this quality away from Yesodei HaTorah to Hilchos Teshuvah. Earlier in this essay we were unable to fathom why Rambam would want to do that. We can take care of the specific answer to that specific question readily and simply. However, we will find that there are some ramifications that will require a little more thought.

First, then, here is a quick answer to a quick question.

There is the mitzvah of *ahavah* and there is the quality of *ahavah* that is entirely divorced from its status as a mitzvah. As a mitzvah, there is no doubt that *ahavah* belongs among the השקפות יסודיות that, as we learned earlier in this essay (footnote 4), determined the content of Yesodei HaTorah for the Rambam. As can be expected, as is indeed demanded, Rambam treats the mitzvah aspect of *ahavah* in Yesodei HaTorah. However, *ahavah* as a motivating factor in the performance of *mitzvos* has nothing at all to do with its standing as a mitzvah. If there were no mitzvah of any kind to love the Ribono shel Olam, *ehrliche Yidden* would still feel boundless *ahavah* for Him. That aspect of *ahavah* fits logically and seamlessly into Rambam's discussion at the end of Hilchos Teshuvah and that is how he uses it there.

There really is no problem.

This insight, however, does nothing to alleviate our difficulty with the definition of the אהבה הראויה that the Rambam also reserved for the Hilchos Teshuvah passage. Why not lay down a correct and all-encompassing definition in Yesodei HaTorah where we are first introduced to the mitzvah? That question becomes even more perplexing when we consider that the Torah apparently offers a definition; we are to love God בכל לבבך ובכל נפשך ובכל מאדך. Now this requirement does make it prominently in the Hilchos Teshuvah passage, once in *halachah* 3 and once in *halachah* 6,[11] but it is not mentioned at all in either the Sefer HaMitzvos or in Hilchos Yesodei HaTorah. Why is it not?

Then there is the fact, noted earlier in this essay, that this phrase or parts of it *do* occur twice more in the Yad, once in Hilchos Yesodei HaTorah 5:7 in the context of laying down our lives in the applicable circumstances for *kiddush HaShem* and once in Berachos 10:3 in the context of *Dayan HaEmes*.

Is there anything that we can understand here?

I think that in the past few paragraphs we have already laid down the principles that will yield a really quite simple explanation.

I am going to argue that the phrase בכל לבבך ובכל נפשך ובכל מאדך has two distinct meanings. One of those two meanings goes with the halachic reading of וְאָהַבְתָּ; the other makes sense in the context of the possible but not mandatory וְאִהַבְתָּ.

In a halachic context the word "בכל" does not at all carry the connotations ascribed to it by the Rambam in the Teshuvah passage.[12] All it does is to expand the halachic range of the base

11. In neither of these two references does the Rambam cite "ובכל מאדך." I do not know why.

12. Here is an example. At Bereishis 31:6 Yaakov assures Rachel and Leah that he had served their father "בכל כחי." Now there is certainly no indication of any sort that Yaakov was in love with his work as a man might be in love with a woman, thus that his mind never thinks of anything else, and so on. Rambam in Hilchos Sechirus 13:12 simply states that הפועל חייב לעבוד בכל כחו שהרי יעקב הצדיק אמר כי בכל כחי. The Torah Temimah determines that the laws governing the hired worker, for example, that he is obliged to eat well and not to starve himself, that, in order to get the requisite amount of sleep, he is not permitted to take another job (during the day) besides the work that he is doing for his master (at night), that he is not permitted to accept *nezirus* upon himself and so on, all derive from the "בכל כחי" clause. "בכל כח" in this context means simply a conscientious and honest application to the job at hand. The limitations placed upon the hired worker to assure punctilious application to his work belong to the same order as the obligation to be מקדש שם שמים and sacrifice one's life when halachically called upon to do so, and to react to sad news with *Dayan HaEmes*. They are simple halachic extensions of the base obligation of *ahavas HaShem*. They have absolutely nothing in common with the lyric descriptions of the אהבה הראויה that Rambam teaches us in Hilchos Teshuvah.

halachah of *ahavas HaShem*. The Rambam had no need to bring those halachic extensions when he deals with the basic mitzvah of *ahavas HaShem*, nor to cite the בכל לבבך... requirement there, because he cites those *halachos*, together with the בכל לבבך... clause, later on in the context to which they belong.

The passage in Hilchos Teshuvah lives in an entirely different context. Its world knows nothing of the formal mitzvah but focuses instead upon the intense, "sky is the limit" experience of the *pi'el*. In that setting the requirement that *ahavah* be expressed בכל לבבך ובכל נפשך ובכל מאדך does not merely expand the range of formal obligations; its mode is the שגעון of which the Rambam speaks so eloquently.

We are now ready to go to the third section, the one that was really our goal from the very beginning. It will tackle the question that is of such primary importance to all of us. How can we grow into true אוהבי השי"ת?

HOW CAN WE GROW INTO TRUE *אוהבי השם יתברך?*

The time has come to bring this essay to a close. Here is what I hope will turn out to be a *mini*-essay on the topic of *ahavah* between the Ribono shel Olam and ourselves. This is surely an issue that is as fundamental to Judaism as anything can be. For us, the story will begin with *parshas* Ha'azinu. That *parshah* provides us with the Ribono shel Olam's view of history. It begins with the story of His "discovery" of *klal Yisrael* in the wilderness (ימצאהו בארץ מדבר). If anything can be described as a song of love, it is this. Let us look at it and try to enter into its spirit.

> ימצאהו בארץ מדבר ובתהו ילל ישמן יסבבנהו יבוננהו יצרנהו כאישון עינו. כנשר יעיר קנו על גוזליו ירחף יפרש כנפיו יקחהו ישאהו על אברתו. ידוד בדד ינחנו ואין עמו אל נכר. ירכבהו על במותי ו{במתיו} ארץ ויאכל תנובת שדי וינקהו דבש מסלע ושמן מחלמיש צור. חמאת בקר וחלב צאן עם חלב כרים ואילים בני בשן ועתודים עם חלב כליות חטה ודם ענב תשתה חמר.

Here we have it. From the very first moment of our relationship with the Ribono shel Olam, He was determined to create a connection of love between Him and us. Let us remember that earlier in this essay we learned from the language of the Rambam in the Sefer HaMitzvos that *ta'anug* = *ahavah*. The openhanded generosity of the Ribono shel Olam's bounty would surely generate *ta'anug*, and *ahavah* would follow.

But, while knowing very little about the Ribono shel Olam, this we do know. Our physical world, honey flowing from stones, oil from flint rocks, cannot be more than the outer form of an inner reality. Always, always there are worlds within worlds, truths within truths. I wrote in the previous paragraph that the Ribono shel Olam was determined that His relationship with us was to be a connection based on love. Well, why was He determined that this should happen? Where is the generator that produces all those delicacies? Ha'azinu promises us that our bloody history will end with all our erstwhile implacable enemies singing our praises (הרנינו גוים עמו). What will they be singing about? It will certainly not be the fatness of our sheep or the redness of our wine. What is the smile *beneath* the smile? What is the story of our story?

Are there sources of *ta'anug = ahavah* other than the physical ones with which we have just now dealt? Of course there are, and we recall them from earlier in this essay when we quoted the Rambam from the Sefer HaMitzvos: המצוה השלישית היא שצונו לאהבתו יתעלה, **וזה שנתבונן ונשכיל מצוותיו ופעולותיו** עד **שנשיגהו ונתענג בהשגתו תכלית התענוג, וזאת** היא האהבה המחויבת. Without, of course, knowing any details, we can still surmise that this, or something very like it, would be the world that undergirds the luxuries of which Ha'azinu speaks.

The best way to get into this *sugia* would be to study some of RaMChal's dicta about the relationship between body and the soul, between *guf* and *neshamah*. After some thought I decided that the most helpful way of bringing these quotes will be to take them from Toras HaNefesh BeMishnas RaMChal by HaRav Binyamin Efrati where the actual words of the RaMChal are accompanied by a few introductory remarks by the author of that *sefer*. Thus in *Perek Alef: Mahus HaNefesh*, we have Section 3 headed כח הנפש.

> נשמה עליונה זו, שהינה מציאות נפשית נבדלת, כל כוחה בא מצד קישרה לעולמות העליונים, ומצד הקשר הזה, משפיעה הנשמה גם על הנפש התחתונה, להעלותה לדרגה רוחנית. כאמור בספר דרך ה' (חלק ג, פ"א ס"ב) "נמצא ... באדם מציאות נפעל נבדל ועליון מאד, ואין תכלית בביאתו באדם אלא לקשרו בשרשים העליונים בכח גדול, ובמציאות הזה נמשך השפע הנשפע על האדם מן המקורות העליונים וממנו לנפש וממנה לגוף ... והנפש העליונה מנהגת התחתונה."

Then, in *Perek Beis: Shleimus HaNefesh* we have Section 1, headed: שלמות הנשמה.

> כאמור בפרק הקודם, מהותה של הנשמה הוא היותם בצלם אלקים, דהיינו הידמותה לבורא.

מהות זה היא מקור שלימותה של הנשמה, באשר **שלימות הנשמה היא התדבקותה במקורה הא-לוהי**, כאמור בספר דעת ותבונות סי' כד: "הנשמה אינה אלא חלק אלו-ה ממעל, הנה **אין תשוקתה ודאי אלא לשוב ולידבק במקורה ולהשיגו**, כטבע כל עלול החושק לעילתו, ואין מנוחתה אלא כשתשיג את זה."

הגדרה זו של השלימות כדביקות בבורא, מוסברת שם (סי' כב) "השלימות הזה הוא שיהיה האדם מתדבק בקדושתו יתברך, ונהנה מהשגת כבודו, בלי שום מונע מפריע ומעכב, ככתוב 'אז תתענג על ה' '(תהלים קמ יד).

And then, in Section 2, there:

עיקרה ופנימיותה של הנשמה הריהי, אפוא שאיפתה לעונג רוחני, באשר כל תכלית בריאת האדם להיטיב לו, והטבה זו הינה העונג הרוחני. כאמור בספר מסילת ישרים (פרק א): "האדם לא נברא אלא להתענג על ה', וליהנות מזיו שכינתו, וזהו התענוג האמיתי והעידון הגדול מכל העידונים שיכולים להמצא."

אשר על כן נבראה הנשמה בשאיפת תענוג, על מנת לבטא שאיפה זו בעונג הרוחני העליון.

Please note the many uses of ע נ ג and its cognates (עידון and so on) in these passages. Earlier in this essay, we found the same expression repeatedly in the Rambam. We have certainly become used to the idea that ענג and *ahavah* function in unison. Now that we have mustered these significant quotes from the RaMChaL, we can formulate our conclusions as follows: The Ribono shel Olam, from the very beginning, wanted to foster an *ahavah* relationship with man, the crowning glory of His creation. *Ahavah* is the state that comes about in the delight that is generated when two halves of a single whole that have been separated from each other find themselves once more together. The Ribono shel Olam knew what He had to do. He would allow a "part" of Himself to be lodged, somewhere, somehow, within physical man, that "part" remaining an eternal stranger in a physical world, yearning, always yearning, to find its way back to its true home.

But it must be clear to all of us that the Ribono shel Olam does not deal in artificialities. He does not position a "part" of Himself in an environment in which it does not, really *cannot*, fit. And, behold! A miracle! The *neshamah* princess does not sulk in a corner surrounded by alien commoners who cannot possibly appreciate her royal grace. Her smile is a winning smile — and indeed she begins to win over the commoners to her royal standards. The *nefesh*, the simple *life force* shared by the animal world, begins to undergo subtle changes. The language of the spirit that earlier had been a meaningless jumble to her begins to become intelligible. A palate that earlier had been gross and indiscriminate, slowly, or not so slowly, becomes more selective. Taste buds learn sophistication, delights come within reach that earlier could not even have been imagined.

And, wonder of wonders, even the body begins to join in. A longing for a return to the sources sets in, encompassing the whole person and the stage is set for a *ta'anug* that cannot even be imagined. True *ahavah* sets in.

Do you know where we have landed? We are back with Rashi to Bereishis 25:22 and finding Yaakov and Eisav in their mother's womb, fighting over the ownership of the "שתי עולמות", *this world and the next*. Rashi does not tell us who won. For that we must go to Tanya Eliyahu Zuta 19:

> אמרו רבותינו בעוד כשהיו יעקב ועשו במעי אמן אמר יעקב לעשו עשו אחי שני אחים אנחנו לאבינו ושני עולמות יש לפנינו העולם הזה והעולם הבא העולם הזה יש בו אכילה ושתיה ומשא מתן ולשאת אשה ולהוליד בנים ובנות אבל העולם הבא אינו כן בכל המדות הללו ואם הוא רצונך טול אתה העוה"ז ואני אטול העוה"ב ומנין שכך הוא שנאמר (בראשית בה) ויאמר יעקב מכרה כיום את בכורתך לי כשם שהיינו אומרים בבטן. באותה שעה נטל עשו בחלקו העוה"ז ויעקב נטל בחלקו העוה"ב.

I think that we are at a point at which we have found *ahavah*'s "seat in life" in the Jewish experience.

The Ribono shel Olam created a world that contained a Gan Eden in which Adam and the *nachash* ranged free. I venture to suggest that alien Gan Eden within the physical world can be interpreted as the equivalent to the "alien" *neshamah,* as we have understood it, in the physical body. The Ribono shel Olam was setting up a dynamic of estrangement and reconciliation. The *nachash* was able to "drive" Adam out of the *gan,* leaving it to the guardianship of the "armed" Keruvim; Eisav was able to take over *Olam HaZeh,* making it very clear — the dreadful scars that we carry on our collective "body" bear ample and eloquent testimony — that we are persona non grata in "his" fiefdom.

But, while it is true that the Keruvim are keeping everybody, including *klal Yisrael,* out of the *gan,* at the same time they are making sure that when we are once more ready to return, the path will lie open before us. The tiny increments of *ahavah* of which we are sometimes capable will one day grow into an avalanche that will crash all barriers.

PART II

Special Days

6.
Chanukah: Longing for Home

A HOME AWAY FROM HOME

What's a good definition of home?

Robert Frost[1] thought that it was the place where, "when you have to go there they have to take you in ... Something you somehow haven't to deserve." It's where you need no excuse for visiting. It's where you belong; where you can draw up the bridge to keep out a hostile world; where you can let down your hair and put up your feet. It's your space, your stage, your kingdom.

Right?

Wrong, wrong, wrong, and wrong again. Profoundly wrong, dangerously wrong, and, above all, Jewishly wrong.

Home is the place in which we are eternal strangers — and where, the more we are at home, the less we are at home.

Sounds strange, does it not?

Let us test the theory against the facts, and if we find it to be correct, let us try to understand its topsy-turvy logic.

It's a strange world of which the Torah speaks. Strange, if you measure it by criteria that are not indigenous to it.

Let's try thinking Jewish.

STRANGERS IN THE LAND

What I own I should be able to sell. If it's mine, I should be able to pass it on to you.

So we would have thought.

The *halachah* of Yovel tells us otherwise, והארץ לא תמכר לצמיתות, the land is not to be sold in perpetuity (VaYikra 25:23).

Well and good, but how does this prove our thesis?

Because the Torah assigns a reason for this inhibition: כי גרים ותושבים אתם עמדי [You cannot ultimately dispose of your real

1. A modern American poet.

property] because you are no more than strangers with Me ..., and as strangers you have no right to disturb the original distribution of the land.

Now the strictures of Yovel apply only under the most optimum conditions of Jewish possession. They require כל יושביה עליה, that all twelve tribes be living in the land at the time (Rambam, Shmita VeYovel 10:8).

Let us imagine the scene: All or most of Israel are in Eretz Yisrael, a Davidic king is on the throne, the Beis HaMikdash is home of the *Shechinah,* prophets walk the streets, the *urim vetumim* on the *kohein gadol's* chest provides direct communication with God.

And then — only then — are we strangers in the land. Absent some of these conditions, when only a few of us are there, let us say, upon another nation's sufferance, we can sell all we want for as long as we want. There is no hint of being strangers, nothing that marks us as in any way different from any other people.

There we have the paradox of which we spoke before: The more we are at home, the less we are at home.

Strange, isn't it?

Or maybe not so strange.

Let us begin by analyzing who we really are.

BAT GALIM

A place-name mentioned in Yeshayahu 10:30, Bat Galim, provides Chazal with an occasion to teach us something about ourselves. It is, they claim, a hint that we are ברתהון דגלואי, which we can paraphrase as "inveterate exiles," a people never quite at home, because our fathers were perennial misfits in the societies in which they found themselves: Abraham had to make a new life in a foreign land, Isaac had to pull up roots to settle in Gerar, and Jacob spent twenty wearying years in Padan Aram.

So what does that make of us?

It makes us into גלואי, too. Our state of exile is endemic to our very being.

Let us define *exile* as a state of longing, a craving for a return to roots, a refusal to trade the spiritual wealth that inheres in anguished alienation for the tinsel comfort of an artificial sense of belonging.

Let us say that Adam was driven from Eden so that the natural state of man might be one of constant hunger for a more perfect state, a truer truth: that we, the Adam of history, are at our best when we are most like him — obsessed with a forever unattainable ideal, an always beguiling, never-changing beyond.

AND BECAUSE OF OUR SINS WE HAVE BEEN EXILED FROM OUR LAND

How so?

Punishment, of course. That is simple, straightforward — and true.

The land's intolerance for sin is another dimension: the instinctive vomiting action that expels the irritant; the refusal to allow anyone to sully the palace of the king.

True enough but, perhaps, not the whole truth.

Perhaps we are distanced from the land in order to reinforce the healthy, Jewish sense of distance. Perhaps our sinning was an indication that we felt too much at home, had lost our sense of the beyond. We are driven into the wilderness of the nations (Yechezkel 20:35) so that, in longing for home, we will relearn how to long for Home.

Exile, then, is the state in which we are to learn the art of feeling homesick.

Is distance, then, a prerequisite for exile?

Yes.

And in one — unique — instance, no!

Yavan exiled us — in Jerusalem.

Our own times have taught us — oh, how thoroughly and dreadfully they have taught us — that one can live in Jerusalem — in *galus*. That, too, has been part of the baggage that we have carried through history — from our Yavan experience. It was there that we learned that when we forget how to live in Jerusalem, we lose Jerusalem — in Jerusalem.

UNDER THE YOKE OF THE NATIONS

Let us examine this a little more closely. When does God subjugate us to the nations? And in what way?

If we read Yirmeyahu, chapter 5, carefully, we can learn that *galus* is an outgrowth of a weakening of *emunah*.

Wander around Jerusalem's streets, observe and gain understanding. Look around. Can you find a man, anyone who practices justices and searches for *emunah*? If so — I will forgive her. It is *emunah* that You, O God, crave. You have punished them but they have not reacted; have brought them to destruction, but they have refused to be instructed. They were obdurate like rocks, refused to repent.

I imagined that they were spiritually impoverished souls, fools who understood nothing of God's ways or His justice.

I decided to make my way to the more sophisticated among them: they would surely understand God's ways and His justice. But they [too] had all together smashed the yoke, slipped off the harness.

Therefore the lion from the jungle [Babylon] will smite them; the wolf from the plains [Media-Persia] will lay them waste; the leopard [Yavan] will lie in wait over their cities, all who attempt to leave will be torn asunder — for their sins are many, their rebellions overwhelming.

It is *emunah* that God craves. The prophet haunts Jerusalem's alleys and byways, hoping, always hoping, that after all there may be something left that is authentically Jewish. Jerusalem might — perhaps — yet be saved. Hope gives way to resignation; resignation slowly begets despair.

The lion, the wolf, the leopard will wreak their bloody depredations.

Why?

Because they are no more than the outer expression of the inner rot. When Jews live and feel un-Jewishly, it is because they have submitted to a cultural hegemony imposed by alien people with alien values. The chains that shackled our poor limbs as we shuffled along the long and dreary road to Bavel; the cruel dominion with which Media-Persia curtailed our freedoms: These were only the tangibles that defined a truth that far transcended them.

We had lived in Jerusalem, the city of *emunah,* but had lost the feel and heft of what *emunah* really means. We lived at home but felt ourselves to be citizens of the distant capitals from which a tinsel glitter exercised its magic lure. We had become Babylonian expatriates wasting away in a Jerusalem that held no charms for us, Median sophisticates doing time among the religious trappings of a life that we despised.

And so we left. Not of our own will, to be sure, but dragged along in irons to experience from close hand what had beckoned so seductively from afar. At Babylon's rivers we would learn the beauty of Zion's songs.

So much for the lion and the wolf.

What of the leopard lying in wait outside our very own city, not even bothering to drag us to its lair?

That was the worst *galus* of all.

In the others, Jerusalem had still been with us — we had only failed to appreciate it. It was there even when we were not, desolate, alone, in ruins, and in tears, waiting, always waiting, for its children to return: a lone star toward which we might always steer, a magnet to the pull of which we needed only to respond.

Not so with Yavan.

Jerusalem herself had disappeared. It was not we who were dragged into exile. It was exile darkly and insidiously, through the seductive grace of beautiful buildings, beautiful statues, beautiful thoughts, and beautiful bodies, that sank its dank and poison tentacles into our very beings.

Yavan went straight for the jugular. How so?

TO KNOW, TO REALLY KNOW

Let us think a little about *da'as*. It stands at the very head of the needs and wants that animate our daily *tefillos*. Clearly, among all of them, it is the most pressing.

And the wording of the *berachah* is striking.

אתה חונן לאדם דעת. It is a matter of *chaninah* of an undeserved gift to which we have no real claim at all.

But why? We have no problem asking for health and wealth, redemption and forgiveness, peace and justice, all without resorting to an invocation of *chaninah*.

Why should *da'as* be different?

Because *da'as* is different.

Health and wealth, redemption and forgiveness, peace and justice, all are qualities that belong in the here and now. They make life pleasant, they make the world into a better place. They are, to be sure, not easily attained, need God's blessing to be fully realized, but they are no strangers to the human condition.

Da'as is different.

May Your mercies, O HaShem, our God, be bestowed upon the righteous, the saintly, the elders of Israel Your people, upon those of their scholars who are left to them, and upon ... the righteous strangers!

Strangers? In a litany of the spiritual elite of our people? How do strangers belong in this list?

Thus Maharal.

His answer is the key to the conundrum that has engaged us here. The list is a list of strangers. All: the righteous and the saintly, the elders and the scholars, all are out of place, all aliens in a physical world. השכל הוא גר בעולם הזה. The very mind is out of place in *Olam HaZeh* (Gevuros HaShem 9).

There is a difference, Maharal (Derech Chaim) teaches, between *chochmah* and *da'as*. *Chochmah* is the knowledge of objects as they appear to us. *Da'as* is the apprehension of their essence.

In this, our physical world, *chochmah* reigns supreme. Its function is to delimit and to delineate, to recognize relationships and to establish laws. Cause and effect, action and reaction all are grist for its mill.

But not the innate sanctity that informs all being. Not God's smile or God's frown, which infuses each event and each experience with the stuff of which eternity is made.

All this lies within the ambit of *da'as*. It is an otherworldly intruder. If we are to attain it, we need God's grace, His *chaninah*.

We can take our analysis a little further.

Why the *Adam* in this *berachah*? Why, אתה חונן לאדם דעת?

An interesting word, *Adam*. Certainly related to *adamah*, earth, presumably because it was from earth that man was formed. But, Maharal (Netzach Yisrael, chapter 13) wonders, can this be so? The whole animal world was also formed from the earth. How does *Adam* define man in particular?

Adamah, Maharal thinks, carries a very special connotation. It is the ground of all being from which, in the end, directly or circuitously, everything derives. It is the ultimate potential.

Adam is much more than an "earth-being." Adam is that one of God's creatures whose value lies never in what he is but always in what he can yet become. He is the eternally unrealized, the one whose justification and ground of being lies ever in the beyond.

And it is we, the Jewish people, who, among all of mankind, are called Adam. אתם קרוין אדם ואין אומות העולם קרוין אדם (Yevamos 61a). Only we, among all mankind, must be the ever unsatisfied, the ever striving.

אתה חונן לאדם דעת. Freely and only as an expression of unbounded *chaninah* do you allow us, Your Adam, to attain *da'as* — that faculty that permits us to live as You would have us live, to strive for that which You would have us strive, and to become, at least in part — but never more than in part — that which You would have us become.

So God gave us a gift: the gift of being the eternal stranger, the one with whom history never quite knows what to do. The one who must — if he is to maintain his integrity — be different.

And Yavan, too, received a gift.

Yavan was granted the gift of beauty. Noach's promise to his oldest son, יפת אלהים ליפת (Bereishis 9:27), found its most exalted and developed expression in Yavan. If our heart quickens to the symmetry [and occasionally the asymmetry] of a work of art, of a tree, of a mathematical equation, of the unchanging, regal, utterly predictable movement of the heavenly bodies, the stars, and their planets, the suns and their acolytes — that is the Yavan within each of us.

It is the faculty of wonder, the sense of the aesthetic that so enriches our lives.

But ultimately, it is a faculty that is doomed to frustration. It is hopelessly entangled with the mark of *hevel*, for that is what Solomon taught: שקר החן והבל היופי (Mishlei 31:30). [Thus, Maharal in Gur Aryeh to Noach.] In the end it leads — nowhere at all because it knows only the surface, never that which is beneath.

Yavan delights in a sunset but has no understanding at all for the Shabbos that it ushers in. It sees perfection in the human body and fails to understand that without the *bris milah* its completeness is an illusion. It understands, and understands well, the phases of the moon but has no sense at all that time, that most circumscribed of all by the seemingly eternal circular motion of the heavenly bodies, can also be sanctified.

Chazal described the *galus* Yavan as חשכה גדולה, a dreadful darkness — much worse than the earlier depredations of Bavel and Media-Persia. Those were bad enough. It is no fun to be smitten by the lion or laid waste by the wolf. But bad as they were, they did not strike at our essence. They left the *Adam* in us, intact. They did not drain us of our longing. They destroyed [or left destroyed] our Temple but did not — what is infinitely worse — defile it.

Slowly, insidiously, Yavan attacked our essence. There were no *misBavlim* and no *misYadnim* but there were — to our dreadful shame — *misYavnim*. We ourselves eroded our inner truth. Yavan could not have destroyed our Jewishness if we had not, on our own, compromised it so thoroughly that it remained vulnerable to the onslaught of their ideas.

Jerusalem, and only Jerusalem, was the right place for *galus* Yavan. It alone among the cities of the world has a soul. ירושלים הבנויה כעיר שחברה לה יחדיו (Tehilim 122:2). When we severed the ties to our inner truth, we severed the עיר שחברה לה יחדיו between the Nether and the Upper Jerusalem.

Absent that connection, Jerusalem can serve as the locus of exile as effectively as Rome or Berlin or New York — only more so.

It is no coincidence that the victory over Yavan took the form of, *The mighty into the hands of the weak, the many into the hands of the few*. These realities were not a part of our rehabilitation but constituted its very being. It was the realization that ours is a different world from that defined and limited by the unbending harmonies of Yavan's aesthetics, which finally brought us home.

We began our musings with a quote from Robert Frost who felt that "home" is the place you somehow haven't to deserve.

How wrong he was.

Perhaps if we live through this Chanukah as we ought to live, we will deserve once more to come home. Home to the home in which we will remain the eternal stranger who is never quite where he ought to be.

Truly at home. גרים ותושבים אתם **עמדי**. With Me!

7.

Purim 1: Yosef and Binyamin Celebrate Purim in Mitzrayim

You know, in a way they really did. Here is a quote from Megilah 16 a and b

> לכלם נתן לאיש חליפות שמלות ולבנימן נתן חמש חליפות. אפשר דבר שנצטער בו אותו צדיק יכשל בו? ... אמר רבי בנימן בר יפת רמז רמז לו שעתיד בן לצאת ממנו שיצא מלפני המלך בחמשה לבושי מלכות שנאמר ומרדכי יצא בלבוש מלכות תכלת וחור ועטרת זהב גדולה ותכריך בוץ וארגמן.

> [By giving only one set of clothing to each of the brothers but five to Binyamin, Yoseph] was hinting that Binyamin was destined to have a descendant (Mordechai, the איש ימיני, the Benjaminite) who would be wearing five royal garments as he left Achashveiro's palace. (Based on Esther 8:15)[1].

Clearly there is much that requires explanation in this mysterious Chazal. Commentators of course did what commentators do and much has been written on the subject. In this essay I want to deal with only one aspect of this mystery.

Why, of all things, would Yosef at just this dramatic moment, be thinking of the Purim story?[2]

We will need to know much more about Purim and about Mordechai. And that means that we will need to know a lot more about Binyamin.

It is always good to start with a challenging question. Our hope to find a satisfying answer will keep us focused. Here then is the question with which I propose to begin our quest. The halachah

1. I advise you not to worry too much about the strange idea that Yosef would have known about Mordechai and the Purim story. The world of Aggada has its own rules. I do not mean that these ought not to be examined, but, in the context of this essay, such an examination would be a fatal distraction.
2. Maharsha (*Chidushei Aggados*) offers an explanation. I plan to use this essay to explore what might perhaps be another possible route to travel.

determines that in a leap-year when there are two months of Adar, Purim is to be celebrated in the second one rather than in the first.

On its face it is difficult to understand why this should be so. Here is why. Two opinions on this matter are recorded in the Gemara. Those who hold that Purim should be celebrated in the first Adar base their opinion on a well-known and widely applied principle that אין מעבירין על המצוות, that a mitzvah that can be done now should not be pushed off into the future.[3] The second opinion, the one that became the halachah, argues that מסמך גאולה לגאולה עדיף, It is preferable to bundle "salvations" as closely together as possible. Pushing off Purim to the second Adar brings it closer to Nisan and therefore to Pesach. The two salvations are now close together.

Here is my problem. Why is "bundling" better? We have two values here that are clashing. One (אין מעבירין על המצוות) is a formal, well-established rule that is derived from the Torah[4]. The other is an apparently vague "preference" (עדיף) for which no explanation is offered. Even Rashi is silent. So, once more, why is bundling better?

This is the question that I suggest we should all keep in mind. I have a feeling that we will not get to an explanation until the end of this essay. We will be making some interesting stops along the way.

THE BEGINNINGS

In the meanwhile let us attend the drama of Rochel's experiences with childbirth. First with Yosef and then with Binyamin.

What were Rachel's reactions when she saw that after so many years and so many tears, God had finally granted her a son?

She was human and so her thoughts turned first to herself. Her standing in society had been restored; the source of her constant embarrassment had been removed. אסף אלהים את חרפתי (from אסף,

3. An example of the application of this principle is recorded in Orech Chaim 25:1. Normally when Tefilin are put on, the של יד are put on before the של ראש. If, when reaching into the bag in which the tefilin are kept one inadvertently comes into contact with the של ראש before the של יד the rule of אין מעבירין is activated and that one is put on first. This is only one among many.

As I wrote above, אין מעבירין is a well established rule.

4. ושמרתם את המצות, מצוה הבאה לידך אל תחמיצנה. See Mechilta to Shemos, 12:17.

to gather in, thus, to inhibit, to limit.[5]) God has contained my shame (Bereishis 30:23).

But she was also our mother, Rachel. She knew her being to be linked absolutely to her partnership with Yaakov in establishing the twelve tribes.

And so she prayed: יוסף ה' לי בן אחר (from יסף, to add) (Bereishis 30:24). She would not be satisfied with just this one. She craved another child.[6]

And, wonder of wonders. The limiting, inhibiting אסף gives way to the expansive, embracing יסף. Unlike begets unlike – and the seemingly impossible becomes the norm.

A prayer is answered. Another child is born.

But this time pain and exhaustion take their toll. Anticipation gives way to a weary acquiescence to a fate that cannot be changed. She has lost her fight, gives up the struggle. She calls the child בן אוני, child of my impotence, my affliction (Bereishis 35:18).

At the extreme moment of fulfillment she has been defeated. What is is, and nothing can be changed.

But the ear of her grieving husband has picked up a smidgen of hope. It is true that און means affliction. But it also means strength.[7]

He is determined that the latter meaning will be the operative one. He calls his son בנימין, child of the right. Power and success are to be his.

And so Binyamin becomes און *from* און, *the symbol of hope wrenched from despair, victory over despondency.*

And in this he has borrowed a little from his brother. און *becomes* ימין *even as* אסף *turns into* יסף.

Rachel's children do not make peace with givens. Nothing is absolute. In seeming defeat lie the seeds of victory.

5. This translation follows the Targum and Ramban. Rashi translates אסף as, has hidden. For the purpose of our presentation in this essay (and only for that purpose. I am obviously not taking sides), I have chosen to follow Ramban. The reason will become obvious as we go along.

6. Rashi explains that having born two sons her contribution to the twelve tribes would at least be on a par with that of Bilhah and Zilpah. In this essay we will be exploring another possibility.

7. Ramban, there.

OF DEFEATS AND CONQUESTS

To turn Rachel's און into Yaakov's און; that is the epic struggle that informs Binyamin's history. Where smallness and greatness are locked in constant, unforgiving conflict there must be unremitting vigilance, unflagging energy. The ידיד ה'[8] must be the fruit of a victory that the זאב יטרף[9] protects in his lair.

A moment of negligence can, and does, produce a moment of weakness in which an entire kingly future can be forfeited.[10] On the other hand, the battle fought bravely and consistently produces a Holy of Holies in which the Shechinah finds a home.[11]

This is the reality of Binyamin's trek through history. Contradictions are overcome and turn into the stuff of destiny.

THE TEARING WOLF

A tearing wolf has victims. Who, in the first place, is the victim of Binyamin's rampages?

The answer is unexpected: it is he himself.

When King David was looking for a suitable place upon which the Beis HaMikdash might be erected, he found a mountain peak that seemed to meet all the requirements. However, he was advised to go to a lower point, this because when Moshe blessed Binyamin he declared that the Divine Presence was to dwell בין כתיפיו, between his shoulders [not the highest point, which would have been the head]. The Gemara explains this requirement with the observation that the noblest-looking part of the ox [presumably because of the rippling muscles and awesome strength massed there] is at the shoulders.[12]

Why an ox? How does the impressive strength of the ox's shoulders have anything to say about Binyamin whom Yaakov

8. The beloved of God. The term that Moshe Rabbeinu used to describe Binyamin in VeZos HaBerachah.

9. The Tearing Wolf. The term that Yaakov used to describe Binyamin in VaYechi.

10. I Shmuel 15:24. Shaul's moment of weakness in allowing himself to be persuaded by the people, lost him his kingship.

11. Megilah 26a. A sliver of land went out from Yehudah's portion and entered that of Binyamin. Every day Binyamin was irked by this and wanted it returned to his portion. In the merit of this craving Binyamin became אושפיזכן לשכינה, host to the Divine Presence. The Holy of Holies was built in Binyamin's portion.

12. Zevachim 54b. See Rashi to Devarim 33:12.

saw as a wolf? It was Yosef, not Binyamin, whom Yaakov described as an ox?

What do we do with this puzzle?

There can be only one answer.

Yosef lives in and through Binyamin. Binyamin has, as it were, a dual existence. In his own right he is a tearing wolf, but he shares the nature of the mighty muscled ox because he has taken upon himself the fulfillment of Yosef's destiny too.

Let us examine this proposition.

It was when Yosef was born that Yaakov said to Lavan, "Permit me to leave so that I may return to my own place, to my land" (Bereishis 30:25). To this Rashi remarks: Yaakov made this request [only] after Eisav's nemesis was born. For it is written, And Yaakov's house shall be like a fire, Yosef's house like a flame. Eisav's house shall be like straw. Fire without a flame cannot travel. Thus only after Yosef (the flame) was born did Yaakov feel that God could now frustrate Eisav's wiles. It was time to go home.

Thus it is clear that Eisav will succumb to Yosef. But while Yehoshua, the first conqueror of Amalek (Eisav's grandson), was indeed descended from Ephraim (Yosef's son), Shaul and Mordechai were Benjaminites

Clearly, then, it is the "Yosef" in Binyamin who functions when he faces down Amalek.

Let us observe the moment when Yosef, as viceroy of Egypt, comes face-to-face with his younger brother. Yosef hastened for his emotions toward his brother overpowered him and he wanted to weep ... (Bereishis 43:30). Rashi explains: Yosef asked Binyamin whether he had any children. When told that there were ten sons and the names that they bore, he asked for the significance of these names. Binyamin answered that each was called by a name that somehow incorporated some aspect of Yosef's nature [נעמן שהיה נעים ביותר] or history [בלע, שנבלע בין האומות]. In effect then, the ten sons of Binyamin were, in a way, Yosef's sons.

This truth is reflected in Sotah 36b: Yosef was destined to produce twelve tribes in just the way that Yaakov did ... but instead ten (of these potential twelve tribes) were born to Binyamin and only two, Ephraim and Menasheh, to Yosef. But, since they were in reality meant to be Yosef's sons, they were all named after him.

Binyamin, the tearing wolf, tore first of all from himself, partly losing himself in his brother's personality.

Where does one find such strength?

THE PORTION OF THE TEARING WOLF

The altar was built upon a base [יסוד] that extended one cubit beyond the actual altar's dimensions. It was upon this base that the blood of the sacrifices was poured. But this base did not run along all four sides of the altar. The eastern side [which lay in Judah's rather than in Binyamin's portion; see below] had no יסוד. The base for sanctity could lie only in the חלקו של טורף, the portion of the tearing [wolf] (Zevachim 53b).

R. Levi bar Chama taught in the name of R. Chama bar Chanina: A sliver of land extended beyond Yehudah's portion [of the Land, which lay to the east of Binyamin] and entered Binyamin's territory [encompassing the eastern areas of the Temple, including the Temple Mount, the Ezras Nashim, and part of the Azarah including even the eastern portion of the altar] and, throughout his life, righteous Binyamin begrudged Judah this portion ... Because of this Binyamin's deserved to become host to the *Shechinah* [the Holy of Holies was situated in his portion] ... (Megilah 26a).

It is not easy to play host to the *Shechinah*. A proud, bombastic person leaves no room for God in his world.[13] Only one who has vacated his personality of any selfhood can make room for the Divine. Only Binyamin who was unable to make peace with the fact that certain aspects of holiness lay outside his domain, who knew longing and craving only for sanctity, was able to retreat into himself sufficiently to produce the requisite space.

Binyamin, Child of the Right. All powerful [ימינך ה' נאדרי בכח]. Strong enough to be weak. Mighty in giving rather than in taking. Host to God's Presence on earth.

13. See Berachos 43b: He who walks with his head held high [בקומה זקופה] ... is considered as though he pushes up against [כאילו דוחק] God's presence on earth [רגלי השכינה].

MASTER OF SILENCE

Rachel understood the efficacy of silence [when she did not reveal Lavan's deception in substituting Leah as Jacob's bride], and because of this her children would understand the efficacy of silence. Binyamin did not tell his father that the brothers had sold Yosef; Shaul did not announce that he had been anointed king; Esther kept silent with regard to her parentage when she was taken to Achashverosh's palace.

Rachel's skills seem to have been exercised by Binyamin and his descendants [Binyamin, Shaul, Mordechai, Esther] rather than by Yosef. If Chazal teach that her "descendants"[14] knew of the efficacy of silence, then it was the Yosef in Binyamin who was meant.

Silence requires strength, מי כמוך באלים ה', Who is like You among those who are able to keep silent (Gittin 56b).[15]

It is the mighty בן ימין, augmented by the oxlike strength of Yosef, who is master of its mysteries.

But the test of true strength is versatility. To be always silent, even when circumstances call for aggressive intervention, is to be slave, not master, of the mode. Thus Mordechai told Esther, כי אם החרש תחרישי לעת כזאת, רווח והצלה יעמוד ליהודים ממקום אחר, For if you insist on keeping silent, even in *such a time*, easing and salvation will come to the Jews from another source... (Esther 4:14).

SOUNDS OF SILENCE

God's ominous silence cradled Jewish destiny in Achashverosh's Shushan. He had, so to speak, withdrawn within Himself. The Gemara (Chulin 139b) finds an inkling for the Purim miracle in the Torah: אסתר מן התורה מנין? ואנכי הסתר אסתיר פני ביום ההוא. Where is the story of Esther hinted at in the Torah? It is in the verse: And I will surely hide [הסתר from סתר, "to be hidden," the root from which the name אסתר is formed] My face on that day. We had apparently been left, flailing, unattached, to our fate, had become the plaything of two buffoons whose intentions — and their

14. Which would normally include Yosef.

15. In this context אלים is to be taken as the mighty ones. Chazal point out that there is a connection between אלים and אלמים, those who cannot speak, hence, the silent ones. It takes the mighty to know how to remain silent.

ability to actualize them — were deadly serious. Two men got together. One had earth to sell; one had a trench to fill (Megilah 14a). What could be simpler? Everything dovetailed so neatly. We were, so it seemed and so it was, lost.

But there are sounds of silence that the attentive ear can discern. Even though I absolutely hide My face from you, nonetheless I will communicate with you through the medium of dreams. [Rashi: Since it says, ואנכי הסתר אסתיר פני **ביום** ההוא, I will hide My face from you on *that day*, the implication is that at night — the time of dreams — the Face is not hidden] (Chagigah 5b).

למנצח על אילת השחר: מה שחר סוף כל הלילה אף אסתר סוף כל הנסים. With Esther the period of the night, the period of prophecy,[16] comes to an end (Yoma 29a). But it is "the end of the *night*." It yet partakes of the mystery of darkness in which the clamor of the noisy day does not completely drown out the divine voice. Prophecy, the clear incisive break in the natural order, is a thing of the past, but the half-blurred, unfocused, dreamlike intimation of a deeper truth can still be tapped.

Such a period in time has its special challenges. The intimacy of darkness, as it were, has to be snatched from encroaching day.

It is a time that calls for Binyamin. He knows the secret of forging the holy out of the profane so he will be able to expand the darkness mode of the night to its farthest reaches.

And so it is Mordechai, the איש ימיני, who recognizes the מלך behind the מלך. In Esther he will find the perfect mold to lend form and function to the boiling mass of his energies. God will yet be found in Shushan, bending to His purpose the very forces that seemed to negate His being.

AND MORDECHAI'S BIDDING — ESTHER DID

What do Chazal really mean when they say that Esther can be discovered in the Torah's prediction that, ואנכי הסתר אסתיר פני ביום ההוא? Certainly the period — one of horrific darkness — can well

16. Maharal explains that the night, when nature is, so to speak, quiescent, rather than the day when it is active and manifest, is the ideal time for miracles and prophecy.

This, in the dimension of time, is the equivalent to the desert in the dimension of space. The greatest miracles occurred in the silence of the wilderness rather than in the hurly-burly of urban life.

be described as one of הסתר פנים. But why Esther the person? If ever there was someone for whom God's presence was a palpable reality in even the most forsaken of conditions, it was Esther. Witness that throughout the terrible years of solitude in the palace, she maintained her *ru'ach hakodesh* until the very moment in which she — for the very first time — entered Achashverosh's presence of her own volition (Megilah 15b).

Why should she, as a person, be marked as a symbol of הסתר פנים?

The association between Mordechai and Esther in bringing about the salvation of Purim presents us with an intriguing conundrum. We have come to recognize Mordechai as the archetypical איש ימיני. Binyamin, of course, is the אושפיזיכן לשכינה, the host of the Divine Presence in Israel, thus the one among Israel's children in whom God's presence is most openly discernible. How, then, does he interact with Esther, the protagonist of the hidden face, one whose mode is the lonesomeness borne of the inability to discern God?

The answer of course is that this lonesomeness, far from being a disability, is a mighty cause for closeness to the Ribono shel Olam. The hidden face is never an end in itself. God hides Himself, so that we may be galvanized into searching for Him. The spiritual, no less than the physical, abhors a vacuum. Esther is the ideal foil for Mordechai. The restless drive that animates the tearing wolf and energizes his never-ending quest for the expansion of the boundaries of sanctity is challenged by the emptiness of the Hidden Face that she typifies.

Mordechai draws Esther into the ambit of "Presence", as surely as his tribe Binyamin fought to convert the profane into the holy, and as surely as the miracle of Purim draws the natural and profane into the ambit of the miraculous and the sacred, and prods encroaching day into the nocturnal mode.

Esther does Mordechai's bidding. She is *talmid* to his *rebbi*, the void demanding to be filled.

אסתר מן התורה מנין, does, indeed refer to the person rather than to the period. The intent of the question is this: Where, in the Torah, do we find a hint for the *rebbi–talmid* relationship that must be the hallmark of Jewish survival in any period of הסתר פנים?

The tragedy of Achashverosh's decree came about when people jettisoned their *emunas chachamim* and joined in the king's banquet, against the advice of their *rabbonim* (Megilah 12a). It was reversed when Esther taught us how to be a *talmid*.

OTHER BATTLES, OTHER CONQUESTS

Now, King Achashverosh levied a tax upon the land and upon the islands (Esther 10:1).

Who really cares? Why should the tax policies of this heathen despot find a place in *kisvei hakodesh*?

Our question is not an idle one. It penetrates to the core of the Purim saga. What is Achashverosh's role in this story? Is he a bit player needed as a foil for the main protagonists, Mordechai and Esther on the one side and Haman on the other, or is he, in some way not immediately apparent, as central to the plot as they? What is the real significance of the fact that: *On that day King Achashverosh gave the house of Haman the Jew-hater to Queen Esther* (Esther 8:1)? Clearly Achashverosh attaches great importance to this gift — he mentions it prominently at 8:7: *See I have given Haman's house to Esther*... But why is this really important? It seems a small enough gesture. Why make an issue of the gift rather than of the fact that Mordechai was elevated to Haman's position of power?

Something here seems to beg for further analysis.

ACHASHVEROSH AND HAMAN

How are we to understand the interplay between these two?

Achashverosh is a Median king, and Jewish subjugation to his hegemony comes under the rubric of the second of the four kingdoms [Babylon, Media-Persia, Greece, and Rome] that were described by Daniel.

But there is something unique here.

Nebuchadnezzar, the Babylonian, has no shadowy Amalek presence lurking behind him. Why does Achashverosh need a Haman to energize his hatred of Israel?

Our quest for an answer takes us back to the very dawn of history.

... AND LET HIM DWELL IN THE TENTS OF SHEM

What did Noach mean when he blessed Yaphes with the words: יפת אלהים ליפת וישכן באהלי שם?

Rashi renders יפת as, ירחיב, to widen, and then goes on to assign the subject, אלהים, to the second phrase, rendering the vav of וישכן, as, "but" [... but may God dwell in the tents of Shem].

Let us see whether the פשוטו של מקרא can allow us to have Yaphes be the subject of the second phrase, too, thus that the entire sentence is part of the blessing that Noach bestows upon this son.

Noach had lain in a drunken stupor in his tent and was discovered by Cham, who promptly calls his two brothers.

Why?

Clearly because he wants them to join him in whatever his father's nakedness and disgrace meant to him.

He does not succeed and Shem and Yaphes act in opposition to his plan.

But they are not equals in this enterprise ויקח שם ויפת את השמלה. ויקח is in the singular, rather than the expected, ויקחו. The initiative came from Shem [*He*, not *they*, took]. Shem takes, but Yaphes just tags along. He permits himself to be drawn into a worthy [Shem-like], rather than an unworthy [Cham-like], exercise.

Instead of *joining* with Cham, he *joins* with Shem.

The story can be seen as a struggle between Cham [from חמם, "to heat" or "to be hot"], the evil one burning with illegitimate desires, and Shem [the Hebrew שם, "name," denotes a significant presence], the solid, strong, and good human being, for the soul of Yaphes [related to יופי, "beauty"], the vacillating protagonist of [neutral] physicality and aesthetics [a function of the physical] who, by his nature, can be drawn to either side. Under the sway of evil, he becomes a tool of evil; when he casts his lot with sanctity he serves nobly — the cause of the sacred.[17]

When Noach wakes up, he realizes precisely what has happened. The roles that Cham and Shem played in their struggle

17. This view of the story, and the interpretation of the three types represented by the three brothers, is based upon Maharal in Gur Aryeh there.

Maharal draws parallels between Noach's three sons and those of Adam [Shem/Shes; Cham/Kayin; Yaphes/Hevel], thus allowing us to universalize the theme of the story as we have done within.

over Yaphes's soul are clear enough to him. He curses the one, blesses the other.

But what to do about Yaphes? Noach knows him to be weak, knows that he will always be a follower, never a leader. He knows that this time he did the right thing, but that it could just as well have gone the other way.

There is only one hope that a caring father would express under such conditions. He would probably word it something like this: My child! You were exposed to a severe test. Cham and Shem were vying for your soul. This time you made the correct decision and found immortality for yourself by opting to follow Shem. There will be many other tests, many other decisions you and your descendants will be called upon to make. Take your lesson from what has happened now. Eschew the shallow blandishments of Cham and make your spiritual home with Shem. Find shelter in his tent.

יפת אלהים ליפת, May God make Yaphes stand [firmly] with wide-spread feet. (The wider the step, the firmer the stance.) וישכן באהלי שם, so that he [Yaphes] may be [permanently] ensconced in the [protective] tents of Shem.

One way to view history is to see it as a continuation of that primeval battle. Will man's innate love of the refined, the harmonious, the aesthetically pleasing, in short, will the Yaphes in man, fall prey to Cham's fiery and destructive passions, or will it be sublimated to lend grace and dignity to the spirituality that is Shem's? Will Yaphes become slave to Cham, or luminous body to Shem's luminous soul?

Only Greek — the most pleasing form of human expression — is fitting body for the Torah's soul (Megilah 9b). Yaphes has much to give. The soaring cadences of his language can captivate our minds and focus them on the Torah's sublimities; the melodious phrasings of his music can delight our hearts and lift us beyond our smallness and our lusts.[18]

They can also destroy — utterly. We all know — too well — what Yaphes, in the grips of Cham, can do to us by means of aesthetics run amok, a culture dragged through all the filth of the mind's ugliest sewers.

Yaphes, the insecure and the unsecured. The weather vane of humanity.

18. Thus, the *shirah* in the Beis HaMikdash.

Yaphes's trek through the ages has known many twists and turns. Koresh [king of Media, descendant of Yaphes] became God's anointed when he brought about the *Shivas Tzion* and thereby became a part of historic Shem's progression toward the realization of God's purpose. Antiochus [from Yavan, descendant of Yaphes], with his blind hatred of the sacred and the pure, advanced historic Cham's vendetta against the sublimity toward which the human spirit can soar.

In neither of these two instances was there an actual "Shem" or "Cham" involved. In both it was more a matter of identifying with historic trends associated with those two prototypes. But there were in the past, and were to be in the future, other times, and other places, in which the original pattern was to be more closely followed.

We shall first glance onward, to the Gogian wars, which are to presage the messianic age, and then come back to Purim, the immediate focus of our interest in this essay.

A complete presentation of the picture that the prophet Yechezkel draws of those climactic events would take us far beyond the scope of this essay. The point that is of interest to us in our present context is that, according to a number of sources (marshaled in the ArtScroll Ezekiel, pages 580– 582), while the majority of the nations who are enumerated at Yechezkel 38:2–6 as fighting under the Gogian flag are of Yaphesite descent, Gog himself will be from Eisav-Edom.

Yaphes under the sway of Cham.

Poor Yaphes! Poor, tragic humanity. So much beauty that could have infused life with dignity and serenity. Such cultural sublimities that, had they but been allowed to, might have lifted man beyond his pathological affinity for the mean and the petty. All wasted. All rotting on the slag heap of history. Yaphes, in the final dreadful convulsions of man's battle against his better self, will have chosen to become Cham's minion.

Yisrael will have to walk alone, unaided, to meet Moshi'ach.

But it was not always so.

Achashverosh — another scion of vacillating Yaphes — fought himself valiantly and won a victory of sorts. The saga of his metamorphosis runs like a subplot through the story of Israel's salvation.

In the end he made the right decision — and won his little piece of immortality.

Back to the questions with which we started this passage. What is so important about the gift of Haman's home to Mordechai? Why the interest in Achashverosh's tax policies?

Mordechai's elevation to power was an act of statesmanship. He was the man of the hour, and from a political standpoint there is no doubt that Achashverosh chose well. It was significant in the short run, but the long thoughtful gaze of history is not caught by it.

The ceding of Haman's house was another matter altogether. This was a value judgment. Mordechai had taken Haman's place as mentor and anchor of this confused and distraught man. Something of Esther's spiritual grandeur must have touched the shallow and murky recesses of his addled mind and — if only for a moment — Noach's dream came true.

Yaphes had joined forces with Shem.

With feet firmly planted, Achashverosh becomes a major actor upon the stage of history. Even the taxes that he levied upon his possessions become a part of Torah.

Binyamin has won another victory.

Another און of frailty has been turned into an און of strength.

HOST TO THE *SHECHINAH*

What is really meant when Binyamin is described as being אושפזיכן לשכינה? The term certainly seems to imply more than the simple fact that it was in Binyamin's portion of the land that the Holy of Holies was situated. Form, after all, is no more than tangible essence, a means by which the eternal soul may be etched in the here and now.

What is *Shechinah* if not the suffusing of the temporal with the supernal, the infusion of light into darkness.

ליהודים היתה אורה..., Light shone for the Yehudim ...

What is Binyamin if not the embodiment of this function?

איש יהודי היה בשושן הבירה

איש ימיני.

ליהודים היתה אורה

I am almost trembling as I write this. Please dear Reader join me in the wonder of it all. I am going to quote myself from a few pages back. I suppose I could have simply given you the page number and sent you back there to read it up. But at this stage of our discoveries we need the truth actually staring us in the face: here and now.

Please read this passage.

למנצח על אילת השחר: מה שחר סוף כל הלילה אף אסתר סוף כל הנסים.

With Esther the period of the night, the period of prophecy,[19] comes to an end (Yoma 29a). But it is "the end of the *night*." It yet partakes of the mystery of darkness in which the clamor of the noisy day does not completely drown out the divine voice. Prophecy, the clear incisive break in the natural order, is a thing of the past, but the half-blurred, unfocused, dreamlike intimation of a deeper truth can still be tapped.

Such a period in time has its special challenges. The intimacy of darkness, as it were, has to be snatched from encroaching day.

It is a time that calls for Binyamin. He knows the secret of forging the holy out of the profane so he will be able to expand the darkness mode of the night to its farthest reaches.

Here it is; black on white. The Purim miracle was brought about by expanding the darkness of the night, the time most hospitable for prophecy, into the שחר, the morning's shine: אילת השחר.

Now glance at the heading of this section: ליהודים היתה אורה. That need not have been stressed had not the anticipated mode been that of darkness. Purim is the story of light crashing the barriers and driving away the darkness.

Except that, as we have just quoted: The intimacy of darkness, as it were, has to be snatched from encroaching day.

This seems to be a new take on עד דלא ידע, is it not?

Please read on.

A פרייליכן פורים everybody! I hope that what you have read in this essay will help you, next Purim, to approach the "battle of the bottle" with new courage. You know, when I wrote this sentence I did not have anything very profound in mind. I thought it was a cute alliteration and that was all. Then it suddenly hit me

19. Maharal explains that the night, when nature is, so to speak, quiescent, rather than the day when it is active and manifest, is the ideal time for miracles and prophecy.

This, in the dimension of time, is the equivalent to the desert in the dimension of space. The greatest miracles occurred in the silence of the wilderness rather than in the hurly-burly of urban life.

like a ton of bricks (or a truck-full of bottles). Purim is the Yom Tov of Binyamin, the embodiment of metamorphoses where the profane can change into the holy and so on and on and on as we have not tired of pointing out in this long and complicated essay. If, among other things, one can turn day into night (at more or less the same time as turning night into day — see above) and an Achashverosh into a *shtickle ba'al teshuvah,* is it not obvious that one can change a bottle into ... what? Nu, what? NU?

Some Purim!

I assume that your minds, dear Readers, are not too addled so that you would have forgotten the promise that I made at the beginning of the essay. Why is "bundling" better. Why is Purim celebrated in the second Adar, the one closer to Pesach?

The two "salvations" that we are bringing together — Purim and Pesach — tell essentially the same story. *Klal Yisrael* finds itself aliens in a foreign country, imprisoned by a malevolent government, enmeshed in a net from which, by any natural standard, there can be no escape. In both instances the Ribono shel Olam intervenes with miracles[20] and brings about that which under the given circumstances can be viewed as a salvation. The only difference between the two is in the type of miracles that were involved. In Mitzrayim there were open miracles, in Shushan there were not. The miracles masqueraded as עולם כמנהגו נוהג, nature simply taking its course.

In as much as the Mitzrayim episode takes place in Nisan, the first month of the year, and Purim falls in Adar, the last month, I believe that we would be justified in seeing an evolution, beginning in Nisan (Pesach) and ending in Adar (Purim). Since we have the Ribono shel Olam running the world we must assume that the movement is progressive rather than regressive. It would follow that a "hidden" miracle is superior to an "open" one.[21]

Is that something that we can understand? I believe that it is.

20. Remember that the *berachah,* ... שעשה **נסים** לאבותינו is recited when the Megilah is read.

21. See Shabbos 53b. There we have a disagreement between Amora'im concerning a person who was so poor that the only way in which he could keep his infant alive was through an open miracle which was indeed granted him. Some believe that this shows how great he was, others feel that it was a disgrace: כמה גרוע אדם זה שנשתנו לו סדרי בראשית.

I do not believe that the issue of an individual person being helped by an open miracle would have any bearing on our discussion here.

An open miracle breaks the laws of nature that normally rule supreme down here. The Ribono shel Olam is all-powerful and can suspend those laws. Nothing limits His powers and the physical laws of the physical world lose their potency. In effect the physicality of the physical world has been temporarily eliminated and, for as long as it takes, it has become one with the upper spheres.

The implications are that "physicality" defies the Ribono shel Olam's interference. Its laws are absolute and brook nothing that smacks of the miraculous. That is not its mode. It can be temporarily pushed aside and put out of business. In effect it can cease to be a player in the current drama. But it will not permit itself to be changed. Immune, as it were, from even Godly intrusion, its integrity remains unimpaired. Its character puts it beyond the Divine reach. It can be ignored but it cannot be transformed.

The hidden miracle rejects such departmentalization. There are simply no limitations of any kind upon the Ribono shel Olam. He is persona grata in the physical world as much as He is in the infinite beyond. Nature bows to His will no less than do the angels.

Nu! Which is the greater?

I am suggesting that the "bundling" of Purim with Pesach has the nature of the closing of a circle. That is the progression of which we spoke earlier. Our national history began with the open miracles but developed to a point at which these were no longer necessary.

לך ה' הגדולה והגבורה והתפארת והנצח וההוד **כי כל בשמים ובארץ**,
לך ה' הממלכה והמתנשא לכל לראש. (דברי הימים א. כט:יא)

Do you understand now why we spent this long and complicated essay tracing the "sleight of hand" that typified Binyamin's refusal to be bound by any givens? Here we have the greatest of them all.

איש יהודי היה בשושן הבירה
ושמו מרדכי ... איש ימיני

8.

Purim 2: Of Masks and Memories

EVERYBODY LOVES PURIM

There really is a bit of everything: history and Hamantaschen; noshing and nostalgia; battles and bottles; friendships renewed and strengthened; the poor taken to our hearts; the seudah securing family bonds; Hallel — this time through reading the Megilah, not the usual form — and heroism; victory and vindication, all bobbing and weaving through the haze of the ultimate in vintage; excitement chasing experience, a jumble of jubilation, mind and emotion — until, slightly addled but not really the worse for wear, we look back on this small oasis in time, with the overwhelming feeling: It's good to be a Jew!

And then, there are the masks ...

Let's talk a little about dressing up. Two faces, two persona, if you will. The one turned outward, relating, communicating, telling the story of one's choice, limited in the range of its outrageous pretensions only by the skills of the makeup artist. A spurious reality [here's a Purim oxymoron for you!] anchored in nothing more substantial than the passing winds of fancy. The other, hidden away, genuine because it is relieved of the necessity of putting on a face for the public, reveling in a moment that is stolen from infinity, in which it is possible to focus, distortion-free, upon the only thing that really counts, a truth that is truer than the average truth, a smile beneath a smile!

Haman was no evil genie conjured out from some wayward bottle, cast arbitrarily upon the shores of history. He was the tangible result of tangible sin; do you remember all the Jews cavorting at Shushan's drinking fest? Israel had erred — terribly — and deserved destruction. Haman is every cancer, overpowering and smothering, gnawing away at the vitals, where the first, deviant cell was implanted by the hapless victim himself.

"Why then," the Gemara asks, "was Israel saved? Does God show favoritism?"

The Gemara's answer casts the Purim story as a great charade: When Israel sinned, their essential being was not involved. They acted out of fear, put on a front to deceive the murderous monsters in whose power they writhed. Inner Israel remained untouched. And so, Haman, too, was not real. A paper ogre, impotent and laughable, with no function other than to shake us out of a dream world wherein we had confused form with essence, had forgotten who we really were.

A little boy knocks at the door to deliver *shlach monos*. In his hand he carries the singularly ferocious mask which should have constituted his costume. The lady of the house, eager to enter into the spirit of the day, asks why he is not wearing the mask. "I tried to, but I got too scared of me!"

There we have it. The tragedy of getting one's persona confused. We all live lives which involve us in various kinds of make-believe. We all know that beneath the veneer of pettiness which the exigencies of life occasionally foist upon us, there is something solid, something worthwhile, something of which we can be proud. The beauty of Purim's masks is that they can so easily be removed. We learn that the way home need not be long or arduous.

Chag Purim Sameach everybody! Chag Purim Sameach.

9.

Purim 3: The World as a Hot Tub

WARMING UP THE FRIGID WATERS

Somehow it does not sit right with us.

Destroy? Erase? An entire people?

We, the children of Abraham, Yitzchak, and Yaakov who know so well how to love, to teach, to care, but nothing at all of hate or vengeance?

On balance this must be the hardest of all *mitzvos*. It clashes with everything for which we stand. How can we turn ourselves inside out and learn to hate where we so want to love? Even the great Shaul was not quite able to do it.

And yet — it's there. DO NOT FORGET! Harsh. Unforgiving. Unforgiving of them — and of ourselves if our nerves fail and we can't drum up the strength to do what has to be done.

With Amalek it is different.

With Amalek we play hardball.

For us it seems to be all theory. For us Amalek is a shadow. It's one of those *mitzvos* we can't do anything about. We don't know who they are. We wouldn't under present circumstances be able even to dream about eradicating anyone.

Why is reading this *parshah* so important? Does it tell us anything at all?

Why do we hate them so? What did they do that is so terrible?

They went for the jugular. They refused to grant us the uniqueness that our ancestry and the Egyptian experience conferred upon us. Everyone trembled before God's people. He had brought a nation to its knees, split a sea, sent manna from heaven—all for us. We are special. We have a mission. We know something of holiness. We can bring God back into history. We can turn history toward God.

And Amalek laughed.

There was a tub of scalding water. No one dared to jump in. A reckless, uncaring fool took the leap. He scalded himself — but cooled it off for everyone else.

Amalek laughed, and the world learned to laugh with him.

Today we can battle Amalek.

The tub is full of icy water. People are repelled by it. Seek comfort elsewhere. We can jump in and warm it up.

The world as a hot tub. What a challenge! What a Purim thought!

10.

Tu BiShevat: Our Cousins the Trees

I would imagine that one of the fondest memories that people who learned here at Ner Israel carry through life is the gorgeous show of color that the Ribono shel Olam puts on for us during the fall. It does not last very long, but for a couple of weeks, at least, it is hard to tear our eyes away from the gorgeous foliage surrounding us on all sides and to focus instead upon the honking and amazing "V" formations of wild geese which wing around overhead.

Most of us hope fervently that the late and sadly missed Rav Gifter read Avos 3:7[1] correctly. He suggested that it is only the person who, in order to be delighted by the beauties of nature, needs to interrupt his learning, who has, so to speak, forfeited his right to live. One who does not see two disparate worlds, but instead integrates his appreciation of the astounding lavishness with which the Ribono shel Olam hands us our aesthetic highs, along with his gratitude that He permits us insights into His beloved Torah, is, on the contrary, very much doing God's will.

With *Tu BiShevat* in the air, our thoughts are, or should be, very much centered upon trees. And if you think that there is nothing very interesting about trees, think again. It cannot be for nothing that the very first recorded prophecy granted to man, the very first message that the Ribono shel Olam conveyed to Adam, centered exclusively upon trees. I wonder whether it was from there that Dovid HaMelech took his cue when he began his Tehilim with the Talmid Chacham being described as *a tree planted near the waters* (Tehilim 1:1). There has got to be a reason. No?

1. [Please note that there is some discrepancy in how this set of *Mishnayos* is divided. In the text that you are using it may be that this *mishnah* is not marked as 7.] Here is the Mishnah's lesson: One who is engrossed in his learning as he walks along the street, and interrupts his studies in order to exclaim: "How beautiful is this tree! How gorgeous this plowed field!" is viewed by Scripture as having forfeited his right to life.

10. *Our Cousins the Trees*

If I had to vote for the single most difficult verse in the Torah to translate, I think it would be Devarim 20:19. *When you lay siege to a city and wage war war against it ... you must not destroy its trees wielding an ax against any food-producing tree.* "כי האדם עץ השדה לבא מפניך במצור."[2]

Try your hands at the very last few words — כי האדם עץ השדה לבוא מפניך במצור. What can they mean? The very diversity that we find among the commentators shows how very difficult it is.

I have a suggestion to make.

There is a quirk in Hebrew that I have not come across in any of the other languages of which I have any knowledge. I will give you two examples. The first comes from Koheles 5:8, where we have a phrase that asserts that even a mighty king who seems to have everything still needs the farmer. Without food his might will dissipate very quickly. But instead of "farmer" the text reads "field". "Field" in this usage stands for "the man of the field." My intuitive sense is that in English we would not speak of a "field" when we mean a "farmer."

Here is another example.

It comes from the speech that Joshua and Calev made when they attempted to dissuade the people from listening to the discouraging report made by the spies. Here is the text: *But do not rebel against God. Do not fear the inhabitants of the land. They have lost their protection. They are our "bread".*

Two expressions require our attention. Why, "our bread"? Nowhere in TaNaCh, as far as I was able to discover, is "bread" used as a metaphor to describe people who are easy to vanquish. Also, their protective cloud needs thought. Which cloud had protected them until now, and why had it now moved away, leaving them vulnerable?

First then, *protective* clouds.

Rashi offers two explanations, of which the second reads, *the shade that the Ribono shel Olam had spread over them has departed.* Why had God spread a protective cloud over the Canaanites and why did it disappear now?

I believe that the answers lie in a Ramban in No'ach in which

2. In this essay I have eliminated all Hebrew words in order to make life easier for those readers who find the Hebrew difficult. In this particular case I was not able to be consistent. Those of you who *are* fluent Hebrew readers need to see the original text in order to appreciate how very difficult the phrase really is. Sorry!

he explains why Eretz Yisrael was given to the Canaanites pending the time when the Jewish People would be ready to take it over.

The Ribono shel Olam's disposition that the land which He intended to give to his children should first fall to the descendants of Canaan was motivated by Canaan's status as a slave to Shem. In this way, Canaan would build up the land, till its fields and build its cities, in order that Abraham's children would find their possessions ready and developed for them when the time would come for them to take possession.

The Ribono shel Olam would surely have wanted to protect the Canaanites in Eretz Yisrael as long as their task was not completed. *However,* once *klal Yisrael* would be ready to enter the land, that protection would no longer be necessary. This is precisely the argument. Since it is now the Ribono shel Olam's wish that we should enter the land, there is nothing that we have to fear from the Canaanites. The period of their indenture to us has ended. There is nothing to prevent us from merely walking in and taking our own.

This insight will also help us to understand the expression, *our bread*. It is analogous to the Koheles verse that we have just discussed. We should interpret "our bread" as "the people who provide us with bread." Yehoshua and Koleiv are telling the people that the Canaanites had been given the land only in order to make it fertile for the Israelites, that is, to provide them with "bread". Because of this, the protection that they had enjoyed until now in order that they could perform their task was no longer needed.

We see that our holy tongue, Hebrew, has an educational element. The Ribono shel Olam wants us to look beyond objects to the people who stand behind them. Simple gratitude demands that we think of the farmer when we see a field and of the baker when we see a loaf. And, once we are focused on this line of thought, we should not forget Gittin 52a where we can listen to R. Yose calling his wife, "My home".

"Whom" do we see when we look at a tree? If, as we have now learned, the world of objects is not self-validating but bids us look beyond them to a truer truth, we ought to expect that something as imposing as a tree should also have a "someone" lurking in its shadow, waiting for us to discover him. Who might this be?

It seems to me that there is no more powerful metaphor for man himself than is the tree. It has its genesis in a seed, buried deep in the dank, dark, worm-infested earth and from those unlikely beginnings it draws its power, its fecundity, the color of its leaves, the beauty of its blossoms and the sweetness of its fruits. It sends out its branches which, in God's good time, send out their own, each really in itself a little tree which, in unison with all the others, becomes a hospitable shelter providing shade and nourishment to those who stand in need.

There is really no need to spell out the referent of this metaphor. The first of the three truths which Avos (3:1) bids us to contemplate if we wish to keep away from sin is our origin in the "putrid drop". Nothing very promising there. And yet, and yet ... think of what can grow out from there! Think of the power and the excellence, the distinction and the sheer beauty of what we can become if we set our minds and energies to it. Think of the blessings which we can confer upon our surroundings, the purity which lies within our grasp, the wisdom that is ours for the taking if we permit, tree-like, the *blessed rains* of the Torah to develop our faculties and stimulate our growth.

If we now go back to the Pasuk with which we started, it seems to me that we can suggest a meaning for the difficult phrase which we isolated above. Let us first be clear that the underlying rationale for the prohibition against hacking down fruit trees is that the Torah forbids us to summarily waste any of God's gifts (Devarim 20:19–20).[3] However, having made this clear, we must still note that there appears to be some redundancy in the text. For the simple prohibition, *and you shall not cut it down*, should really have been enough. The graphic, *Do not destroy its trees by swinging an ax against them* seems to engage us at a different level. We are confronted with a picture of one of us wantonly wielding an ax, exercising brute force against this defenseless loveliness.

You cannot, the Torah seems to be saying, remain untouched by this cruel destruction. כי האדם עץ השדה, the tree is too close to man, it *is* in fact the "man," and the step between felling the kindly tree and felling your brother is too small. The tree is sufficiently

3. Here is the Hebrew verse together with a translation. כי תצור על עיר ימים רבים ... לא תשחית את עצה לנדח עליו גרזן כי ממנו תאכל ואותו לא תכרת כי האדם עץ השדה לבא מפניך במצור. *When you besiege a city for many days ... do not destroy its trees by swinging an ax against them for from it you will eat and you shall not cut it down ...* For the time being we will leave the final phrase, ... כי האדם untranslated because at this point we have not yet decided what precisely it is telling us.

like your brother that לבא מפניך במצור; you should regard the tree as within the besieged city.[4] Just as you are unable, at this point, to kill the people in the city because they are protected behind their walls, so should your insightful sensitivity put the tree out of bounds for you. Although it stands exposed before you, you should look upon it as though it were behind the shielding wall.

Next time we see a beautiful tree, let us contemplate the potential that lies within each of us.

I wish all of you, my fellow "trees," that we may merit Dovid HaMelech's blessing:

והיה כעץ שתול על פלגי מים אשר פריו יתן בעתו
ועלהו לא יבול וכל אשר יעשה יצליח

He will be like a tree planted near the waters,
That yields its fruit in season,
Whose leaves never wilt,
And whatever it produces thrives.

4. A word is in place here regarding the suggestion that I am making for the translation of this difficult phrase. Firstly let us agree that the phrase *is* difficult. A glance at the many different possibilities put forward by the various commentators makes that very clear. Under the circumstances, and given that as far as I know there are no halachic implications, I felt that as long as it is clear to all my readers that what I am suggesting is just that, a suggestion and nothing more, I am on safe ground.

I wrote this essay many years ago and only now I dug it out because I hoped that some of you readers might enjoy a little material to stimulate your thinking about the rather mysterious *Tu BiShevat*. Still I was not about to put it in a book without rechecking what I had written then.

When I got to this phrase I began to feel some misgivings. It sounded like a very thunderous silence. Why not "listen" to that silence and forget about the whole idea? I had pretty much decided on that course when it occurred to me that I had never consulted the Hirsch Chumash on this matter.

Here is what I found: *For the tree of the field is the existence of man; [hence it is also] to go into the siege before you.* The commentary reads in part as follows: Do not cut down the fruit trees of the besieged city, for the fruit trees constitute the existence of man and therefore are included in the siege; i.e. they are part and parcel of what you are trying to obtain by the siege … *They are part of the besieged city.*

Please note that I am not claiming that Rav Hirsch's interpretation of the *sugia* is in any way similar to mine. It is not. But, so it seems to me, he is translating this final phrase almost precisely as I have done.

11.

Water Walls at Yam Suf

SEA PLAGUES

על הים לקו ...

רבי יוסי הגלילי אומר: מנין אתה אומר שלקו המצרים במצרים עשר מכות
ועל הים לקו חמשים מכות ...[1]

The R. Yose HaGlili passage that we put at the head of this essay appears toward the end of the first part of the Haggadah and I suspect that, by the time you reach it at your seder, chatzos is fast approaching. Probably you do not have the time to pay it too much attention. Writing an essay is different. There are no threatening deadlines. We have all the time in the world to examine this little-understood sugia and, believe me, we will need all of that time and then some. We will find that the study of the events at the Yam Suf will open some very exciting gates for us.

The first, and so it seems to me the most blatant, problem is that though each of the three Tana'im who discuss the relative severity of the "sea plagues" when compared to the "Mitzrayim plagues" agree that the former were harsher by a factor of five, these plagues are not even mentioned in the Torah.

EXCURSUS

A word is in place concerning the expressions אצבע and יד upon which the derashos are based.[2]

1. In my research for this section I made extensive use of Rav Kasher's *Haggadah Sheleimah*, R. Aryeh Kaplan's *The Living Torah*, and the Mesorah translation of both TaNaCh and Shas. We ought all to be grateful to some wonderful people who put in a great deal of effort to provide us with *sifrei ezer* that make sources available that we might otherwise have missed.
2. In my research for this section I made extensive use of Rav Kasher's *Haggadah Sheleimah*, R. Aryeh Kaplan's *The Living Torah*, and the Mesorah translation of both TaNaCh and Shas. We ought all to be grateful to some wonderful people who put in a great deal of effort to provide us with *sifrei ezer* that make sources available that we might otherwise have missed.

First, אצבע: In *lashon hakodesh* the term has two possible meanings. It can be used generically, describing each of the five digits that are parts of our hands and feet, but it is also the proper name of the "index finger" or "forefinger," the one nearest the thumb, that is normally used for pointing things out.

The אצבע that is the subject of the discussion in this section is the one that is part of the phrase, אצבע אלהים היא, which the magicians used to describe the third plague (the lice) to Pharaoh. In spite of the fact that its referent seems to be only that plague and not any of the others, our sugia evidently assumes that it is a description of all the plagues.[3]

Now which of the two meanings is assumed here? Is it "a finger" or is it "the 'index' finger"? It seems to me that our sugia, which associates the word with the number ten, must be assuming the first of the two [a finger]. It is as though the magicians were describing the group of the ten plagues as a "finger's worth" of trouble. If you engage "a finger," you get ten plagues and consequently, if you engage the entire hand, you get fifty. No special function is attached to this finger.

Now the Rambam (*Moreh Nevuchim* 1:66) in discussing the phrase כתובים ב"אצבע" אלהים (Shemos 31:18) argues that in that phrase, אצבע is the equivalent of "His will and His desire" (כתובים בחפץ אלהים כלומר ברצונו וחפצו). That definition is clearly predicated upon the second meaning. The index finger "indicates" this meaning. Our context, where it describes the inability of the magicians to duplicate this plague, would certainly be using this meaning. "With this plague God is indicating to us that He, and none other, is the source of our discomfiture!"

It is my distinct impression that throughout the Torah אצבע is used with this second meaning. (See Shemos 29:12 as an example and see Kesubos 5b and Rashi there.)

It seems perfectly clear that the meaning that our sugia attaches to the term אצבע (a digit that brought about ten plagues) does not accord with the פשוטו של מקרא (an act clearly perpetrated by God).

We have the same problem with the sugia's use of יד in the phrase, וירא ישראל את היד הגדולה. It seems very clear that the *yad hagedolah* that is cited could very easily refer simply to the

3. For an explanation, please see *Haggadah Sheleimah*, page נג, number רפט.

awesome power involved in splitting the sea. There seems no need at all to use it as intending to jack up the number of "sea plagues" to fifty. If proof were needed, we have Yehoshua 4:21–24, which makes this very plain.

Here is a quote:

> ויאמר אל בני ישראל לאמר אשר ישאלון בניכם מחר את אבותם לאמר מה האבנים האלה.
> והודעתם את בניכם לאמר ביבשה עבר ישראל את הירדן הזה.
> אשר הוביש ידוד אלהיכם את מי הירדן מפניכם עד עברכם כאשר עשה ידוד אלהיכם לים סוף אשר הוביש מפנינו עד עברנו.
> למען דעת כל עמי הארץ **את יד ידוד כי חזקה היא** למען יראתם את ידוד אלהיכם כל הימים.

Yehoshua uses *yad* to describe the splitting of the Yarden, although there is obviously no intention of any kind to indicate any number of "plagues" that were involved there.

* * *

I sincerely hope that you have taken the time to read this Excursus. The technicalities with which it deals may seem picayune, but I earnestly beg you to consider that in more instances than we care to admit, it is in just such technicalities that the treasure lies buried.

Here is the purpose of the Excursus. Immediately before it I had written that these plagues are not even mentioned in the Torah. I anticipated an argument: We do have the change from "אצבע" to "יד" and that is pretty clear. The fact is that even besides the issues that we discussed in the Excursus, there are also other problems with this derivation. As a result of all this, Rav Kasher (page נג, number רפ"ט) quotes both Ritva and Avudraham that הכתובים כאן הם סמך בלבד, **והקבלה היא העיקר**. Tradition, not text, is the carrier here.

Moreover, even if all that we have now worked out were not true — even if the use that the sugia makes of "אצבע" and "יד" were textually incontrovertible — even then we would be faced with a grating mystery. Why, in view of the fact that each of the "Mitzrayim plagues" is described by the Torah in such loving detail, are we denied all knowledge of what actually happened at the sea? We have no idea at all of what form of suffering these plagues imposed upon the Egyptians. Why keep it all so secret?

We notice the same puzzling silence concerning the ביזת הים, the unimaginable wealth that passed from the Egyptians to us at the sea.[4] Once more the existence of such spoils is firmly entrenched in our tradition, and once more the text is totally silent.[5] Why?

We get an inescapable impression that somehow the events that accompanied the splitting of the sea are not for publication. They were entrusted to the oral tradition but banished from the written record. Why?

אל מוציאם ממצרים כתועפות ראם לו (במדבר כ"ג כ"ב)

FAST FORWARD TO BIL'AM'S TAKE ON YETZIAS MITZRAYIM.

IT SEEMS A LITTLE STRANGE THAT WE SHOULD HAVE TO LEARN THE "*ALEF BEIS*" OF WHAT REALLY HAPPENED TO US AT THE MOST FREIGHTED MOMENT OF OUR HISTORY, FROM AN ANTI-SEMITE LIKE BIL'AM. BUT THEN WE MUST REMEMBER THAT EVEN WE SEEM TO HAVE BEEN PRETTY OBTUSE[6] DURING OUR FORTY YEARS OF DESERT WANDERING ...

Am I right? Were we really obtuse? And if we were, how did this come about? All in all *Yidden* seem to have pretty good brains. Why could we not wrap our minds around the changes that Yetzias Mitzrayim had wrought in our standing? How is it possible that after forty years of attending Moshe Rabbeinu's yeshiva we were still *kvetching* about the *mon*? We were on the doorstep of Eretz Yisrael. And here we were at it again, grumbling precisely as we had done decades earlier back in BeShalach when, as only recently emancipated slaves, we could really not have been expected to know any better. Had nothing changed in the last thirty-eight years?

4. Please take the time to study Pesachim 119a carefully. A relatively simple surface seems to hide some very profound secrets in its roiling depths.

5. Except for the intriguing, וַיַּסַּע at Shemos 15:22. Please see Rashi there.

6. I am aware that the generation that wandered through the wilderness for forty years is often called the דור דעה ; see, for example, VaYikra Rabba 9:1, "ודרדע [דה"י א ב] זה דור המדבר שכולו דעה." I do not really know what that term really means. However, irrespective of what precisely it is meant to convey, that cannot alter Devarim 9:7 and 8. זכור אל תשכח את אשר הקצפת את ידוד אלהיך במדבר למן היום אשר יצאת מארץ מצרים עד באכם עד המקום הזה ממרים הייתם עם ידוד. At least at the peshat level there appears to have been some major obtuseness at play.

Let us learn a little שב שמעתתא. The segment that I am about to quote is taken from the long Hakdamah.

ובמדרש אמרו שהכריח הקב"ה אותנו ע"י כפיית ההר שלא תסור התורה ממנו לעולמים, דבאונס כתיב לא יוכל לשלחה כל ימיו, גם המן שאכלו במדבר היה לכונה זו, כמ"ש בספר המגיד לב"י, שהמן שאכלו ישראל היה הכרחי לקבל התורה בלי שום בחירה. ובילקוט ראובני פרשת בשלח וז"ל יפיפיה ג' קצ"ה, הוא שר התורה, הוא המטיר המן לישראל והם אמרו נפשנו קצ"ה, להודיע שקצו ומאסו במן ובתורה ע"ש. וזה היה להם הכרח לקבל תורה, כי המן בא משר התורה והוא לחם אבירים שמלאכי השרת נזונין. **שוב לא היה להם שום נטיה ותאוה חומרית, רק תקוע היה בלבם אהבת התורה והמצות**, וזה נשאר לדורות למשכילים, אשר עליהם נאמר אדם כי ימות באהל:

Apparently there was method to our madness. The *mon* was a life-altering food. שוב לא היה להם שום נטיה ותאוה חומרית, רק תקוע היה בלבם אהבת התורה והמצות. I can see why people would not have wanted to enter into such a permanent suspension of free will. After forty years of miraculous living, "normalcy" might well have appeared an attractive prospect.[7]

Let us get back to Bil'am's prophecies and discover some of these tensions lurking between the lines of that strange story.

The prophecies, spoken as poetry rather than as prose, are not easy to decipher. We will not be exploring their meaning formally since that is not the focus of our essay. However, there is one phrase that draws attention to itself by appearing twice,[8] once each in the second and third prophecies. One gets the feeling that passing on that one would mean that we are missing something very fundamental. Since it is directly concerned with Yetzias Mitzrayim, it is of vital interest to us in the present context. Here it is:

7. I can imagine that some of us might be quite happy when the tekiah sounds after Ne'ilah. In a sense it could be regarded as a relief that we can finally put the tensions of the Aseres Yemei Teshuvah behind us.

Whether or not the following is true, I do not know. But I remember hearing or reading, that during the "*mon*" years we lived in constant hunger. Chazal teach that the mon was לחם הנבלע באברים, that it was absorbed by the body without entering the stomach. It is the food entering the stomach that somehow triggers the mechanism by which hunger is assuaged. That would not have happened while we were being sustained by the *mon*. The point was that our concentration upon Torah was so great and unceasing that the hunger never bothered us.

That is not an easy way to live!

8. At BeMidbar 23:23 and 24:8. The two sentences in which the phrase occurs are not completely congruent. There are minor differences between them. We will not discuss these formally in this essay. As it is, things are complicated enough. I intend to touch upon them lightly as they become relevant to our discussion.

אֵל מוֹצִיאָם[9] מִמִּצְרָיִם כְּתוֹעֲפֹת רְאֵם לוֹ

[Please note that we have supplied the נקודות on this phrase. These נקודות will take on great significance as we go along. Also, please note that "תוֹעֲפֹת רְאֵם" are joined in the cantillation mark(s) with a מרכא טפחה. this thoroughly combines them and precludes a reading that we would have punctuated כתועפת, ראם לו. that possibility will also interest us as we go along.

What does *to'afos* mean and what does *re'eim* mean? And further, given the *mercha tipchah* (combining) cantillation mark(s), what do the two expressions mean in combination?

We begin with רְאֵם. From Devarim 33:17, וקרני ראם קרניו, it appears to be the name of an animal with horns. I suppose that any number of animals could qualify. My *Even Shoshan* dictionary has "oryx" so I am willing to stick with that, though I have my doubts. The oryx's horns are extremely long and straight, famous for their beauty more than for their power.[9] Since the Devarim passage goes on to tell us that the *re'eim* uses his horns to gore the nations, I would have been more inclined to choose some other horned animal.

For our purposes in this essay, the choice does not make much difference. I am planning to follow Rashi (in his first explanation) that ראם does not at all refer to any animal. It is to be taken as an alternative spelling of רם (from ר ו ם), meaning high or exalted.

Now that is not quite the improbable stretch that it would seem. R. Avraham Bakrat (*Sefer Zikaron*),[10] one of the premier Rashi expositors, defends the interpretation. He writes:

> ואין לך לתמוה על זה, שכן מצינו שנראה האלף בתיבת וְרָאֲמָה וישבה תחתיה (זכריה י"ד י') במקום וא"ו ועין הפעל שבשרש רום.

Ergo, the replacement of the "ו" of ר ו ם with an "א" is legitimate.

Now, while it is true that since I discovered the *Sefer Zikaron* in the last couple of years I have become a chasid of his no-nonsense approach to the interpretation of Rashi, I must admit to an initial shock. It is true that in the Zecharyah passage an א is indeed inserted, but, watch the nikud! Here is the phrase: וְרָאֲמָה וישבה תחתיה. The komatz of רָם is maintained. But in the

9. This is probably a mistake. I just saw Wikipedia, which writes: The horns are lethal — the oryx has been known to kill lions with them

10. He was one of the victims of the Spanish expulsion in the fifteenth century.

Balak passage, the reading is רְאֵם! Where do we find רְאֵם meaning anything other than an oryx?

We will return to this really serious question a little later. The time has now come to try to tackle the very difficult *to'afos*.

For our purpose in this essay, I will attempt a marriage between Ramban and Rav Samson Raphael Hirsch. As a first step I will quote the Hirsch commentary to Bereishis 1:20 on ועוף יעופף:

By comparing יָגֵעַ and יגע (יָגֵעַ: tired: יגע: to engage in tiring work, to strive, to labor), we can understand the relation of עָיֵף (tired) to עוף. The eye can barely perceive the repeated movements of the wings. The meaning of עוף, then, is to strive, to advance without letup as opposed to one who walks, who advances step by step.

In his commentary to Balak on *to'afos* he writes:

> From the root, י ע ף which is identical with ע י ף and ע ו ף (see commentary Bereishis 1:20) — denotes *constant* striving to ascend to the heights.

So much for Rav Samson Raphael Hirsch. The Ramban in his Iyov commentary (first volume of Kisvei HaRamban, page עח) renders וכסף תועפות לך as, *Your money will appear to you as so many mountains....* It will be as though your possessions are stacked on the peaks of the highest mountains.

The sense of the Balak passage would be as follows: אל מוציאם ממצרים. The result of the Ribono shel Olam taking us out of Egypt was that His supremacy would be mountain-like in its height and therefore limitless (as for practical purposes are the highest mountain peaks) (ראם=רום).

Now, if that is indeed the meaning of this difficult phrase, it seems to me that this would preclude the *mercha tipchah* cantillation mark(s). Rather than combining *to'afos* with ראם (which would be fine if the meaning had been "the strength of the oryx") it would have been better to combine "ראם" with "לו", thus: כתועפות (mountain-like) is ראם לו (ascendancy to Him). We would have expected cantillation marks that would yield, כתועפות, ראם לו.

The theory sounds great, but the facts seem unhelpful and refuse to cooperate. We read רְאֵם instead of ראמה , and the cantillation marks are *mercha tipchah*.

A DETOUR BEFORE WE CAN ZERO IN ON WHAT I BELIEVE TO BE A POSSIBLE SOLUTION

I suppose that if my suggested marriage between the Ramban and Rav Samson Raphael Hirsch is a good shiduch, we ought to translate תועפות ראם as *The altitude at which He functions* (ראם לו) *is birdlike, thus for all purposes unlimited (as the highest mountains appear to us), because of the unceasing activity of its tireless wings* (כתועפות). As a translation it is a bit of a clunker, but it does reflect the meanings that I have suggested. We will grit our teeth and use it (though as a kindness to me and also to you, my readers, we will shorten it to *the altitude…*)

Let us remember the context within which it occurs. אל מוציאם ממצרים כתועפות ראם לו. The meaning of that sentence appears to be that the Ribono shel Olam "won the right" (כביכול) to be described as One Who enjoys mountain-like ascendancy, by taking us out of Egypt.

Apparently something extremely significant happened on that fifteenth day of Nisan. What exactly was that?

The following longish quote is taken from my discussion of Pesach in my recent book *Awake at the Wheel*:

> Let us go treasure hunting in the *parshiyos* of *Yetzias Mitzrayim* and see whether we can penetrate the surface. There really must be more to it than the story that we learned as children.
>
> We begin with Shemos 12:23: *HaShem will pass through to smite Egypt, and He will see the blood that is on the lintel and the two doorposts; and HaShem will pass over the entrance and He will not permit the destroyer to enter your homes to smite.*
>
> On *He will not permit* Rashi comments: *He will not permit him (i.e., withhold from him) the ability to come.* We are not to translate, *He will withhold permission,* but, *He will withhold the ability.* Maharal explains Rashi's thinking. The text need not stress the obvious. The story itself makes clear that the Destroyer (*mashchis*), whoever he might be, would not have *permission* to enter the Jewish homes. If anything needed saying, it must be that he did not even have the ability. The Jewish homes were simply closed to him.
>
> Is there really a difference? Why would the withholding

of permission not be sufficient? What are the implications? What are we being taught here?

I have the feeling that this question needs to be tackled in a broader context. We will set this question aside for the moment and take a little detour. We will return to the original question a little further along in this essay.

The story of the plagues that were unleashed upon the Egyptians contains an element that, to the best of my knowledge, does not figure, at least not as prominently, in other contexts. I refer to the *miracles* WITHIN *the miracles* that were an apparently important feature of the Egyptian saga.

The plagues of blood and darkness provide examples.

For the plague of blood, we have Tanchuma, VaEira, which reports that if an Egyptian and a Jew were to simultaneously drink from the same cup, the Jew would drink water, while the Egyptian drank blood. In one form or another, this same thought is repeated in many different midrashim. A number of commentators[11] make a similar point in their comments to the plague of darkness. As they read the text, things went far beyond the fact that darkness did not descend upon the areas inhabited by Jews. They interpret the words *in their lodgings* in the phrase that *All benei Yisrael had light in their lodgings* to refer to the *Egyptian* homes. The very rooms that for the Egyptians were stuffed with masses of impenetrable darkness remained unaffected for the Jews in that same place. For them, the very same rooms that imprisoned the Egyptians in suffocating darkness remained as bright and welcoming as always.

Let us not be grabby. Let us live with the fact that we cannot have the slightest understanding of the ways in which these impossible-to-imagine situations were brought about. But, even if we are willing to give up on the "How?" we cannot oblige on the "Why?" The Ribono shel Olam is not a conjurer, intent upon wowing His audience with yet another rabbit drawn from some impossible hat. If it happened thus, we must conclude that the Yetzias Mitzrayim that the Ribono shel Olam wanted could not have happened

11. See, for example, Rashbam and Chizkuni.

otherwise. Something vital to the entire enterprise would have been missing.

What is that?

What is the story beneath the story?

What was it that Yetzias Mitzrayim needed to be that required that the physically impossible should somehow come about? What is Pesach all about? When we get right down to it, was there not a more efficient way to determine who inhabited the house than passing over those that had been marked by the blood? What is so great about passing over and why should the entire Yom Tov owe its name to that particular aspect of an event that surely could have been viewed and honored in many different ways?

The answer to these questions comes in chapter 9 of *Awake at the Wheel.* Here is a quote from that chapter:

> You will recall that I bundled two seemingly disparate issues together. I wondered why the *mashchis* was denied not only permission to enter the Jewish homes but also the very ability to do so, and I also found it noteworthy that the *miracle* WITHIN *the miracle*[12] played such a significant role in the drama of the plagues.
>
> I think that on the basis of what we have learned, we have the answer. Influenced by the language that I found useful in posing the problems earlier [chapter 8 of *Awake at the Wheel*], we have discovered the "story beneath the story." *Our emancipation from Egyptian slavery has implications way beyond the fact that a slave people was finally freed after two hundred years of unrelieved servitude. It speaks of freedom from the cloying shackles of physicality. An alien people, denizen of a higher, nobler, holier world, suddenly take up center stage in human affairs. History will have to learn some new skills and play with them by new rules.*
>
> *Or, better still, not play with them at all.*
>
> Neither *mashchis* nor plague can touch them. For them, the delegated *mashchis* simply does not exist. What is blood

12. The fact that the liquid in the beaker was both blood and water at the same timehy the Egyptian homes were both dark and light depending on who was doing the looking,

for the Egyptians simply is *not* blood for them. It is sparkling, refreshing water. Egyptian darkness is Jewish light.

At the moment in which the Ribono shel Olam "passed over" the Jewish homes, He marked us as His portion. That is a freedom beneath a freedom... .

The Pesach Offering with its attendant *Passing Over* defines our peoplehood more clearly than does any other event in our history.

AFTER THIS LENGTHY DETOUR WE ARE READY TO RETURN TO OUR ARGUMENT

Apparently, Yetzias Mitzrayim "gave" the Ribono shel Olam a "boost" in, of all things, altitude, כביכול. Why, of all possible qualities, stress height?

Because, so I believe, on the second day of Creation a division was made between the (אשר מתחת לרקיע) מים התחתונים and the (אשר מעל לרקיע) מים העליונים, the division between the physical and the spiritual is expressed in terms of height. The Ribono shel Olam had finally lifted His chosen people (ולקחתי אתכם לי לעם) up to Himself. By "passing over" them, by demonstrating that the *mashchis* had no power over them, by making it clear that Egyptian blood was Jewish water and Egyptian darkness was Jewish light (and, as we shall see later in this essay, that the same water that was busy drowning the Egyptians was at the same time a solid wall enclosing us as we crossed the sea on dry land), God taught us that we belonged among the *elyonim* and that we were immune from dangers that lurked among the *tachtonim*. We, כביכול, together with the Ribono shel Olam, would occupy the "high" ground. There would be no "need" for Him to "lower" Himself to the physical world to maintain the relationship that He had "craved."

!כתועפות ראם לו, The altitude ... !

And that was Bil'am's problem. He was an expert, and highly successful, prophet. Get him to curse your enemies, and invariably you would be home free. He commanded astronomical fees because, invariably, he delivered. But there was a catch, the one limiting factor in his otherwise stellar reach. That reach was not "stellar." Our well-known physical world was the playing field upon which he excelled and therefore succeeded. He could not reach the stars. *Klal Yisrael,* ensconced as it was among the *elyonim,* lay beyond his range. As Egyptian blood was water for the Israelites, as their darkness was light, so a Midianite curse was a blessing for us. Balak's well-laid plan was doomed never to even get off the ground.

The drama of the talking ass was not just a filler to make the story more exciting. It was a preview of what lay in wait for him.

How so?

Bil'am had no problem dealing with a talking donkey, but he could not see the angel. Donkeys were a part of Bil'am's world; angels were not. But angels and *yidden* hobnob comfortably in one another's company. On חברים מקשיבים לקולך in Shir HaShirim 8:13 Rashi remarks, מלאכי השרת **חביריך** בני אלהים **דוגמתך**. Before he ever reached Balak, Bil'am must have known that things would not work out, and why they could not work out.

HOW "ANGELIC" ARE WE REALLY?

However, the Balak/Bil'am interaction is a lot more subtle than simply stating: Jews equal angels and, as they say in Israel, *gamarnu!* That equivalence is very far from being absolute. There is a twist to the story that must leave us with a very sobering taste.

We all know the story. Bil'am fails in his mission and an understandably frustrated Balak packs him off. However, before he leaves, Bil'am hands Balak what appears to be a consolation prize. איעצך, Let me give you some advice. As Chazal (cited by Rashi) read this, he is about to hand Balak a fail-safe plot that will destroy Israel as surely as his failed curses would have done. The Ribono shel Olam hates lechery. Why not turn the Moabite and Midianite women loose upon the Jews and their moral turpitude will soon enough "drive" God from their midst. Left floundering, they will simply disappear from history's stage.

It is all very crude, and unfortunately very predictable. Bil'am would not be the last anti-Semite who devotes thought and creativity to our destruction. Most of them, though, do not make it into the Torah. Why should this incident, which to all appearances has no connection to the main Balak/Bil'am drama, be recorded? Of course we could concede that it belongs here to provide the background to the Pinchos involvement and development. But that, too, could have been recorded without revealing Bil'am as the source of the idea.

This may not be a major problem but, so it seems to me, it deserves some serious thought.

Here are the results.

My premise was, of course, totally in error. From Balak and Bil'am's perspective, this piece of devilish advice turned out to be the crowning glory of the story. It was an absolutely brilliant strategy that, at the very last moment, when everything seemed lost, pulled the fat from the fire. Balak, it turns out, got most of what he wanted, and it did not cost him a penny.

Sanhedrin 105b teaches that כולם חזרו לקללה חוץ מבתי כנסיות ומבתי מדרשות. It is worthwhile to quote Rashi here: כל הברכות של בלעם חזרו לקללה **כמו שהיה כוונתו מתחילה**.

In the light of what we have just learned, it seems clear to me that Bil'am had learned his lesson from the failure of his mission and, earlier, from his confrontation with the donkey. It was clear to him that as long as Israel conformed to its "*elyonim*" status, they could not be harmed by any of the arrows in his limited quiver. He was certainly no more powerful than the *mashchis* who had accompanied the Ribono shel Olam on that fateful night in Egypt, and who was simply unable to enter the Jewish homes (= did in reality not exist relative to the Israelites).

Bereft of any appropriate weapons, there was really just one tactic that held out any kind of promise. If it was the Israelite's *elyonim* status that put them beyond his clutches, then if they could be dragged down from their pedestal and turned into denizens of the *tachtonim* world, the path would be opened for a resurrection of the curses.

Bil'am was very clever. His stratagem worked like a dream.[13]

BACK TO תופעות ראם

Earlier in this essay we threw in our lot with Rashi's first interpretation. We voted oryxes out and limitless altitudes in. We felt encouraged by *Sefer Zikaron* who assured us that the apparently unexplainable א in ראם was really no cause for worry. The prophet

13. Why it did not work for the בתי כנסיות and בתי מדרשות is a fascinating story. We will leave that for another time. This essay is complicated enough as it is.

Zecharyah, too, had inserted an א in the phrase וראמה תחתיה. All was well.

Still, we left that section with a depressing sense of discomfort. In Zecharyah the word is read as רָאֲם with the komatz in tact. Here we have to deal with רְאֵם and that is a very different story. Moreover, as we demonstrated above, the cantillation marks as they appear in Balak seemed inappropriate to Rashi's understanding.

We have reached a point at which it has become possible to tentatively offer a cautious solution.[14]

In the section of this essay that deals with the Balak/Bil'am story, we have become acquainted with very real limitations that circumscribed Bil'am's prophecies. We were able to observe his astounding command over the "תחת השמש" world, but learned to recognize his utter helplessness "למעלה מן השמש." With donkeys he could deal; angels were beyond him.

EXCURSUS

Whether or not there was any overt סיעתא דשמיא involved, I cannot say, but I decided to take a look at Rav Samson Raphael Hirsch on Bereishis 24:4, אשר מחזה שד-י יחזה, נפל וגלוי עינים. I admit that I felt a bit like Bil'am, נפל וגלוי עינים, *he who has fallen down yet has [his] eyes unveiled*. I had felt prostrated by my impotence in backing up my idea, and at that precise moment I was granted what, for me, amounted to a vision.

Rav Samson Raphael Hirsch (in the English translation) renders מחזה שד-י יחזה as, *who beholds what* שד-י *allows to behold*. Here is the background to this translation. In the course of his commentary, the Rav directs us to Bereishis 17:1 where he discusses the name שד-י. The issue centers upon the root word from which this name is derived. Is it from ש ד ד, *to lay waste* or from the word די, *sufficient* constructed with the relative pronoun ש. The Rav notes there that our Sages tend to support the latter opinion.

14. There is a good reason for my hesitation made obvious by my use of the qualifiers "tentative" and "cautious." I have never come across anything that even approaches or that is vaguely similar to the solution that I am about to offer. It may be entirely illegitimate for reasons of which I am unaware. Still, I offer it for what it is worth. While I can offer no support for it, I am also unaware of anything that contradicts it. Please use your sharply honed judgment.

To these comments the Rav appends a wonderfully developed disquisition on the Ribono shel Olam as He Who said (and continues to say) "Enough!" to His creation. He demonstrates that it is the "Enough!" principle that makes the finite form of our universe possible. Without that severe exhortation, everything would simply continue expanding into infinity.

At BeMidbar 24:4 (but not before) Bil'am borrows that name to describe his entry into the world of prophecy. He, too, functions under a stern "Enough!" There are strict limitations to what he is permitted to see. However, as he launches into his third prophecy (מה טובו...) he is overwhelmed by the realization that he has entered into forbidden territory. The "שד-י" principle under which he normally functions should have blocked entry.[15] It did not. He is, so to speak, beaten to the ground because of his illicit incursion (נפל) but nevertheless his eyes are opened.

This third prophecy was very, very special. It took place under a unique dispensation.

Earlier in this Excursus we noted that Bil'am did not use these expressions in the first and second vision. Please note the following sentence carefully: These earlier two prophecies involved no formal trespass. Whatever [!!!] he saw there fell within his remit. That, as we shall now see when we return to the essay, included the phrase כתועפות ראם לו.

* * *

Here comes my suggested solution.

Let us remember that the Torah was given to us without any symbols indicating the vowel sounds. From the word ראם as it is written in the Torah, there is absolutely no telling whether it is to be pronounced רְאֵם or רָאָם. Now we have spent a lot of time demonstrating that the רָאָם sense of the word in the present context was totally beyond Bil'am's, and certainly beyond Balak's, grasp. It seems likely that when the Ribono shel Olam "placed" the words into Bil'am's mouth, He did so without the vowel indi-

15. Please see footnote 15. As stated there, we are not going to enter into the nature of the בתי כנסיות and בתי מדרשות that placed them in a category of their own. For our purposes here, it is enough to say that it is in these places that the *Shechinah* dwells among us, and this places them into the category of the *elyonim* from which Bil'am should have been categorically excluded.

cators. Unable to grasp the רְאֵם meaning,[16] Bil'am was left with no alternative. He understood, articulated, and passed on to Balak the only word that he could associate with this spelling — and got stuck with the oryx. Once the vowel indicators were introduced, the word was spelled as Bil'am had pronounced it; it was the only truth contained in the historical record. There was, however, a truth beneath that truth, and that was the true import of the Ribono shel Olam's message to Balak.

For the purpose of this essay, we have reached the end of our thoughts on the Balak/Bil'am drama.

That was a pretty hefty detour in an essay that, judging from the title, purports to explore the mysterious sea plagues that harassed the Egyptians as they floundered in the Reed Sea's waters. What have we gained from our trip? Was the distraction worthwhile?

The answer is, "Yes! It was; in spades." Before too long, we will explain how.

BACK TO THE SEA

In the first section of this essay we were troubled about the secrecy that seems to shroud the events that tradition attaches to kri'as Yam Suf. We know that there were plagues; we know that there were spoils; but, as far as the written record is concerned, none of this might have happened.

We wondered why.

We made a very hefty detour. What did it yield and how will it help us solve our problems?

First things come first. Our goal was to confirm for ourselves that on the basis of the contract that Yaakov made with Eisav while they were still in the womb, *klal Yisrael* was to belong among the "*elyonim*," really aliens in this our physical world. We were not to have the privileges that come with citizenship,[17] but

16. This holds true for even the second time that the phrase appears, which is in the third (מה טובו) section. Although we have earlier established that for that prophecy Bil'am was permitted by special fiat to cross the line (מחזה שד-י יחזה), that was only to the extent that he was permitted a peek into the בתי כנסיות and the בתי מד־רשות. The problematic תועפות ראם occurs in the context of Yetzias Mitzrayim (א-ל מוציאם ממצרים) and in that context the blackout was in full force.

17. For example, אסור ליהנות מעולם הזה בלי ברכה, a stricture not binding among non-Jewish people.

then, in no way were we to be necessarily subordinate to its realities, or subject to its dangers.[18] This was a fact that Bil'am had to discover the hard way. Balak's grand plan simply foundered upon Bil'am's impotence when it came to the Jews.[19]

These insights will now help us as we return to the shores of the Reed Sea. There we will now find an example of the נס בתוך נס in a much more blatant, really a much more shocking, form than in the earlier examples we cited.

Here are eight verses from Shemos 14:22–29.

22. ויבאו בני ישראל בתוך הים ביבשה **והמים להם חומה מימינם ומשמאלם**:
23. וירדפו מצרים ויבאו אחריהם כל סוס פרעה רכבו ופרשיו אל תוך הים:
24. ויהי באשמרת הבקר וישקף ידוד אל מחנה מצרים בעמוד אש וענן ויהם את מחנה מצרים:
25. ויסר את אפן מרכבתיו וינהגהו בכבדת ויאמר מצרים אנוסה מפני ישראל כי ידוד נלחם להם במצרים:
26. **ויאמר ידוד אל משה נטה את ידך על הים וישבו המים על מצרים על רכבו ועל פרשיו:**
27. **ויט משה את ידו על הים וישב הים לפנות בקר לאיתנו ומצרים נסים לקראתו וינער ידוד את מצרים בתוך הים:**
28. **וישבו המים ויכסו את הרכב ואת הפרשים לכל חיל פרעה הבאים אחריהם בים לא נשאר בהם עד אחד:**
29. ובני ישראל הלכו ביבשה בתוך הים **והמים להם חמה מימינם ומשמאלם**:

Please note the repetition of the phrase that we have bolded. We need to examine what is being said, why it is significant, and why it is repeated.

On the surface, the message that the words send seems simple enough. The waters that had just now ceased to flow hardened and turned into two walls (water walls) standing to either side of the Israelites. We are not told why these walls were needed and we are going to have to think about that, but that does not change the message. Whatever happened at or in the sea was blocked off from inquisitive eyes by two, probably massive, walls.

18. For example, נס בתוך נס: the blood that the Egyptian drank was water for us. The darkness that enveloped him was light for us. The *mashchis* charged with taking the Egyptian firstborns was not only forbidden to enter our homes but was unable to do so. In practice, he simply did not exist for us.

19. Earlier in this essay we wrote that Bil'am had no problem dealing with a talking donkey but he could not see the angel. Donkeys were a part of Bil'am's world; angels were not. But angels and *Yidden* hobnob comfortably in one another's company. On חברים מקשיבים לקולך in Shir HaShirim 8:13 Rashi remarks, מלאכי השרת חביריך בני אלהים דוגמתך. Before he ever reached Balak, Bil'am must have intuited that things would not work out, and, beyond that, why they could not work out.

Now why is this change of water into solid walls significant? The following is a quote from the Maharal in his *Chidushei Aggados* to Nidah 31a, page 160.

> ודבר זה יש לך להבין ממה שהתבאר במקום אחר כי משה היה משוי מן המים, והיה נקרא משה על שם מן המים משיתיהו, כי המים הם חמריים ביותר עד שאין בהם צורה כלל. ואין דבר שהוא רחוק מן הצורה כמו המים, **ויורה זה שם מים שהוא לשון רבים בכל מקום, ולא תמצא בהם לשון יחיד בשום מקום. וזה מפני כי היחוד הוא בצורה ואילו המים רחוקים מן הצורה, ולפיכך אין בהם אחדות ולא יקראו רק בלשון רבים. וכמו שמורה על זה השם כך מורה עליהם מהות שלהם, שהרי אין המים דבר מקוים והם נגרים ונשפכים כדכתיב (דברים ט"ו) על הארץ תשפכנו כמים, ואין לך דבר נשפך ונמס יותר מן המים דכתיב (יושע ז') וימס לבב העם ויהי למים**, אבל הצורה הוא דבר מקוים, כמו שידוע מענין הצורה. ולפיכך היה משה משוי מן המים, [כי] משה היה נבדל לגמרי מן החמרי עד שהיה מסולק ונבדל ממנו לגמרי, ולכך היה משוי ויוצא מן המים.

Maharal's assertion that water is the quintessential *chomer* recurs in one form or another throughout his writings. It can in no sense be regarded as in any way peripheral to his philosophy. As the section that I have bolded makes clear, the very ambiguity that inheres in water's liquidity (the plural form, *mayim*) is a vital element in its makeup. All this is a given in Maharal's thought world.

Imagine now this water turning into solid walls, real walls that can scrape your knees. The significance of such an event cannot be overestimated. It literally (or almost literally) turns the physical world on its head. "Water walls" are not simply walls. They are nothing less than "otherworldly."

Big things, *very* big things are happening here.

We will be discussing these walls a little later in this essay. In the meantime we need to address our third question: Why repeat the phrase ... והמים להם חומה?

I indicated earlier that we were about to come across a נס בתוך נס that jacks up the implications of this miraculous concept to a new level of wonder. We have reached the point at which we can make that happen.

Please glance at the BeShalach verses that we cited earlier. You will see that the phrase appears first in verse 22 and then is repeated in verse 29. A lot has happened between those two verses. In the earlier one the Israelites are seen entering the sea. The miracle of the division of the waters has already occurred (*neis*) and, as logic demands, the narrative is picked up once more. The trek through the sea begins. Of course we do not yet understand why the walls were necessary, but we can curb our curiosity. In the meanwhile the sheer marvel of what is happening before our eyes is more than enough to capture our interest.

Verse 29, the second mention of the phrase, is a different story altogether. Verse 27 had, so to speak, liquefied the "water walls" and brought the newly available water crashing down upon the Egyptians. Verse 28 had offered a graphic description of the horrors to which the Egyptians had been exposed by the swirling waves. What then could verse 29, *The children of Israel walked over dry land in the midst of the sea, and the water formed walls for them to their right and to their left*, possibly mean?

Ibn Ezra and S'forno believe that different parts of the sea are being described. The waters were drowning the Egyptians in the part of the sea that the Jews had already passed. Where they were still crossing, the "water walls" remained firm and solid.

Rashi and Ramban are both silent. This leads me to suspect[20] that in their minds this was a replay of the miracles in Egypt (נס בתוך נס) where the blood that the Egyptians were forced to drink was water for the Jews; the darkness that the Egyptians had to endure was light for the Jews. Here, too, the water that drowned the Egyptians was at the same time a solid wall for us.

We are about to head into the section that will finally bring this long and complicated essay to a close. Before we get to that I just want to point out the following. I am postulating that here we are dealing with a נס בתוך נס (only more so) in a way that is comparable to the *dam* and the *choshech* of Mitzrayim. That is indeed my position. Still, there is a major difference and it is that difference that will take center stage in the following section. In the two examples from the earlier plagues, it was the Egyptians who dealt with the miracle (blood that had been formed from water; darkness that had replaced regular light). The Jews enjoyed regular water and regular light; in other words, relative to them, nothing miraculous had happened.

Here we have the opposite. At the point with which verse 29 deals, it is the Egyptians who are drowning in the (nonmiraculous)

20. The rest of the essay is going to be based upon this assumption. Please note that I cannot guarantee its correctness. However, my intuition tells me that had Rashi and Ramban understood the passage as did Ibn Ezra and S'forno, one would have supposed that they (or at least Ramban) would have spelled this out.

water whereas the Jews are being protected by the miraculous "water walls."

Come! Please join me for the home stretch.

THE OTHERWORLDLINESS OF KRI'AS YAM SUF

I want to argue that the twenty-first of Nisan, the day on which the waters split and a dry seabed welcomed Israel into its embrace, is the day upon which God's promise that ולקחתי אתכם לי לעם was fulfilled. The fifteenth of Nisan, the day that we left Mitzrayim (במדבר 33:3) "ביד רמה לעיני כל מצרים", cannot really be viewed as such; as Rashi to verse 4 makes clear, we were allowed to leave only because the Egyptians were טרודים באבלם, caught up in their mourning as they buried their future in the graves of their firstborn. Had everything been normal, they would soon enough have put an end to our flight. It was only at the sea, where Egypt's might was truly smashed, that we finally and firmly began to exist as an independent and unique nation.[21]

In what sense were we unique? In the sense that according to plan A, from the moment that we had crossed the sea until and including our entry into Eretz Yisrael, nothing, nothing at all in both our national and our individual lives would conform with nature's strictures. From the split sea we entered the desert where subsistence of some two million people depended upon a miraculous well and food from heaven. Protection was supplied by the ענני כבוד. From there we arrived at Sinai, with all that that experience implies. The Mishkan came next. It provided the Ribono shel Olam with a dwelling place among His beloved people (please see Shemos 29:46, לשכני בתוכם and Ramban there) and that Presence remained a fixture for some eight hundred years until the destruction of the First Temple. Had it not been for the

21. I suspect that this can explain an oddity in the listing of the מסעות. In verse 8 we read, ... ויסעו מפי החירות ויעברו בתוך הים המדברה. Why המדברה? That is not one of the place-names. I want to suggest that the reason why the Ribono shel Olam chose to have us travel through the wilderness on our way to Sinai and Eretz Yisrael was so that we would have to live miraculously. This would underline the fact that we did not really have any rights in this our physical world since we belong to the *elyonim*.

The meaning of the verse is that we crossed the Reed Sea (thus becoming a free nation) in order to have us land in the wilderness, a place where life as it is normally lived down here would be impossible. Nonetheless, God would miraculously keep us alive.

debacle[22] of the meraglim, we would have entered Eretz Yisrael only days after setting out from the Sinai desert.[23] That entry would have taken place without having to resort to any fighting.

Had all this worked out, Moshe Rabbeinu would have led us into the land and the pre-Messianic period of our history would have been completed.

We can only guess what life would have been like in Eretz Yisrael had we entered under those conditions. We can get some idea from Kesubos 111b, וא"ר חייא בר יוסף עתידה א"י שתוציא גלוסקאות וכלי מילת.[24]

This brief survey, superficial as it surely is, should surely convince us that when we are talking about *klal Yisrael,* we are talking about a people whose place should rightfully be among the *elyonim*. The Torah's descriptions that we have just now followed confirm the ideas that we traced in the Balak/Bil'am drama.

That established, I wish to argue that among all these miraculous happenings, kri'as Yam Suf is special. Here is how. People need to eat and drink. If you (or, You) decide to lead them through the desert, something has to be done about that. If You are the Ribono shel Olam, You will deliver food and drink. If You are intent upon shepherding a caravan consisting of two million souls to Eretz Yisrael, You will pull out all stops to hasten the trip as much as possible. In short, the miracles that we adumbrated answered immediate needs. That is one level.

I believe that kri'as Yam Suf is different. It is true that if Your caravan is blocked by a sea with a vicious army hard upon it in hot pursuit, You had better split the sea. To that extent it was no different from any of the other miracles. But at kri'as Yam Suf there was more, much, much more.

In the first place there are the walls formed by the water. Apart from the fact that even at this late stage we still have no idea concerning their function, there is also the *tzurah/chomer* dichotomy[25]

22. Dictionary meaning: A sudden and ignominious failure; a fiasco.

23. Please see Devarim 1:2, ... אחד עשר יום מחורב and Rashi there. We reached the borders of Eretz Yisrael in just three days.

24. We can have only the vaguest of vague ideas of what this might mean. Here is a quote from Maharal, Nesiv HaAvodah 17: ורצה לומר לעתיד כאשר לא יהיה עוד קללת האדמה שהיה בשביל חטא האדם, אז תקבל האדמה השפע מן הש"י בשלימות הגמור והכל יהיה יוצא בשלימות עד שלא יהיה צריך שום תיקון.

25. Here is a tip offered by one dictionary. Dichotomy is derived from the modern Latin and Greek *dikhotomia,* literally "cutting in two." Dichotomy is usually used to

of which we spoke earlier in this essay that leaves me no peace. What precisely are we being told by handing us a detail that seemingly contributes nothing that would be necessary toward the salvation that the Ribono shel Olam wanted to achieve and which nevertheless teases us with such difficult-to-solve riddles?

Then we have a number of traditions preserved in midrashim that introduce dimensions to the experience of crossing through the sea that seem entirely irrelevant to the main purpose of the miracle as revealed in the Torah — the salvation of *klal Yisrael* from the bloodlust of the Egyptians.[26]

Here is a quote from Shemos Rabba 21:10.

דרש ר׳ נהוראי היתה בת ישראל עוברת בים ובנה בידה ובוכה ופושטת ידה ונוטלת תפוח או רמון מתוך הים ונותנת לו שנאמר (תהלים קו) ויוליכם בתהומות כמדבר מה במדבר לא חסרו כלום אף בתהומות לא חסרו כלום הוא שמשה אמר להם זה ארבעים שנה ה׳ אלהיך עמך לא חסרת דבר **שלא היו חסרים אלא להזכיר דבר והוא נברא לפניהם** רבי שמעון אומר **אפילו דבור לא היו חסרין אלא מי שהיה מהרהר בלבו דבר והוא נעשה** שנאמר (שם עח) וינסו אל בלבבם לשאל אוכל לנפשם.

Here is another from Midrash Tanchuma to BeShalach 10:

ויצאו להם כדי מים מתוקין מתוך מלוחין וקפאו המים ונעשו ככלי זכוכית.

Now the precise meaning of these descriptions, whether they are meant to be understood literally or symbolically, need not concern us in the present context. Here we are concerned with the underlying approach that Chazal took toward kri'as Yam Suf. Very clearly they are teaching us that this event was not to be viewed as simply a means of escaping from the Egyptians. None of these luxuries, and others like them, was necessary for that.

Can we have some idea of what Chazal are teaching us here?

I think we can. Here we go!

Apples and pomegranates waiting to be fished from the waters so that crying children might be pacified? Crystal beakers formed miraculously the better to enjoy the sweet waters that were suddenly produced from the salt water that was indigenous to the sea? It all sounded strange to me, but still there was something vaguely familiar in the description.

describe two contradicting elements of the same person or thing.

26. ויושע ידוד ביום ההוא את ישראל מיד מצרים וירא ישראל את מצרים מת על שפת הים. וירא ישראל את היד הגדלה אשר עשה ידוד במצרים וייראו העם את ידוד ויאמינו בידוד ובמשה עבדו.

Suddenly everything clicked. Earlier we quoted the Gemara in Kesubos that the time would come when finished cakes and beautiful clothes would grow, ready made, out of the soil of Eretz Yisrael. Maharal (see footnote 6) had taught us that this was to be part of the *shleimus* that would be the hallmark of the Messianic era. The "ארורה האדמה" that had been pronounced in Eden would at that time have run its course. Newly blessed earth will be unstinting in its gifts. Why bother people with the drudgery of the oven and the sewing needle? Let nature hand them the finished cake and the perfect jacket. Let them get on with life as it was meant to be lived.

I think I understand now why the walls to the right and left of us were needed, and, moreover, I think I understand why just the "impossible" "water walls" (*chomer* metamorphosed into *tzurah*) were ideal for that purpose.

I think that the ideal venue for the formation of an "*elyonim* nation" is the world of the "*elyonim*" and finally I believe that with all those mysterious descriptions of how the split sea would behave, Chazal were telling us that the area of the Reed Sea was, for the time it took for us to get across, turned into "Messiah" country.

Of course walls were needed to block off the prying eyes of the curious. Special eyes, Jewish eyes, were needed to witness this greatest of all miracles. And, if we are talking walls, what better material for them than *chomer* turned to *tzurah,* which is really only another way of saying the unrealized, the lacking, finally finding its *shleimus.* The walls that defined the area that had allowed the future to crash into the present were more than simply barriers. They were the "Rashi" on the sugia. "*Kinderlech,*" they called out, "do you realize what we are? We are *chomer* turned to *tzurah,* inadequacy having finally attained perfection. This is what is in store for you! You, too, have it in you to grow into mighty walls,[27] unbending in the קומה זקופה that marks you as a ממלכת כהנים."[28]

Indeed big things, very big things were happening!

We are finally ready to return to the question with which we set this essay rolling. Here is a short quote:

27. Remember אום אני חומה.

28. Remember ואולך אתכם קוממיות (VaYikra 26:13 and see Rashi there) that is the final and decisive definition of the result of Yetzias Mitzrayim.

Why, in view of the fact that each of the "Mitzrayim plagues" is described by the Torah in such loving detail, are we denied all knowledge of what actually happened at the sea? We have no idea at all of what form of suffering these plagues imposed upon the Egyptians. Why keep it all so secret?

We notice the same puzzling silence concerning the ביזת הים, the unimaginable wealth that passed from the Egyptians to us at the sea. Once more the existence of such spoils is firmly entrenched in our tradition and once more the text is totally silent. Why?

We get an inescapable impression that somehow the events that accompanied the splitting of the sea are not for publication. They were entrusted to the oral tradition but banished from the written record. Why?

I believe that the answer is indirectly spelled out in Maharal's Gevuros HaShem 16. In that chapter Maharal wonders why, when the Torah tells us of Moshe Rabbeinu's birth, the names of his family members are not given. It is not the Levite Amram who takes Levi's daughter Yocheved as his wife but an *Ish Levi* who takes a *Bas Levi*. Miriam's name is also not given; she is introduced as *achoso*.[29] What is the Ribono shel Olam communicating to us?

Here is an excerpt from the Maharal:

ולא הזכיר הכתוב שם עמרם ושם יוכבד לכתוב וילך איש מבית לוי ושמו עמרם ויקח את בת לוי ושמה יוכבד, שזה מורה על מעלת משה שהוא נבדל במעלתו מכל אדם על פני האדמה, ולפיכך לא זכר אצל אביו ואמו רק שם סתם לא שם פרטי, כי שם הפרטי מורה על איש מיוחד, ומפני שהאב והאם הוא סבה לבן ואם היה עמרם ויוכבד סבה למשה במה שהם בני אדם פרטיים, אז היה גם כן משה אשר הם סבה אליו אדם פרטי זה, והפרטי זה אינו נבדל מן הכלל, כי הפרטי זה הוא חלק הכל ואז לא היה מעלת משה נבדל מכל אדם, לכך הזכיר אביו ואמו בשם הפשוט לא בשם הפרטי זה. ואמר וילך איש מבית לוי לומר כי היה תולדות משה עליו השלום מעמרם ויוכבד לא במה שהוא פרטי זה רק במה שהוא איש בלבד.

We are beginning to get some sort of a sense of the uniqueness of Moshe Rabbeinu. But there is more, much more, to come, and what is to come feeds straight into the issues with which we have been grappling throughout this essay.

Let us read on.

29. Later in the Torah the names are of course given, but that is only after Moshe Rabbeinu has already been born.

ועוד כי כל פרטי הוא מצד החמרי כאשר ידוע מענין הפרטי, שאין בדבר שהוא נבדל מן החומרי פרטי, ומשה שהיה נבדל לגמרי לא נולד בסבת פרטית כלל, ולכך לא נאמר אצלו שם פרטי רק כתב שם איש שהוא שם לכל איש ואינו שם פרטי מיוחד **וזה מורה על מדריגה נבדלת אלהית.** ועוד שאם זכר שמם העצמי, היה משמע כי בשביל עמרם מצד שהוא אדם פרטי זה בא ממנו הגואל לעולם, שכך היה משמע וילך עמרם ויקח יוכבד, רצונו לומר מצד שהם בני אדם פרטיים נולד משה, ומשמע כי עמרם ויוכבד עיקר בלדת משה כמו כל אדם שמוליד בן שהוא נולד בשביל האב, שאם לא היה האב הזה לא היה הבן, **ומפני שמשה רבינו עליו השלום היה מוכן לגאולה משׁשת ימי בראשית, ולא היה צריך רק להביאו לעולם והכנתו כבר היה, ואם לא היה לוי ויוכבד היה בא על ידי אחר**, ואם כתב וילך עמרם היה משמע אם לא היה עמרם זה לא בא הגואל לעולם כי אין שני עמרם בעולם, **ולפיכך כתיב וילך איש כי יש אנשים הרבה בעולם ואם אין זה יש אחר והבן זה גם כן.**

And then there is the crowning section. It explains why Moshe Rabbeinu and his family came from *Shevet Levi*.

ולפיכך היה ראוי לצאת מהשבט הזה הגואל אותם מן השיעבוד וכל זה מפני קדושת השבט הזה. כי כבר אמרנו לך למעלה, **שהשיעבוד הוא שייך דוקא לחומר שהוא מוכן להשתעבד בו ולהיות מתפעל וזה נתבאר למעלה**, אמנם שבט לוי מפני שהיה קדוש, ומי שהוא קדוש הוא נבדל ממעשה החומר, כמו שנתבאר לך זה למעלה, וכל זמן שהיו כלל ישראל בשיעבוד לא היה ראוי לשבט לוי להיות הם מושלים על המצרים, מכל מקום זכות עצמם וקדושתם הועיל שלא היה ראוי שיהיו מושלים מצרים על שבט לוי הקדוש והנבדל, ואיך יהיה מושל עליהם החומר הגרוע הזה הם המצריים, עד שהיו ישראל ראוים להגאל, **ואז הוציא הקב"ה הגואל משבט מושלים הוא שבט לוי אשר הוא קדוש ונבדל, ואז היה מושל על החומר הם מצרים אשר נמשלו לחומר דכתיב (יחזקאל כ"ג) אשר בשר חמורים בשרם, ולפיכך יצא משבט לוי משה רבינו עליו השלום אשר הוא הצורה השלימה והוא נבדל מן החומר כאשר יתבאר**, היה אדם נבדל מן החומר כמו משה רבינו עליו השלום, והוא היה ראוי להיות מושל על מצרים כדכתיב (שמות ז') ראה נתתיך אלהים לפרעה וגו.

Let us summarize.

The soul of the story of Yetzias Mitzrayim appears to be the victory of *tzurah* over *chomer*. Moshe Rabbeinu as Moshe Rabbeinu is pure *tzurah*, essentially unconnected with his parents. They were the means by which he made his appearance in this world, but it could equally well have been anybody else. Moreover, it was no coincidence that he belonged to *Shevet Levi*. Mitzrayim is absolute *chomer* (בשר חמורים בשרם) and is handed over to a tribe that is קדוש ונבדל (apparently, *tzurah*).

It turns out that the "water walls" were absolutely in character with everything else that was happening. If we are right in the various suggestions that we have made (that the splitting of the sea and the Egyptians drowning in that very water [*chomer*] is to be regarded as a piece of *Olam HaBa* crashing temporarily, and as a onetime phenomenon, into our physical world), then a better marker to demarcate the area in which this would take place could not be imagined. The "water walls" (*chomer* turned to *tzurah*) are of one piece with Moshe Rabbeinu.

We began this essay by asking why no details of the "sea plagues" or the "sea spoils" are given. I suggest that they are omitted for the same reason that the details of the parentage and family connections of Moshe Rabbeinu are omitted when he is introduced to us. In the world of *tzurah*, all of this becomes unimportant. It is the idea that is all-powerful.

In the same way that when Moshe Rabbeinu first comes upon the scene, the specific identity of his parents is of no interest to us (it in no way defines his essence), so, at the Yam Suf — once the world of the elyonim, the world of the *tzurah* takes over temporarily — it makes no difference which particular plague discomfited the Egyptians or even that plagues were imposed upon them,[30] or which particular ornaments constituted the spoils that finally paid the Israelites for the slavery of two hundred and ten years or, indeed, that such compensation was exacted.[31]

The "water walls" said it all. For a brief historical moment the "hardening" of the *rakia* on the second day of Creation gave way to the original "softness" that had preceded it.[32] "Yes!" *K'rias*

30. If you have access to the חדושי הגרי"ז הלוי על תנ"ך, you might want to examine his take on the role that the plagues played at Yetzias Mitzrayim. He demonstrates that rather than being a means of breaking Pharaoh's will and forcing him to free the slaves, they were punitive in nature. That is certainly why the plagues were in place even at the sea after the Israelites had already been set free.

31. Now that we have thought along these lines, it strikes me that this may be hinted from the very beginning at the Bris Bein HaBesarim. Here are the relevant pesukim (Bereishis 15:13 and 14): ידע תדע כי גר יהיה זרעך בארץ לא להם, ועבדום וענו אותם ארבע מאות שנה. **וגם** את הגוי אשר יעבדו דן אנכי ואחרי כן יצאו ברכוש גדול. I thought that I would research the weight of the expression "וגם." Does it indicate a lowering of significance? My search program showed two hundred and forty-nine uses of the word in TaNaCh and that put paid to my plan.

Still, I imagine that for most of us our favorite "וגם" is וגם חרבונה זכור לטוב and that certainly seems to bear out our theory. Apparently neither the punishment of the plagues nor the compensation attained through the spoils, can compete with the גר יהיה זרעך.

32. If you have access to my recent book, *For Rashi's Thoughtful Students*, you might want to glance through chapter 8 (pages 94–99). There we discuss the creation of the second day, יהי רקיע בתוך המים. Rashi notes that "יהי רקיע" is to be understood as "יתחזק הרקיע." The implications of this change are discussed in that chapter.

Yam Suf was, and still is, saying. "For God's *yidden* the *Olamos HaElyonim* are a very real reality."

Here I am going to quote a passage from that chapter that impacts directly upon our interest here:

> Our sources speak of a hierarchy of many different "worlds" each of them drawing energy from the one above it while energizing the one beneath. Together they form a seamless continuum. Now these worlds are all nonphysical and, at least in theory, we can grasp the fact that such a model exists. With the creation of our physical universe a mighty question mark reverberated in the infinity that preceded it. Can a physical entity become a part of that whole? Can it blend effortlessly into that other, non-physical reality?
>
> Apparently there is a two-part answer. "Yes, it can! but, at the same time, "It cannot happen without a struggle!"
>
> The "Yes, it can" became enshrined in the reality of the "soft" expanse of the first day. The borders were, so to speak, porous. Access between the two forms of "world" would have been possible and uncomplicated. But that ideal can become the real reality only in an ideal physical world. That ideal does not come about overnight. On the second day the stranger appeared in the serene world of the "worlds." It was a chunk of physicality that would (or perhaps would not) fit in.

12.

The Three Weeks: Who Is a Jew

Who is a Jew?

Yes, yes, we know the answer well enough; have tried our hardest to share it with all who would listen; have felt secure that, for us at least, the matter is settled.

But let us ask again. Is the halachic answer, that we know so well, the only one? Are there, inside and outside of the halachic context, other definitions? Could there be gradations in the degree of Jewishness to which we might rightfully lay claim?

Well, let us change the question a little.

What is a Jew? What makes a Jew, Jewish?

Chasam Sofer has an astounding answer: A Jew — even one whose birth fulfills all halachic requirements — remains Jewish only as long as the Jewish people are willing to accept him as a confrère[1] in their eternal covenant with God!

His radical suggestion is made in explanation of a halachic opinion that tefillin written by an *apikores* are to be burned (Shulchan Aruch, Orech Chaim 39:4). How, he wonders, can the sanctity of such tefillin be thus compromised?

His answer: *It appears to me that* klal Yisrael *has the authority to read such rebels out of the [Jewish] nation, rendering them absolute non-Jews ... excluded totally from the covenant of Israel.*

As simple as that! The *apikores* has opted out of Jewish peoplehood. Written by an honorary non-Jew, his tefillin lack the status of *kisvei hakodesh* and are consigned to the flames.

We are Jewish, then, to the extent that we can claim legitimate standing within the covenantal community that came into being when God made a *bris* with the *avos*. That standing is conditional, is not guaranteed to everyone who was born of a

1. This is French term that has been co-opted into English. Frère is French for brother; a confrère is someone who thinks and feels and often acts as I do. In a way he is "joined" to me.

Jewish mother. It can be forfeited by an intolerable flouting of covenantal obligations.

A sobering thought!

Now, on the basis of what we have learned, we may legitimately wonder whether there are gradations to Jewishness. Are there values that are so central to the *bris* that they brook no compromise at all? That denigration of such values, while not denying Jewishness absolutely, as is the case of the *apikores*, nevertheless mark one as somehow less a *ben bris*?

We move back in history, return to the very dawn of our peoplehood. The *Meraglim* with their devastating tidings have returned. The people, erstwhile slaves, unschooled in the skills of war, are terrified at what lies ahead. They weep through the night and, through their tears, in their fears, turn against Moshe and Aharon. With typical slave mentality they crave the predictability of servitude, prefer it to the unknowable challenges of freedom. Across the centuries we can almost hear the grief that must have animated their dreadful cry: *Let us appoint a new leadership, and return to Egypt!*

They had failed — and must have known it.

God sees no hope. A new beginning must be made. He will send a plague, wipe out a people too weak to rise to the call of a beckoning destiny, and re-create a nation capable of understanding Him — through Moshe.

And Moshe prays.

Now, we would have thought that, if ever there was a time to invoke the memory of the *avos*, this was the moment. What greater, more potent advocacy could be offered than that these weaklings are, after all, children of giants — buffeted, it is true, by centuries of slavery, sapped of the dynamism that once had animated their fathers, but withal, a soul within them, a seed waiting to burst into flower, a core of goodness, solid and strong, upon which a future might be built?

But, on this score, Moshe is silent. When earlier at the tragedy of the Golden Calf, he had begged God's forgiveness, it had been on the strength of *bris avos*: *O remember Avraham, Yitzchak, and Yisrael Your servants ...* Now, it is as though the *avos* do not exist for him.

Why?

Ramban explains: *Moshe does not invoke* zechus avos *in the prayer that he offers up on this occasion, indeed, he does not mention the* avos *at all. The reason is as follows: The land [of Israel] had been given to the* avos *and it was from them that the [present generation] had inherited it. Now [the people] were rebelling against their ancestors, were spurning the very gift for which the* avos *had sacrificed so much. How then could Moshe invoke the oath that God had made to the* avos *when the children were saying, "We have no interest in it!"*

"The oath that God had made to the *avos*." That is the covenant. It is the *bris avos* that, *Tosafos* (Shabbos 55a) teaches, is immutable and can protect long after *zechus avos* has been rendered impotent by our waywardness.

Rendered immutable? Then why could Moshe not invoke it?

The answer is inescapable. The covenant is unconditional, God's commitment under it, unwavering — for those who do not reject its very essence and assumptions. We may sin so badly that *zechus avos* becomes impotent and withal can still remain members in good standing of the covenantal community. But let us disavow the very essence of the *bris*, disparage that value that for the covenantor-*avos*[2] was the paramount component of their commitment, then indeed the binding, embracing, protecting ties of *bris* are loosened. Even Moshe, at a moment of true desperation, in which the future of his beloved *klal Yisrael* hung in the balance, dared not invoke it. By not loving the land enough, the degree to which they were indeed true children of the *avos* — in the spiritual, not the biological sense — was called into question. His Jews were not acting Jewishly!

To test the degree of our Jewishness, then, we must measure our attachment to Eretz Yisrael.

By what yardstick is love to be measured?

Intense love, by its very nature, is narrowly focused. Love diffused is, necessarily, love diminished.

Exhausted and broken, the Levites of old sit at Babylon's rivers. Their souls had once resonated to the sweet songs of Zion; they cannot discover that music within themselves on foreign soil. They were in Babylon but not of Babylon. They were the prototypes of the true exile. They did not say, "Let us sing the song of HaShem so that the bitterness of exile might be mitigated, so that we might build a home away from home." They

2. A covenantor is a person who is bound by the provisions made in a covenant.

jealously savored their terrible longings, would not make peace with a reality that they could not change.

There is a remarkable passage in Maharal that we should study carefully, for it has much to teach us.

Shemos 12:40 tells us that *Israel's stay, the time that they had spent in Egypt, was four hundred and thirty years.* Rashi, mindful of the fact that the Israelites had been in Egypt only about two hundred years, comments: [They were in Egypt] after they lived as strangers in [other] lands that were not theirs.

The difficulty is obvious: How can the Torah talk of a stay in Egypt if, in fact, other countries were also involved?

Maharal offers this answer:

> Since it was their destiny to go down to Egypt and to be enslaved there, they were comparable to a person whose main domicile is in a certain land, who, although he will occasionally leave it to live in another country, will, provided that it his intention to return, be considered an inhabitant of his own land. It is as though he were living there all along. Thus, although originally Israel did not actually live in Egypt, still, since God had decreed that they be enslaved there, it is considered to be their actual home. [They were "in Egypt" even while they lived in other countries.]
>
> ... For, were you to take a clod of earth and throw it into the air, you would surely not maintain that this clod of earth belongs there. Clearly its place is down below ...

Today, the situation is reversed. Our land, the place where we belong, is not any "Egypt" but Eretz Yisrael. Away from it we are a clod of earth suspended in the sky — a pitiful, ludicrous misfit, dangling unanchored and unbeautiful — in nothingness!

Is this how we feel about our exile? About ourselves?

We are bidden to study our history so that we may move forward along the paths of our destiny, secure that we will not repeat the mistakes of the past.

When, in the books of Ezra and Nehemiah, we study the resettling of Judea after the Babylonian exile, we are struck by the loving detail in which the names of individuals and families who returned from Babylon are listed. Those who wrote these books must have known that it would not take long before these carefully preserved records would turn into meaningless strings of names; the individuals and accomplishments that stood behind them and gave them body, lost in the mists of centuries.

Why, then, record them?

Surely this can only be understood as follows.

The initial rigors of the captivity had long since been forgotten. Large, vibrant Jewish communities had sprung up in Babylon. The Jews enjoyed wealth and power and had been granted a great deal of autonomy in the running of their internal affairs. Great courage and determination were required to leave the comforts of such an exile for the desolation of a ruined land. Many could not find it within themselves to take such a momentous step. Those who did are the shining heroes of our past. They won the right to be granted a measure of eternity by being inscribed in *kisvei hakodesh*.

But all is not well. Ezra finds the tribe of Levi too sparsely represented among the returning pioneers. *I then scrutinized the people and the* kohanim, *but I could find no Levites there* (Ezra 8:15). While Scripture ascribes no explanation for the Levites' poor showing, tradition passes a harsh judgment: *Why were the Levites punished, in that they were no longer to receive the tithes [which had originally been given to them]? Because they did not go up [to Judea] in Ezra's days* (Yevamos 86b).

Is it not strange that just the Levites, the Torah teachers of the nation, should have failed this crucial test? A scant seven decades earlier it had been they who, in utter despondency, could not, or better, would not, bring themselves to sing God's song on foreign soil.

Had they then become acclimatized to exile so swiftly? How could it have happened that, in their love of the land, they lagged so far behind their brothers?

Perhaps, after all, it is not so hard to understand. The highly developed infrastructure of Torah-learning institutions that years later was to produce the Babylonian Hillel, the Rebbe of all future generations in *klal Yisrael*, must already in those early years have begun to take shape. Ezra himself, we are taught, came up to Judea later than he would otherwise have done because he refused to leave Babylon as long as his teacher, Baruch ben Neriah, was alive. We would be wrong to assume that this Rebbe-*talmid* relationship functioned in a vacuum. It lies in the nature of things that the exiles would have made sure, as their very first concern, that there were *chadorim* and *yeshivos* so that Torah would be preserved among them.

It would, of course, have been the Levites who were the life force that animated these efforts.

Could this then not perhaps explain the apparently inexplicable? The Levites felt the need to return to the land less than did their brothers. Within the four *amos* of *halachah* there was such a sense of purpose and sanctity that somehow the pain of *galus* was not felt so acutely.

When they were exiled to Babylon, the Shechinah *accompanied them ... And, where is it to be found? Abbaye answered, "In the synagogue at Hutzal and in the Shaf VeYashiv synagogue of Nehardai*[3] (Megilah 29a). And Rabbi Elazar HaKapor taught: The synagogues and study halls of Babylon will one day be established in Eretz Yisrael (*there*). If all this was true and could be experienced so many centuries later, it surely stands to reason that in the earlier years, with prophets and divine inspiration still among them, it would have taken a sharp sense of discrimination, indeed, to be able to see the advantage that the waste swampland of Judea held over the Beis HaMidrash in Babylon.

And yet, the Levites were judged wrong. There is theory and practice, *aggadah* and *halachah*. In punishing them, Ezra proclaimed that it is not good enough to meet the exiled *Shechinah* in the Beis HaMidrash in Babylon, when the desolate land craves the return of its children (VaYikra 26:43).

So does history speak to us. Are we listening?

These three weeks provide us with a chance to look into ourselves and ask some pointed questions.

3. Both of these places were located in Babylon. That, one would suppose, might well have persuaded some people that they might as well stay back in Babylon.

IN RECOGNITION OF A

GENEROUS CONTRIBUTION

IN MEMORY

OF

Dr. Richard

&

Regina Weinberger

OF

VIENNA, AUSTRIA

AND

BALTIMORE, MARYLAND

מציבים אנו בזה

את כבוד

הרב שמואל אלחנן

ב"ר מאיר לייב בראג זצ"ל

ר"ח טבת תשע"ג

ת.נ.צ.ב.ה.

He knew many secrets And lived by them.
He knew that we all crave respect
And treated everyone, great and small, like a king.
He knew that students love teachers who love them,
And he was unstinting in the love he showed each
of the many, many who called him "Rebbi."
There was another secret that he had mastered.
He knew how to turn dross into gold.
He could and did take students, who showed little
aptitude and less interest in their studies,
And by his deft touch and faultless educational intuition
Made first class Benei Torah out of them.
The pride of the Yeshivos that they subsequently entered.
He knew the power of a well-placed compliment;
knew how to make a student feel on top of the world,
But for himself, great Talmid Chacham though he was,
A simple "Es Kumt Mir Gornisht"
Ended the matter.
There was of course one glory in which he did bask.
The great immortal Rav Avigdor Miller זצ"ל
found in him the ideal life-partner for his daughter.
Greatness found greatness; and, yes, sanctity found sanctity.

יהא זכרו ברוך

IN MEMORY

OF

OUR BELOVED

HUSBAND, FATHER,

AND

TEACHER

Solomon Ralph Bijou

HE LIT A LIGHT IN OUR HEARTS

THAT

WILL GUIDE US AND OUR CHILDREN

THROUGHOUT OUR LIVES.

—FROM HIS WIFE,

CHILDREN, GRANDCHILDREN,

AND

GREAT-GRANDCHILDREN

THERE ARE MANY PEOPLE WHO OWE

THEIR LIVES TO

THE LOVING CONCERN OF

Ezra & Zekia Shasho

OF BLESSED MEMORY.

WE GRATEFULLY RECALL THEIR GOODNESS AND

THE WONDERFUL EXAMPLE THAT THEY SET.

THEY, AS ALSO

THEIR BELOVED DAUGHTER

Frieda Kredy

AND THEIR BELOVED SON

Egal Shasho

OF BLESSED MEMORY,

WILL FOREVER LIVE ON IN OUR HEARTS.

—BY THEIR CHILDREN,

GRANDCHILDREN, AND FAMILY

Albert Hamway זצ"ל

UNDERSTOOD WHAT JEWISH LIVING

WAS ALL ABOUT.

IN FARAWAY JAPAN HE RAISED HIS CHILDREN

WITH A LOVE FOR THEIR TRADITION.

THEY EACH BUILT

WARM AND LOVING JEWISH HOMES,

PASSING ON TO THEIR CHILDREN AND

THEY TO THEIRS THE FLAME

WHICH THEIR FATHER HAD PASSED TO THEM.

HE IS REMEMBERED WITH LOVE BY

HIS WIFE, HIS CHILDREN,

GRANDCHILDREN,

AND GREAT-GRANDCHILDREN.

מציבים אנו בזה

מזכרת נצח

לאבינו מורנו היקר

ר' לטמן

בן ר' חיים דוב בער ז"ל

איש צנוע

שכל חייו רק כצבי

לעשות רצון אבינו שבשמים

ולאמנו מורתנו היקרה

רות רבקה לאה

בת ר' אברהם ע"ה

יהא זכרם ברוך

IN LOVING MEMORY

OF

OUR PARENTS

Mollie

AND

Sam E. Levy

TWO WONDERFUL PEOPLE

ONE LOVING HEART

Ally & Marlow Dayon

Knew how life was supposed to be lived
Quietly and modestly
They went about their acts of caring
Helping where help was needed
Coaxing smiles from broken hearts
With their colorful and bubbly natures
Their door was always open
As were also their minds
Theirs was the wisdom of the heart
They enjoyed life and enjoyed each other
We miss them sadly but our pride
in who our parents were softens our pain
By their daughter Sharon Grossberg
And their sons
Irwin, Richard and Jeffery Dayon

WITH A SMILE ON HIS WISE FACE

AND NOVHARDOK MUSSAR IN HIS HEART

HaRav Chaim Mordechai Weinkrantz זצ"ל

UNDERSTOOD US ALL SO WELL, SO VERY WELL.

NO PROBLEM,

BUT HIS WISDOM FOUND A SOLUTION.

NO PAIN, BUT HIS EMPATHY

WAS A HEALING BALM.

CHILD OF A CULTURE VERY DIFFERENT

FROM OUR OWN, HE NEVERTHELESS FOUND

COMMONALITY IN HIS AND OUR

JEWISH HEARTS.

WE WILL NEVER FORGET THE BOOKS

WHICH HE SO DILIGENTLY TAUGHT US,

NOR THE LIFE LESSONS

FOR WHICH HE WAS A LIVING TEXT.

—THE MONDAY SHIUR

IN LOVING MEMORY OF

Esther & Isaac Mezrahi

Pillars of our community, they always knew what had to be done and, profoundly creative, found ways to do it. Above all they were a team. One heart animated them both, one soul breathed life into their dreams. After father passed on, mother kept the flame burning for eighteen more years. May their memory be a blessing for us, our children, and grandchildren.

IN LOVING MEMORY
OF MY BELOVED PARENTS, AND MORE,
MY GOOD AND PRECIOUS FRIENDS

Jack & Jeanette Feldman

They were generous, warmhearted, and gentle. You could not meet them without being touched by their goodness.